David Sinclair is the author of several previous biographies, including *Edgar Alan Poe* and *Two Georges: The Making of the Modern Monarchy*. His latest book *Hall of Mirrors* is a fascinating study of the Treaty of Versailles and its legacy. David Sinclair has enjoyed a long career as a Fleet Street journalist and newspaper executive, most recently as executive editor of the *Financial Mail on Sunday*.

His website address is
www.novo.com/davidsinclair

THE POUND

A Biography

David Sinclair

ARROW

Published in the United Kingdom in 2001 by Arrow Books

1 3 5 7 9 10 8 6 4 2

Copyright © David Sinclair 2000

First published in the United Kingdom in 2000 by Century

Arrow Books
The Random House Group Ltd
20 Vauxhall Bridge Road, London SW1V 2SA

Random House Australia (Pty) Limited
20 Alfred Street, Milsons Point, Sydney,
New South Wales 2061, Australia

Random House New Zealand Limited
18 Poland Road, Glenfield
Auckland 10, New Zealand

Random House (Pty) Limited
Endulini, 5a Jubilee Road, Parktown 2193, South Africa

The Random House Group Ltd Reg. No. 954009

www.randomhouse.co.uk

A CIP catalogue record for this book is available from the British Library

Papers used by Random House are natural, recyclable products made from
wood grown in sustainable forests. The manufacturing processes conform
to the environmental regulations of the country of origin

Typeset in Bodoni by SX Composing DTP, Rayleigh, Essex
Printed and bound in Denmark by Nørhaven A/S, Viborg

ISBN 0 09 940606 3

Contents

Introduction   1

1   Anyone Got a Pound?   9
2:   Pounds, Shillings and Pence   24
3   Coins of the Realm   41
4   Danegeld to Domesday   59
5   Hard Currency   78
6   Taxing Times   95
7   Coining It   110
8   Toil and Trouble   126
9   The Good, The Bad and The Ugly   141
10 Money Makes the World Go Round   156
11 Bankers' Hours   171
12 Paper Chase   189
13 The People's Pound   208
14 Sterling Work   227
15 Cashing In   247
16 The Last Days of the Pound?   267

Chronology: Key Dates for the Pound   287
What a Pound Was Worth   290
Index   293

Introduction

The symbol of Britain's national wealth today is a small, gold-coloured coin weighing just nine and a half grams and made from a mixture of copper, nickel and zinc. It is an insignificant-looking disc, the pound sterling, and it no longer counts for very much. Time was when an income of £300 a year could support a gentleman of leisure in some style, with his own house, servants, a carriage and a horse. But that was a couple of centuries ago. Today, £300 is not too far above the sum the average British worker earns each week. A pound is just another coin to rattle in the pocket or the purse.

It was a very different story in the fifteenth century, when the very first pound coin came into use. Large and heavy with real gold, it formed the centrepiece of what has been described as the finest, best executed and most handsome coinage in Europe.

Of course, in the late Middle Ages not too many people would have been carrying pound coins in their pouches. The wages earned by a skilled stonemason, for instance, were about eightpence a day, so that his annual income would probably not have been much more than ten pounds. He paid his rent in silver pennies, or indeed, often cut the coins into halves and quarters to buy his meagre supplies of food, fuel and clothing. If the stonemason had ever seen a gold pound, it would only have been because he was working for the king, or an aristocratic landowner, the church or one of a new breed of merchants who were making fortunes in trade with continental Europe.

But like the pound, even the silver coins used daily by ordinary people – pennies, groats, perhaps shillings if they were rich or thrifty enough – were valuable items in their own right, made from varying quantities of fine silver mixed with base metals such as copper to increase their durability. Money, in those days, had tangible worth, related, in theory at least, to its bullion content – unlike today's currencies, the notional values of which are arrived at as a result of complex calculations based on economic output, balance of trade, interest rates, capital movements, liquidity and so on.

In late mediaeval England the new pound coin, with its half-ounce of fine gold, became the standard against which the currency of the kingdom and that of other countries was measured. The pound's worth depended on not only the amount of fine gold the coin contained but also the relative value of gold against that of silver. Gold had long been the most prized of precious metals, and it was therefore natural that it should be adopted as the absolute measure of value when the use of money began to develop among ancient civilisations some 700 years before the birth of Christ. However, in the absence of notional money, the only way to establish the absolute value of gold was to compare it with the next most precious metal, which was silver.

Thus began what is known to economists as the bimetallic monetary system, under which gold and silver were made into coins on the basis of a legally determined weight relationship between them. In other words, an ounce of gold would be worth a set number of ounces of silver. That is how the monetary pound first came into being, not as a coin but as the measure of weight. In classical measures a pound was the equivalent of twelve ounces and twelve ounces of silver were considered to be worth one ounce of gold. It was logical, therefore, to gauge quantities of silver coins in pounds.

For centuries the gold–silver ratio had been abitrary, fixed not by any commercial assessment of gold's value on the basis of its availability but merely according to the prejudices of ruling authorities in various parts of the civilised world. By the time the first pound coin was minted, though, prevailing economic thought in Europe – established by a French bishop and royal adviser named Nicholas Oresme – held that the value of money was dependent upon the total amount of bullion, both gold and silver, known to be in circulation. It was perhaps the earliest expression of a theory that in the eighteenth century would, with refinements, become known as the Gold Standard, in which the pound sterling would play a crucial role.

When the British government officially adopted the Gold Standard early in the nineteenth century, however, the pound – whose value was fixed at 123.7 grains of gold – had already travelled a long way in its fall from the grace of its earliest days. Over the years, the bimetallic system had proved both to have serious flaws and to be unequal to the vast expansion of trade

3

that had followed the discovery of new lands from the late fifteenth century onwards and the arrival of the Industrial Revolution. At the same time the whole concept of what money is had moved on, as new generations of economists gradually rejected the dominance of bullion in determining the worth of currency and argued instead that cash was merely a token of value based on other factors.

In fact, within less than a hundred years of the pound coin's appearance the noted astronomer Copernicus had applied his scientific brain to the currency question and had proposed that the real measure of value rested not with the quantity of bullion in the coinage but with the actual numbers of coins in circulation. That was a sixteenth-century expression of the theory, fashionable closer to our own times, that manipulation of the money supply was the main determinant of currency values.

The object of such theorising was an attempt to stabilise currencies in the light of bimetallism's shortcomings, of which there were three important ones.

First, a currency based on bullion was prey to instant inflation because its intrinsic worth made it tempting for users to shave slivers of precious metal from it before passing it on. It was a way of hoarding wealth, since once you had obtained enough gold or silver by this means you could have it melted down and either recast as new coinage or made into plate or jewellery. The coins mistreated in that way, however, immediately lost value because their intrinsic worth was reduced with their weight of silver. The face value of a single penny would remain the same, but the number of pennies required to make a pound weight would obviously increase, because they were lighter, so in overall terms the currency had been devalued. That led to price inflation, for in order to pay for something costing a shilling – which was also a weight before it became a coin – you might have to give nine pence instead of the usual full-weight five.

Skimming of coins was a problem with bullion currency from its earliest days. In some periods of history it became so prevalent that even single coins were not accepted because the recipient lost out with each underweight one he took. The poor generally suffered from such inflation more than the rich, simply because they had fewer coins to exchange. If a wage of sixpence a day was paid in skimmed pennies, it amounted to a pay cut. But even the wealthy classes, right up to monarchs themselves, could be victims of underweight coinage. They might insist that rents and taxes were paid by weight rather than face value, but they might equally find that the light pennies were refused by the soldiers, craftsmen and merchants they in turn had to pay. When it came to sums of hundreds or thousands of pounds, as in the case of royal revenues, the loss could be substantial.

The second serious problem with bimetallic coinage was caused by the monetary authorities themselves, usually the kings and emperors who held autocratic power determined the gold–silver ratio and caused the currency to be minted. As civilisations progressed, the business of government became more complicated and more expensive. Monarchs were almost always short of money with which to defend or expand their realms, to buy support, to administer justice and to keep themselves in the manner they felt they deserved as God's anointed. Their great temptation was to increase the supply of ready money by deliberately debasing the coinage, or reducing its bullion content.

In terms of the English pound, it was worth at various times anything between 225 and 300 silver pennies, as the penny's silver content went from a standard twenty-two and a half grains to eighteen, or twelve or even just a little more than ten grains at one point, as monarchs sought to increase their cash flow. It was a short-term and ultimately self-defeating policy. The kings could get away with it for a while in domestic terms by lowering the amount of silver required to buy gold, or by reducing the fineness of the bullion in the coins. But when it came to overseas trade they often found that their debased currency would not be accepted. Worse still, the money supply they had sought to manipulate in their favour eventually began to work against them as large quantities of debased English money were exported in return for better quality foreign gold or silver. Provided enough coins were offered in the exchange, foreign buyers were willing to collect them for melting down and recycling as their own full-value currencies. The English sellers, meanwhile, were happy to accept full-weight coins from abroad as a better store of value.

Which brings us to the third great disadvantage of bullion-based currencies, first identified by the classical Greek writer Aristophanes and restated in Elizabethan England by an astute financier named Thomas Gresham, thereby becoming known as 'Gresham's Law'. This 'law' suggests – and it has often been proved true – that in any monetary system subject to debasement, the best-quality coins will always disappear because their holders will be unwilling to pass them on, preferring to hoard them as a hedge against inflation, while habitually using the bad coinage in their everyday transactions. It is a phenomenon that made it very difficult to maintain a permanent standard of value in bullion coinage, because the minute people began to doubt its integrity as a result of skimming, counterfeiting or the hint of debasement, the coins with the highest bullion content would begin to be withdrawn from circulation. We see Gresham's Law in action even today, when coins and banknotes really are no more than transient tokens: the most battered ten-pound note or the damaged penny are the ones we tend to pass on first even though in absolute terms they are 'worth' as much as perfect examples.

It is surprising that the bimetallic system lasted as long as it did, given its serious deficiencies and the repeated currency crises they gave rise to. The pound sterling was to suffer many vicissitudes on its journey of transformation from the handsome, half-ounce gold piece that began its life to the inconsequential, brassy little coin that may prove to be its last manifestation in the face of the all-powerful US dollar and the enigmatic newcomer of the European single currency, the euro. Perhaps the wonder is that it survived at all, given the staggering changes that have occurred in economic activity, theory and practice over half a millennium. Yet even as conservative 'sound money' advocates were fighting successive rearguard actions to maintain the link between currency and bullion, the pound was adapting itself to conditions in which it would be the international markets of trade and finance that would determine value rather than the gold or silver content of coins. In fact, it was the pound, as the currency that created and maintained the British Empire, which helped to establish those markets, perhaps unwittingly participating in its own eventual demise.

The little coin that now jingles among our small change could turn out to be the last we see of the pound, but even if it does cease to exist generations to come will marvel at its long and unique history. For when that first beautiful gold piece was tipped out of its mould the pound had already been a potent financial force for some five centuries, while the roots of the system that produced it stretched back even further, into the depths of early Anglo-Saxon England.

1

Anyone Got a Pound?

Now money . . . was invented chiefly for the purpose of exchange: and consequently the proper and principal use of money is its consumption or alienation whereby it is sunk in exchange. Hence it is by its very nature unlawful to take payment for the use of money lent.

Thomas Aquinas, *On Usury*, c. 1269–71

As battles went, it was not much of an encounter. To the man who won it, however, and who received the crown of England on a featureless Leicestershire hillside, the battle of Bosworth Field seemed like an endorsement from God.

The victor of Bosworth was a twenty-four-year-old Welshman – or at least the remote descendant of a line of ancient Cymric princes – named Henry Tudor, Earl of Richmond. He had little real claim to the English throne, but on that late summer day, 22 August 1485, he seized it by force as the hated King Richard III was abandoned by much of his reluctant army, unhorsed and beaten to death. Tradition has it that the king's battered crown was retrieved by Lord Stanley, who placed it on the handsome head of Henry Tudor and was subsequently rewarded by being named first Earl of Derby.

In fact, Henry had proclaimed himself king the day before the battle. His victory he took as a mark of divine approval, since God's will was about all he could advance in support of his cause. His mother was a great-great-granddaughter of King Edward III, who had reigned more than a century earlier, yet there had been many diversions in the hereditary line since then and others in the royal houses of York and Lancaster had better connections to the crown. It was Henry's good fortune, however, not only to have killed the king but also that Richard III had left no heir. To many among a nobility tired of the internecine strife of the Wars of the Roses, and disgusted by the bloody rule of the Yorkist Richard, the emergence of the Lancastrian Henry signalled a new beginning – especially when the new king shrewdly united the factions by marrying Elizabeth of York.

The optimism attending the accession of King Henry VII proved to be fully justified. He and his successors, Henry VIII and Elizabeth I, made the Tudor dynasty probably the most successful and certainly the most celebrated royal line in English history. His own reign brought the country peace, stability and systems of administration and justice that helped to place it in the forefront of European powers, and ultimately to ease its transition from the mediaeval to the modern world.

But perhaps his most lasting memorial is the unit of currency that would dominate all others for nearly 500 years: the pound.

Henry VII ordered the minting of the very first pound coin in 1489. Until that time the pound had been merely a money of account, a convenient book-keeping device representing the value by weight of quantities of silver pennies, the coins in which most cash transactions were carried out. Precisely how many pennies made up a pound depended upon their weight, which varied markedly over the centuries, but by Henry's reign the acknowledged standard was 240 pence to a pound. No one, though, had yet thought of turning the money of account into a coin that could be used instead of pound bags of pennies.

The penny had served most monetary purposes perfectly well, for the simple reason that cash had been of relatively little importance to most of the English population. It was only when the systems of barter, payment in kind and the complex feudal arrangement of rights and personal obligations began to be replaced by money wages and purchases that the demand for coins became widespread. Even then it was by no means universal.

At the beginning of the thirteenth century, for instance, agricultural labourers – those who were not serfs – were being paid a penny a day, but that would often be augmented by supplies of food and drink from their employers to meet the basic needs of life. Any cash the workers used was spent mainly on such things as rent, fuel and clothing, and the amounts involved were small. In fact, where there was real demand for coins it was generally for fractions of a penny. That was why, in August 1279, the first quarter-penny coin, the farthing, had been introduced, followed a year later by a halfpenny. Both were silver but the farthings were so small that people usually lost them and they were discontinued until new minting techniques allowed them to be revived in 1613. The halfpenny was more popular and would survive in silver form for some 400 years.

Where substantial amounts of ready money really counted was among the upper classes who owned land and property, and who would have been involved in larger transactions covering rents and taxes as well as payments to the people who worked or provided services for them. And, of course, nobody had greater needs than the king himself, not only a one-man government with the right to levy taxes but also by far the most substantial land and property owner in the country and therefore also its most important employer.

However, even the large sums received and spent by the monarch, government officials, the aristocracy and the propertied classes could usually be dealt with by the traditional penny. Transactions were not particularly frequent and when they did take place the units of account – the shilling, the mark and, of course, the pound – into which the pennies were consolidated by weight, were considered equal to the task.

Things started to change towards the end of the thirteenth century when rising demand caused by a steadily growing population began to cause significant increases in the cost of living, or what we now call price inflation. At the same time the accelerating development of a monetary economy led to the creation of new classes of merchants, shopkeepers and traders, whose livelihoods depended on cash sales. There was also a growing export trade that required cash purchase of commodities such as wool. Records show that between the 1220s and 1280s, the number of silver pennies in circulation more than quadrupled to keep pace with the demand for currency. Production of the coins was beginning to outrun the supplies of silver available, so in 1280 there appeared a larger denomination silver piece, known as a groat and worth four pence. Demand continued to grow, however, and the authorities finally had to resort to gold for the coinage, issuing in 1344 the florin (equivalent to six shillings of silver in weight or seventy-two pence), then in 1412 a coin known as the 'noble' (at eighty pence), and in 1465 the gold 'ryal' – the highest value yet at ten shillings in weight, or half a pound of pennies.

No doubt a pound coin would have appeared in due course, except for the fact that by then both gold and silver were in very short supply as a result of a century of plagues and wars across Europe. The silver content of the English penny had already been drastically reduced in an effort to maintain the required numbers of coins in circulation and the ryal, which contained 120 grains of fine gold, was the best that could be achieved with the limited supplies of bullion available. Even so, the demand for coins continued to exceed the amounts circulating, so that even foreign coinage became sought after as a means of exchange throughout England.

Such was the situation inherited by Henry Tudor in 1485, but he was well equipped for the task of restoring financial stability. For a start, money to him represented security in a very direct way. His early life had been full of insecurity. As a member of the house of Lancaster he grew up in the custody of the Yorkists, who seized the throne from Henry VI in 1461. Ten years later, after the Roses battle of Tewkesbury, the teenaged future head of the Tudor clan was spirited away by his uncle to the friendly ducal court of Brittany, where he would remain in exile until the French-backed invasion that eventually placed the English crown on his head. For more than twenty years he had been denied his patrimony and forced to rely on the charity of others, not always benign. Hardly surprising, then, that even as king he should feel vulnerable, an impression that could only be reinforced by the Yorkist plots that swirled round him after his accession. Henry VII saw money as power, the power to raise armies against his enemies and to ensure the loyalty of aristocratic supporters who could only too easily be bought by the other side.

At the same time the king – unusually for a monarch of the period – had a shrewd financial brain and in some respects shared the sort of philosophy that propelled Margaret Thatcher towards becoming prime minister in 1979. Allowing for historical differences, the conditions in which they took power were remarkably similar. Both inherited a country in the latter stages of a long period of stagnation, punctuated by short-lived bouts of optimism and economic boom, and more or less equally unsuccessful attempts to make the good times permanent. In Thatcher's case, Britain had failed fully to recover from two world wars that had robbed it of empire, economic power and self-confidence. Henry took over an England seemingly still paralysed by the shock of the Black Death and reeling from the uncertainties of the Wars of the Roses. Each responded by relying heavily on monetary and fiscal policy, by establishing a cult of personality, by promoting a sustained expansion of trade, and by reforming the systems and practices under which the country operated.

Both were what might be termed 'progressive conservatives', superimposing new ideas on traditional values and determined that the existing machinery of state, rather than being replaced, should simply become more efficient and cost effective. Like Thatcher, Henry Tudor adopted a 'kitchen cabinet' approach to government, taking only a small circle of trusted advisers into his confidence and sometimes treating even his own supporters with a certain degree of suspicion. Equally, Henry believed in the creation of a meritocracy, promoting men of ability, integrity and loyalty even if they did not come from the old ruling classes. And, in a sense, the late fifteenth-century king and the late twentieth-century prime minister shared the same fate, both securing their places in history at the expense of their personal popularity, especially towards the end of their careers.

But the most striking similarity between them was their commitment to sound money as the key to successful government and economic stability. When Henry VII came to the throne England's trading condition was relatively good, both domestically and internationally, but in spite of that the currency was in a poor state. The political infighting between supporters of the noble houses of York and Lancaster had weakened the monarchy's grip on the money supply and made coin production uncertain in terms of both quantity and quality. The foreign coins which had been obtained in exchange for goods or English money were circulating widely – partly to make up for a shortfall from English mints and also because of the continuing debasement practised in repeated recoinages. People who wished either to trade or to save against sudden changes in political fortune felt more comfortable with coins issued by continental mints.

Henry VII, having dealt in the second year of his reign with the little local difficulties of rebellions by the pretenders Lambert Simnel and Perkin Warbeck, calculated that an early return to mastery of the mints would be an astute move politically and economically. It would help to rebuild respect for the crown among the people and, for those who still harboured their own royal ambitions, it was a sign that this king intended to be firmly in charge. To rulers on the Continent, the creation of new, high-quality coins would demonstrate that England once again saw itself as an economic force to be reckoned with.

The choice of the new denomination was no accident either. Not for Henry Tudor a penny or groat. He started at the top. People had been counting money in pounds for at least 500 years and now they would have a coin to represent that almost mystical sum. Containing 240 grains of gold and bearing the image of the monarch, the pound coin was oficially called a 'sovereign' and it was worth twenty shillings or 240 silver pennies. This was serious money. The gold sovereign and the pound it represented – and later came to be called – would survive many incarnations in the future, but their nominal value would remain constant for nearly 500 years, until 1971, when Britain converted its currency to the decimal system at a hundred pennies to the pound.

With bullion supplies still restricted, obtaining the gold for the ambitious new pound coin was a problem. Henry solved it by reforming the system under which new coinage was produced.

In the days of money based on precious metals, old coins were taken to regional mints licensed by the crown, where they were melted down and the gold and silver extracted to be recycled in the new currency. People could also take gold and silver jewellery to be converted into coins. The mint-masters, or moneyers, charged a fee, of which part was paid to the royal treasury and the rest made up the mints' profits. In 1489 the going rate for moneyers was ninety pence (or seven shillings and sixpence) per pound of gold and eighteen pence (one shilling and sixpence) for silver.

To encourage people to have their gold recycled the king reduced the mint charges to just thirty pence, or two shillings and sixpence, per pound. The premium for silver, too, was lowered, to a shilling, so that new silver pennies and groats could be produced. Henry also issued a proclamation prohibiting the circulation of foreign groats and half-groats, which encouraged people to visit their local mints to have those coins melted down and recycled as new English money. These measures resulted in a vast increase in output from the moneyers, so that by 1504 it was feasible for the king to issue a new, smaller denomination silver coin for everyday use. This was called the 'testoon' and was worth twelve pence, making it the forerunner of the shilling coin, which has survived into these decimalised days as the five-pence piece.

This recoinage placed the English currency alongside the best in continental Europe and helped to restore confidence at home in both the coinage and the monarchy. From the point of view of the king it also had great practical advantages, making it considerably easier for him to collect new taxes and customs duties he wished to impose. Instead of his officials having carefully to weigh out bags of silver, they could confidently accept sovereigns and shillings.

That pressing reason apart, however, Henry VII saw the acquisition of money as a path to glory both for himself – as a man clearly concerned with what posterity's view of him would be – and for the new monarchy he was determined to construct. During his exile he had seen the power and splendour of European courts, particularly that of France, and he understood public opinion well enough to know that royal pomp and ceremony were deeply appreciated as expressions of national pride. England was not to be seen as a mere offshore island. On his pound and other coins Henry placed an artistically accomplished likeness of himself wearing the closed crown symbolic of an emperor rather than the traditional open one signifying the warrior prince. His court became more glittering and more populous than those of his predecessors. As just one example, the number of high-born personal attendants at Court doubled in the course of the reign – and overall, royal expenditure rose by about the same amount.

In addition, of course, there was the business of government, for which the king was held to be personally responsible. The defence of the realm was a primary role and one that was becoming increasingly expensive as the idea of professionalism took hold among the soldiery even if, as yet, the regular army did not exist. With its static population, England lacked manpower, which meant that foreign mercenaries had to be hired for most military operations, while the navy remained a less than adequate force to guard an island state. In the wake of civil strife, lawlessness was a serious problem, so that systems of enforcement and punishment had to be strengthened. During the Wars of the Roses the judicial system had fallen into disrepute, subject as it was to factionalism and political pressure.

There was no hope of establishing law and order unless the courts were seen to be fair, so a programme of reconstruction was necessary from the highest court to the humblest local tribunal. The operation and supervision of the system required a bureaucracy, as did the many other tasks that became the business of central government during the transition from feudal to modern state. All of this – good for both the country and the position of the monarchy – was expensive.

But Henry VII was just the man to identify the needs and to raise the funds to satisfy them. Though he surrounded himself with trusted advisers and officials – as well he might, given the nature of his accession and the abundance of powerful forces intent on bringing him down – he took personal charge of the exchequer, spending hours studying account books and signing off every page himself. His attention to detail became legendary.

But the most striking thing about the king's approach to finance was its remarkable modernity. With a vision almost unmatched among contemporary rulers, he was committed to the idea of a cash economy. His predecessors had granted castles, lands and rights to game, waterways or timber in return for services rendered by local lords, especially the provision of troops at moments of crisis, and conversely much of the revenue they could depend on had been in commodities such as fuel and foodstuffs or in services. Henry VII would have none of it. Though his recorded gross revenues from the royal Duchy of Lancaster were only marginally greater than they had been for Henry V in the early years of the fifteenth century, Henry VII managed to increase the cash yield by more than half through the skilful exploitation of the resources at his disposal. With his understanding of asset values and his capacity for maximising them, he maintained demesne revenues at nearly forty per cent of the total royal income at a time when other European monarchies could count on perhaps only a tenth of that.

When it came to rewarding loyal office holders or political and military allies, the king's approach bordered on meanness, a fact that was not lost on some of his beneficiaries and helped to diminish his reputation in the last years of his reign. With the mind of an accountant, he carefully calculated the cost–benefit ratio of any grants of pensions, land, sinecures or annuities, with the result that royal patronage was too often a cause of resentment rather than gratitude. And although Henry liked to promote the brightest and best among his retinue to positions of responsibility, his desire for financial gain led him to offer other offices to the highest bidder – among them the jobs of Attorney-General and Speaker of the House of Commons. Nor were the buyers permitted to use their positions as profitably as they might have hoped for. The king's sharp eye soon fell upon attempts at corruption or diversion of funds. He was determined that any windfalls should come his way.

The same head for figures naturally turned its attention to taxation as well. If people wanted effective government, strong defences and a stable, unifying monarchy able to compete with rival European courts, they could hardly expect not to pay for them. England was becoming prosperous again, with agriculture booming and exports of both farm and industrial products rising steadily. During the twenty-four years of Henry's reign, for instance, the value of English cloth sold abroad increased by almost two-thirds. Such an expansion of trade was an opportunity too good to miss. The king gradually put up customs and excise duties by half, and raised the level of direct taxation on income and consumption by a similar amount. For an increasingly burdened populace there was to be no gain without pain. It had need of its new pound coins to meet its growing bills.

Meanwhile, Henry devised a fiscal innovation that paid dividends politically as well as in terms of revenue. If subjects who served or pleased him were to receive favours, he reasoned, it seemed only right that those who opposed or annoyed him should suffer penalties. The traditional way was to imprison or execute such malefactors and seize their lands and properties. Henry VII used that method often, issuing no fewer than 138 Acts of Attainder convicting opponents, perceived or real, of treason – and even when the king later changed his mind, there was no guarantee that the victim was still alive to enjoy his freedom or that he or his family would get back all their property. But these were for serious cases only. For relatively petty offences, and with the daily perusal of his accounts always in his thoughts, Henry decided that wayward peers should be heavily fined. It was quicker and it yielded hard cash.

Thus in 1507 the Kentish nobleman Lord Bergavenny suffered a huge financial penalty of £70,650, imposed by the court of the King's Bench, for allegedly maintaining an illegal private militia. It was the exact sum – five pounds each for 471 men over a period of thirty months – that his lordship had paid to twenty-five gentlemen, four clergymen, a cobbler, a tinker and 440 yeomen at a rate of five pounds per man per month between June 1504 and December 1506.

Clearly this was a splendid money-raising operation, so much so that the king even offered discounts to those who pleaded guilty to whatever offence it was thought profitable to charge them with. But his talent for business also produced an ingenious refinement of the scheme. Not content with extracting cash from men who displeased him, he laid financial burdens on those who just might. Henry demanded that powerful provincial nobles sign loyalty bonds against the possibility that they would turn against him or act in a manner contrary to his interests. The sums for which the bonds were written varied from one hundred to ten thousand pounds, presumably depending on the wealth of the man involved and the risk of his misbehaviour. At the merest hint of a slight, the king could sue the offender under common law for the amount of his bond and the money simply dropped into the royal purse. Because the action was a civil one, the facts of the alleged wrongdoing did not have to be proved, only that the debt existed in law. The verdict was a foregone conclusion and the offender had little choice but to pay up.

When Henry VII died in 1509, the treasury coffers were brimming with gold and the revenues from the royal estates were healthier than they had been for years. He was conscious of being the founder of a new dynasty and he wanted it to succeed him on a firm financial footing. Historians will argue that the Tudor period saw England in better condition than it had been at any time since the Romans had withdrawn more than 1000 years before. Equally, economists will suggest that during the century or so of the Tudor dynasty the seeds were sown that would eventually transform Britain into the world's first economic superpower. Finance was very much the driving force of the Tudor century.

But while people appreciated the pound, the shilling and the general improvement in the coinage brought about by Henry VII, some of his creative economic policies did little to endear him to his subjects. As the contemporary historian and papal tax collector Polydore Vergil put it, the people eventually began to think that they were suffering not on account of their own sins but because of the greed of their monarch. 'It is not indeed clear', Vergil commented, 'that at the start it was greed; but afterwards greed did become apparent.'

He was probably right. Towards the end of his life Henry fell prey to an illness that seemed to affect his mind, making him paranoid, uncommunicative and excessively mean. Money had always been an obsession, but now the pursuit of it was the only thing that drove him. It was a sad end for a man who had done so much to improve political and economic conditions in his country – for the man who first made the old pound the modern, potent force it would remain over many centuries.

In the same year that he revealed his splendid coin, King Henry launched a new warship. It was also called the *Sovereign* and the coincidence serves as a symbol of the voyage upon which the English currency was embarking. There would be extremely rough waters to navigate, but the pound would sail on proudly for half a millennium and continue to fight for its survival.

Yet even when Henry VII introduced it as a coin, the pound had come a very long way from its humble origins.

2

Pounds, Shillings and Pence

One pound of gold is worth seventy-two solidi of gold. One uncia is worth six solidi. A third of a gold solidus is worth five silver solidi.

Laws of the Visigoths on Coinage, AD 681

Quite when the word 'pound' came into the English language as a description for a sum of money is not clear. We know that by the early tenth century AD the term was used for accounting purposes in the collection of rents, taxes and fines levied by the monarch, but some historians suspect it might have occurred even earlier, during the reign of King Alfred, who refined the Saxon currency system no fewer than three times. What is certain, though, is that people in those days did not talk generally about pounds in

24

financial transactions in the way they would later.

As a unit of weight, the word pound stretches far back into the ancient world, appearing as *pondus* in Latin, as *pfund* among the Germanic tribes and as *pund* in Old Norse and subsequently in Old English. The Latin word simply meant a 'weight' and was probably used originally to describe any object, such as a stone or a piece of metal, that could serve as the agreed measure of a quantity of, say, wheat. It remained in the vernacular even when a mathematical system emerged and, in the case of the Roman Empire, the unit of weight was called a '*libra*' and represented twelve '*unciae*', or ounces. That is the reason why the English currency unit became a pound but was designated by the letter 'L' – which was to become the now familiar £ sign – derived from the initial letter of libra.

In Roman calculations twelve was a magic number, used not only in weight but also to designate length and, so far as the currency was concerned, to express the ratio of value by weight between silver and the more precious gold. Thus, for the Romans and, by extension their empire, one ounce of gold was always worth twelve ounces of silver. That relationship between the basic currency unit, the silver '*denarius*', and gold coins such as the '*aureus*' or the '*solidus*' was always maintained, though the number of coins required to make up the relative weights might vary, depending on the demand for coinage and the available supplies of bullion. If gold was scarce, for example, the bullion content of the solidus might be reduced, so that it would take seventy-two coins to make up a libra rather than the more usual sixty. The bullion content of the silver denarius would also be reduced, from its customary twenty-three and a quarter grains to twenty-one and seven-eighths in order to maintain the twelve-for-one-ratio, or else its numerical value against a solidus would be reduced from forty-eight to forty. The gold standard, as we would call it now, was always one to twelve of silver.

While the Roman Empire existed this monetary system naturally became general throughout occupied Europe. Britannia was late in falling under imperial domination, but even before the arrival of Julius Caesar on its shores in 55 BC the more sophisticated Celtic tribes inhabiting the islands had learned from their continental cousins in the Roman provinces the usefulness of money and were carrying out transactions in coinage made not only from gold and silver but also bronze and an alloy known as potin, a mixture of copper and tin. In spite of Caesar's dismissive observation that the barbarians knew no better than to offer sword blades as payment, there is reason to suspect that part of the reason for the full-scale invasion that followed him during the first century AD lay in the prospect of easily transportable spoils in the form of hard cash.

For the next 400 years, the Britons would be accustomed to an economic structure that owed much to the exchange of money. The libra, solidus and denarius became so much part of the culture that £.s.d. – as shorthand for pounds, shillings and pence – would symbolise a peculiarly English currency system until the latter years of the twentieth century, when revaluation on a decimal basis brought Britain into line with its European neighbours, the shilling disappeared and the d. became a p.

The Roman monetary structure served Britain well. Trade expanded rapidly, not only with the rest of the empire but also with Arab countries, and the islands enjoyed a degree of sustained prosperity they would not see again until the Middle

Ages. Archaeological research has uncovered splendid villas, which reveal that native Britons could live as well as their Roman masters if they knew how to take advantage of the opportunities offered by association with the ancient superpower.

That all changed during the fifth century, when Rome's energy finally ran out and fierce, land-hungry tribes from the north and east overran Europe. By about 435 the last Romans and their wealthy British supporters were dead, had fled or were in hiding, and the invading Angles, Saxons and Jutes were carving up the country among themselves as they wiped out the surviving Celts, or enslaved them, or drove them north and west into the unwelcoming highlands and across the sea to their fellows in Ireland and Brittany.

Though they are generally regarded as bloodthirsty barbarians, these newcomers were in fact principally farmers from the plains of Germany, deeply respectful of the land and with a firm social structure based on lordship and kin. The cult of the warrior was certainly strong, but their way of life was essentially agrarian, in large family settlements presided over by hereditary chieftains. What this sort of society had absolutely no need of was money as a medium of exchange, so that for the next 200 years there was in Britain – alone among the former Roman provinces – no coinage in general use. Barter became once again the standard transaction. Taxes did not apply in the extended family community and debts or fines for lawbreaking would often be paid by obligation or in blood. If in tilling their fields the settlers turned up hoards buried by their former occupants, the gold, silver or copper coins were simply used as ornaments.

27

Societies rarely remain static for long, though. As the invading tribes established their territories and their lives became settled, the population began to increase and more complex structures started to emerge, partly as a result of economic pressure. There were simply more mouths to feed, which meant demand for greater agricultural production and an impetus to trade overseas when domestic resources could not meet developing needs. There is plenty of evidence that, before the middle of the sixth century, the Saxons of southern England were in regular contact with the Frankish peoples just twenty miles away across the Channel – and they, of course, had continued to use something like the Roman currency system. In fact, Frankish influence did lead to the first minting of coins in England since the departure of the Romans, probably during the 580s, when King Aethelberht of Kent married the Christian Princess Bertha, daughter of the King of Paris. Bertha was accompanied to England by a certain Bishop Liudhard, and it was he who caused the tiny coins to be produced in London. They were few in number, however, and they seem to have been used only as gifts, rather like medals.

It was another churchman, the first Bishop of London, who made the next attempt at reintroducing the English to money, between the years 604 and 616. By that time the speed of social change was accelerating as Christianity spread across the country following the mission of St Augustine in 597. Conversion of the pagan kings – of whom Aethelberht had been the first – and their followers meant far more than fundamental changes in religious practice. The Christian church placed great store by education and it was not long before literacy became fairly common among the upper classes under the tutelage of monks. The use of the written word helped to make society more complex, more questioning and more inclined to look beyond the horizons of farm and family. It also changed the nature of transactions among clans, which could now be recorded. Even in what we refer to as the Dark Ages, England was beginning dimly to perceive how useful a currency could be as a means of doing business.

One man who clearly saw the possibilities was Bishop Mellitus, who issued gold coins in London. His motivation may have been at least partly religious. He had been a member of one of the missionary teams sent by the pope to redeem the heathen, but after early success – which resulted in the creation of the first cathedral at Canterbury and the first church of St Paul on what was then the highest point in London – there was a good deal of backsliding among the Saxon princes. Aethelberht's own son, Eadbald, reverted to the old religion and many others became lukewarm if not downright hostile. It could be that Mellitus saw the introduction of gold pieces as a civilising influence, or else a straightforward bribe to keep the rulers tied to the faith. But he was forced to flee a pagan backlash in 616, living in Gaul for three years until he returned as Archbishop of Canterbury after the then King Eadbald had been persuaded of the error of his ways.

Nevertheless the seeds of an early cash economy had been sown, and by 630 various tribal kings were producing their own gold coinage in quite large numbers. The supplies of gold were not infinite, however, and within thirty-five years the moneyers were having to mix it with silver to meet growing demand. By the turn of the century gold was no longer being used and the coins produced were made of an alloy of silver and base metal.

The age of the silver penny was at hand.

Not that there was anything called a penny just yet. The coins of the seven main Saxon kingdoms into which England was divided had a variety of names reflecting very different cultural influences. The smallest denomination, often made from brass, was known as a 'styca'. This might relate to the Saxon word 'sticce', which was a measure of magnitude, but more probably it derives from a term used in many languages for a cutting tool – perhaps especially the Arabic 'zicca', since Arabs were the most advanced and skilful coiners of the period. Styca itself appears to be Gothic in origin, and it is known that the Gothic peoples of central and eastern Europe used Arab or Arabian-style coins – some had no choice, since this was the time when the Mohammedan armies were moving westwards. The derivation is reinforced by the fact that the dies then used by moneyers were not very regular and the shape of the finished coins was achieved using shears.

Then there was the 'sceat', or scat, probably the most widely used coin, generally made of silver and therefore to be considered as the direct predecessor of the penny. The name appears to come from Old Norse and is related to the word for herring. It has been suggested that the term arises from the Norsemen's willingness to accept payments in fish. And why not? Other transactions involved such commodities as livestock or quantities of corn and ancient Scandinavian society was rather more maritime than agrarian. At all events, sceat is a word that crops up frequently in relation to money during the seventh and eighth centuries, and it is interesting to speculate on whether the more modern English slang word 'scads', meaning 'lots of', refers back to the Saxon coin.

Other currency units included the 'thrimsa' (worth three sceats and possibly derived from the Latin *trium*), the 'ora' (obviously referring to gold), the 'mancus' and the 'dirhem' (Arab again, the former meaning simply 'coined money', the latter an actual coin). The thrimsa was fairly short-lived and may have been the name given to the early gold coins of the tribal kings. As to the others, they were probably used mostly as monies of account rather than coins, although it is known that mancusses did circulate in the northern English kingdoms during the seventh and eighth centuries, and it is likely that dirhems did appear as a result of trade with the Frankish empire, where Arab coins circulated freely as a result of the Moorish occupation of Spain and southern France. As for the ora, its value was reckoned at sixteen grains of fine gold, or the equivalent of five silver sceats, but in most early English texts this amount is referred to as a 'scilling'.

At the beginning of the eighth century the 'new' English had progressed from having no coinage at all to achieving the relatively complex outline of a currency system that would survive, with a few changes, far into the future. What benefits did currency bring our English forebears?

Money has four basic purposes: as a unit of account, as a medium of exchange, as a standard against which the value of things can be measured and as a store of value that can be saved for the future. The earliest form of ready money, recorded in China about 1200 BC, was the shell of a mollusc called a cowrie. You could buy and sell goods for a certain number of cowrie shells, which was more efficient than the barter system, and presumably you could save any you received and build up a store for future purchases. Where the system proved lacking was as a standard of value. The shells themselves had little or no intrinsic worth so the number that would buy an ox, for instance, would be purely notional in that it was based on supply and demand in the oxen market rather than on the supply of money. That made the economic system very one-sided, with the balance in favour of the producer against the consumer. How could you know if you were getting a fair deal?

Six centuries later the Lydians of Asia Minor had a better idea when they started producing coins made from electrum, a natural amalgam of gold and silver. Precious metals had long been made into desirable objects capable of being used as a medium of exchange, but these could be unwieldy and were difficult to judge in purely economic terms because the intrinsic value was affected by the beauty and craftsmanship of the object. Ingots of pure gold and silver had been traded for centuries, so it was a logical step to take the metals and melt them down into small coins which both had a worth of their own and could be used to establish the market value of commodities, goods and services.

Trade was the spur, of course. Throughout the civilised world societies were developing beyond the point where they could sustain themselves through agriculture alone. They needed to buy and sell not only commodities such as wool but also manufactured products to provide employment and a means of living for growing populations. The ancient Babylonians, the Romans and even the agrarian Saxons had established factories turning out clothing, pottery, brooches, weapons and so on. But industry needs expanding markets if it is to prosper and markets rely on an efficient medium of exchange and value. In short, they need money.

Having invented metal money, the Lydians opted for fixed coin weights in fine gold and silver, but maintaining that standard took no account of market forces and led to the problem of what to do when the supply of bullion ran low or price inflation occurred. The way round that was to mix gold or silver with base metals so that the bullion weight could be varied according to prevailing economic conditions, thus making the use of money more flexible, and to develop a fixed relationship of value between the precious metals. In the Persian empire it was thirteen and a third silver for one gold, while the ancient Macedonians chose ten for one. The Romans settled on a ratio of twelve silver for one gold, while the Arab empire had a decimal system that translated in European terms to about six and a half for one. Among the Gothic tribes of northern and eastern Europe the ratio was eight for one.

Under such systems any domestic coin could be judged in relation to any other: you simply needed more or fewer to keep to the ratio. The bullion weights also made it easy to use coins internationally, since they could be related to the prevailing gold–silver ratios. Money met its four economic criteria and, for the authorities who controlled it, there was the added bonus of charging a fee for the minting of coins – typically between ten and twelve per cent of the bullion weight – and thereby not only making a profit but also manipulating the basic value of the coinage to suit themselves.

Saxon England, as a latecomer in monetary terms, had no such standard. The sceat and the stycca, the dirhem and the mancus were essentially regional in character, sometimes made from silver, sometimes from copper or brass, and founded on different value systems – Roman, Arabic or Gothic. Broad differences in value made exchange difficult, especially in overseas trade. There is evidence that the Frankish empire, for instance, was suspicious of English coins, while some sources suggest that Arab merchants simply refused to accept them (which may explain why the dirhem was used in the prime trading area of the south-east). What was needed was a unified standard and a coinage that would be recognised anywhere in the known world.

Before that could happen, of course, England itself had to achieve a degree of unity. It needed an overlord with the military and political skills to bind the seven kingdoms together and create a power to rival the Frankish empire under Charlemagne. In the middle of the eighth century such a leader emerged.

King Offa of Mercia is one of the most shadowy yet most important figures of the later Dark Ages. Chiefly remembered for the great Offa's Dyke, the seventy-mile earthwork he had built to let the Welsh know where his kingdom began, this ruler had the vision, the ambition and the will – not to mention the ego – to create a putative English state more than half a century before the title 'Rex Anglorum' could really be applied with confidence. Relatively little is known about him. No contemporary chronicler recorded the details of his reign and a lot of what we can discover is the stuff of legend and folk memory. Probably it would not be stretching the truth to describe Offa as a power-hungry thug. 'You know very well how much blood he shed,' observed the monastic commentator Alcuin of York in one of his letters. Yet this was the man who, among other achievements, created the currency that would see England, subsequently Britain, through the next 1200 years – the

English penny and, by extension, the English pound.

The massive structure of Offa's Dyke gives us a clue to the king's pretensions. He was not content to be just another tribal warlord and in fact he is thought to have been the first English monarch to claim kingship by divine right. He certainly regarded himself as the equal of the greatest European leader and statesman of the age, the Emperor Charlemagne. But the engineering and more particularly the detailed design that produced the Dyke tend to show the king as a man with a keen interest in matters technical as well as political. That side of him would be reflected in his coinage, along with an appreciation of artistic merit.

It might have been the Franks who actually gave Offa the idea for the penny. Charlemagne's father, the quaintly named Pepin The Short, had in 752 begun to mint a small silver coin known as the denier – after the Roman denarius – which soon started to circulate in large numbers. Since the Franks were the main customers of English exporters, this new currency attracted a good deal of interest. By the time Offa seized the throne of Mercia in the English midlands after a civil war in 757, demand was growing for a standard currency that could easily be exchanged with the denier.

Having gained what was then the most influential Saxon kingdom, Offa immediately set about bringing the others under his control and, as if to emphasise his importance, he also began to issue new coinage bearing his image. Even his early attempts demonstrate technical skill and artistic sensibility. They were small, thick coins, containing between sixteen and twenty grains of silver, and were considered, by the Mercians at least, a great improvement on the old sceat.

What these coins were actually called is unclear, but the word 'penning', perhaps with the original meaning of 'a bond', was in use at the time and in the laws of King Ine of Wessex, written about 694, the coin of the smallest denomination is officially referred to as a penny. This might have been just local usage, though by the early eighth century the word is known to have been current in northern France, the most immediate destination of English trading ships.

The first indisputable penny appeared in Kent about ten years into Offa's reign. It has been ascribed to King Heaberht of Kent but was certainly minted on the instructions of Offa, who was the king's overlord. It was larger and flatter than the original Mercian coin and had a fixed weight of twenty-two and a half grains of silver. This was the prototype of the English coinage that would be in general use by the time of Offa's death in 796 and would remain the standard means of exchange for five centuries afterwards.

The quality and beauty of these pennies – and there would be many variations inspired by Offa – are unique in Anglo-Saxon coinage. The king supervised or possibly suggested the designs and personally controlled the minting process, which was carried out by moneyers whose names frequently appeared on the coins. The extraordinary degree of standardisation suggests that the number of mints was limited, the main one probably being at Canterbury, where some contemporary coins were also issued by the archbishop.

One particularly fine coin bearing Offa's name also features a highly artistic if somewhat unflattering portrait of him as a mop-headed man with unusually large ears. Earlier moneyers had made little attempt at portraiture, settling for crude representations of male heads and often symbolic devices such as a quiver of arrows. For the sake of his personal vanity and public glorification, Offa had clearly employed an artist of considerable talent – a tradition that would be followed by most later monarchs or their agents up to the present day.

A striking feature of Offa's currency is its almost total reliance on the new penny. Some halfpenny pieces were minted for him and a few gold coins were also produced, but these appear to have been short-lived. The reason for this is obscure, since documents of the period refer to a variation of the Arab mancus as a unit of account, worth about twenty pence, and the scilling (later shilling) weight of one twentieth of a pound, or five pennies, is also in evidence, though no equivalent coin existed.

Unlike his European neighbours Offa chose a system of value on a scale between six and a half and six and two-thirds for one, almost identical to the Arab system. Though Arab coins circulated widely in the north of France it was only in the far south, which had been occupied by the Saracens, where the Arab ratio was prevalent. The likeliest explanation for Offa's choice of ratio is that it would have made English pennies most easily exchangeable for the Arab mancus, which appears to have been the only gold coin freely circulating in Britain at the time.

Even more directly, Arab influence is seen in a silver coin of the eighth century minted for King Aethelberht II of the East Angles – a contemporary of Offa and ultimately a victim of the Mercian's ruthless ambition – and resembling the Arabs' half-dirhem, though the East Anglians called it a sceat or a penny.

But there is another possible reason for adoption of the

Arab scale, one that casts a fascinating cloud of mystery over the origins of the English currency. It concerns a coin that later became known as 'Offa's dinar' (a dirhem by another name) and it raises the question of how closely Arabs were involved in the production of what would become the traditional money of England.

This coin is one of a very small number known to have been struck in gold in England and bears the legend 'Offa Rex'. It also carries a series of inscriptions that have little to do with a Christian Saxon king. For a start the moneyer noted in Arabic, 'In the name of God. This dinar was struck in the year 157', which equates to 774 AD in the western calendar. The Arabic lines continue: 'Mahomet is the messenger of God, who sent him with the doctrine and true faith to prevail over every other religion' and 'There is no other God than one God – He has no equal'. The few other gold coins of the period carried the names of the moneyers, among them Pendraed and Ciolheard, though in neither case did Offa's name or likeness appear on them. This has led to suggestions that the king relied heavily for his new coinage on Arab moneyers and even claims that he embraced Islam.

It is true that the Arabs were in the forefront of science, technology and art, and that as a result their coinage was far superior to any produced in Europe. It has also been found that moneyers with Arab-sounding names were operating in England during the seventh and eighth centuries, though their numbers may have been greatly exaggerated. But this does not mean there were no English mints capable of producing the new coinage. The techniques for cutting the steel dies in which coins were formed, and for refining gold and silver to the precise quantities required, could have been learned from Arab masters by English apprentices, as the work of Pendraed and Ciolheard testify – although it is true that later kings were obliged to import continental experts when they wished to improve the coinage. And even if Offa's dinar was made by an Arab, why did a king who insisted on supervising every stage of production permit an English coin to appear with Arabic inscriptions?

Two explanations other than Arab provenance are possible, though neither is entirely plausible.

One is that the famous dinar was simply copied from the Arab coins then circulating widely and produced as an incentive for Moorish merchants to trade with the English, hence the Arabic inscription. That seems a little far-fetched. If there was commerce between England and the Arab world it is unlikely to have been substantial enough to warrant special coinage. The first bilateral trade deal in English history was concluded between Offa and Charlemagne, which surely indicates where the bulk of imports and exports lay. In any case Offa had so improved the English currency that any reluctance to accept it on the part of Arabian traders had presumably been overcome, especially since the value ascribed to it followed the traditional Arab ratio.

Another possibility is that the dinar was struck for ceremonial purposes. In that case, for whose benefit was it? One of the Offa legends suggests that the king made a visit to Rome late in his reign, did homage to the pope and agreed to donate the sum of 365 mancusses each year as thanks to St Peter for the blessings granted to his kingdom. Tradition has this as the origin of the Romesceat, later known as Peter's Pence, which became a sort of papal tax levied on England. Was Offa's dinar, at sixty grains of fine gold, struck for the purpose of making that payment? Well, if it was, adding Arabic inscriptions was hardly the best way of impressing the pontiff. Moreover, another tradition has Romesceat going back to King Ine of Wessex, which would seem more likely in view of the fact that by Offa's time the sceat had been replaced by the penny almost everywhere except in Scandinavian-leaning Northumbria. Finally, there are serious doubts about the veracity of the Offa story based on his character and his view of himself in the political firmament. As the self-declared equal of Charlemagne the 'Rex Totius Anglorum Patriae' was unlikely to submit to a papacy that had already acknowledged the sovereignty of the Frankish emperor.

So this remarkable coin must remain a mystery, an exotic curiosity in the history of the English currency that began with the obscure King Offa. By the time of his death at the end of the eighth century his countrymen – at least those who were free men and had a reasonable standard of living – had become accustomed to using money in going about their everyday business and England had begun to establish itself as an important trading nation. It had also started to suffer the first incursions by a new wave of invaders, the Vikings, whose presence would help to provoke the next important development in the history of the penny and the pound.

As Abbot Alcuin noted, the end of Offa's reign marked 'not a strengthening of his kingdom, but its ruin'. English money, on the other hand, would go from strength to strength.

3

Coins of the Realm

This year was Ipswich plundered; and very soon afterwards was ealdorman Britnoth slain at Maldon. In this same year it was resolved that tribute should be given, for the first time, to the Danes, for the great terror they occasioned by the sea-coast. That was first ten thousand pounds.

Anglo-Saxon Chronicle, AD 991

If the history of the penny we still use in England today begins with King Offa, that of the pound owes a great deal to the arrival of the Vikings on British shores shortly before Offa's death. The Norsemen's attempts to conquer the islands, and the ultimately successful efforts by the Anglo-Saxons to stop them, led to a vast expansion of the money supply and the emergence of regular cash transactions that were probably greater than any that had been made before. Large sums were obviously required for defence and the recovery of lands and property laid waste, but on top of that was the policy of trying to buy off the invaders with huge amounts of cash. For the best part of 300 years the English economy would be ruled by ever-increasing demands for money with which either to repulse or appease the fierce and skilful warriors who threatened to turn Britain into a Scandinavian province.

At first it seemed like nothing more than piracy. The earliest Viking raid appears to have been at Portland, on the south coast, in 786, carried out by a strong Norwegian war party. In historical terms it was a minor incident, but by the time Offa died ten years later such incursions were becoming more regular, and the Norsemen were establishing settlements in Ireland and the far north of Scotland. They needed land. The loose alliance among the three Scandinavian peoples – Norwegians, Swedes and the dominant Danes – was in danger of breaking down because of disputes over living space and many chieftains saw emigration as the best option. Some turned eastwards to Russia, others settled in what is now Germany and other parts of the Frankish empire. For increasing numbers, however, it was the fertile islands of Britain that held the greatest attraction.

The Anglo-Saxons were ill prepared for the coming onslaught. The forced unity of Offa's reign was falling apart as the kingdoms of Mercia and Wessex battled for supremacy and the Northumbrians, who had never submitted to Offa, fought to maintain their independence. For the next two decades a series of more or less obscure kings rose and fell, until in 825 King Egbert of Wessex inflicted a heavy defeat on Mercian armies and began the conquest of the entire region. Four years later

Egbert's military prowess gained him the acknowledged over-lordship of Northumbria and it looked as if there would be a new 'Rex Anglorum', since Kent, Sussex, Surrey and Essex were already under his effective control. But none of the documents of the period refer to Egbert as King of England, only of the West Saxons and Kentishmen, and it is likely that his power outside Wessex was very limited. His overlordships appear to have been essentially ceremonial and even in Mercia, which was under his direct control for some time, a rebellion seems to have resulted in the restoration of an independent king named Wiglaf, previously deposed by Egbert.

Meanwhile the Viking menace was growing. A substantial force wreaked havoc on the Isle of Sheppey in Kent in 835 and there were further serious raids in 841 and the following year, again in Kent but also in East Anglia and at Southampton. The King of Northumbria was killed by an invading force in 844 and an important battle against the Danes in the Dorset region is recorded in 845. By the next decade there were 'heathen' forces camped in the Midlands and Northumbria, and the first recorded naval battle in English history took place off Sandwich in Kent, when a Viking fleet was defeated. Danish armies were now wintering in England, ready for the next campaigning season. In 851 a force of probably several thousand men, landed from 350 ships, sacked Canterbury and stormed London before they were driven off by the Wessex army of King Aethelwulf, Egbert's son. For the next fifteen years, however, the Vikings kept coming back and each year they gained more ground and established more camps.

For the English the fighting and the spreading ravages of the Danes were becoming expensive and the situation soon grew worse. A serious invasion force apparently led by one Ivar The Boneless landed in East Anglia in 865 and proceeded to fight, rape and pillage its way round the country. Their plan of campaign, such as it was, involved securing strong defensive positions, and spreading terror and destruction throughout the surrounding areas until the inhabitants bribed them to stop. The *Anglo Saxon Chronicle* notes for 865: 'This year sat the heathen army in the isle of Thanet, and made peace with the men of Kent, who promised money therewith.' Not enough, as it turned out, because the Danes broke the agreement and under cover of night 'stole up the country, and overran all Kent eastward'.

That incident exemplifies the self-defeating nature of the bribery policy that seems to have emerged under the guidance of local Church leaders. Seeing that their terror tactics worked, the Vikings merely spread their violent activities more widely and increased their demands for money in areas where they were already practising extortion. On the other hand it is difficult to see what else the unfortunate victims could have done. Northumbria and Mercia were wracked by civil wars, which severely weakened their capacity to respond to the invaders, and even in the reasonably united Wessex and its southern dependencies a line of short-lived kings – all the sons of Aethelwulf – made it almost impossible to maintain a coherent strategy of defence. It would be left to Aethelwulf's fourth son, King Alfred, to subdue the Danish threat and lay the true foundations of the future English state, including its national currency.

The beginning of the new reign in 871 was inauspicious, to say the least. Wessex was fighting the Danes on all fronts with not much success and Alfred took the crown when his elder brother died during what became known as the 'year of battles'. On the very day of the dead king's funeral at Wimborne in Dorset, Saxon troops suffered a heavy defeat and a month later Alfred himself had to flee with the remnants of his army. A further year of disasters followed and the king was forced into the by now traditional bribe in order to prevent the Danes from invading Wessex. The uneasy peace lasted only a year or two and in 878 the foreigners fell upon Alfred's kingdom again, occupying Hampshire and Wiltshire. The king was driven back to the Somerset marshes, where the story of his famous incompetence at baking cakes is set but where he also raised an army that smashed the Danish force and gave Alfred the power to conclude a peace treaty.

England was now split into two states along a line running roughly from London to Chester. The greater part, from East Anglia to the Scottish lowlands, was firmly under Danish control, but the two ancient and most powerful Anglo-Saxon kingdoms of Mercia and Wessex were saved from Viking occupation. To bind the survivors together, Alfred arranged for the marriage of his daughter to the Mercian king and set about consolidating what he referred to, for the first time in history, as Angelcynn – the forerunner of 'Englaland', which eventually became England.

Alfred remains the only British monarch to merit the title 'The Great' and he earned it by much more than his stand against the Danish invaders. Apart from being a military man, he was an intellectual with an interest and considerable skills in geography, science, literature, education and economics. He created something approaching a standing army, recognising the needs of the agricultural economy by organising it so that in normal times only half its soldiers would be on duty. He is regarded as the founder of the English navy, having supervised the building of large warships with up to sixty oars in recognition of the fact that the country's best defence against future invasion was the sea that surrounded it. He created a network of well-planned fortified towns, known as burhs, setting the pattern of urbanisation that would so influence the course of English history. The modern cities of Oxford, Chichester, Winchester and Exeter, among others, owe their origins to this period.

All this required money, of course, as did repairing the homes, churches and monasteries devastated by the fighting. Amazingly, the output of the rural economy appears not to have been disrupted too seriously by the wars against the Vikings, and the mints at Winchester and Canterbury must have been operating continuously to finance the national defence. So must the London mint, although its coinage varied depending upon whether the Saxons or the Danes were occupying it at the time. Having gained control of these mints, Alfred added five more and set about a large-scale reconstruction of the currency. For this there was a political as well as an economic motive.

The Danes in the north and east used the old Gothic currency system, as did areas now under Saxon control that had previously been occupied by the invaders. For a time Alfred allowed that to continue, though he minted new silver pennies and other coins, which have become known as 'offering pieces', sent to Rome by the king to help support the papacy under the system of Peter's Pence apparently established during the eighth century and by this time, apparently, an accepted 'tax'.

The early new pennies were light in weight, about fifteen grains of fine silver, and carried a bust of Alfred on the face. They were clearly designed to be acceptable to the Danes since a table of monetary values was included in the Anglo-Danish peace treaty. The shilling of account was valued at five pence and there is also the mention of another measure, the mark, worth 150 pence.

The mark was to become an increasingly important monetary unit during the Middle Ages under the pressure of price and wage inflation, which would lead to dramatic increases in the money supply and therefore a need for additional units of account. The shilling became unwieldy beyond a certain point and the pound was reserved for very large sums, so the mark came somewhere in the middle.

Like so many other terms for monies of account, the origin of the mark is uncertain but there is a case for suggesting that it began – perhaps in its Old Norse form 'mork' – as a measure of the legal weight ratio of silver to gold, which in the Gothic monetary system was eight for one. That would make it the direct ancestor of the pound. Later it was used simply to express a weight of gold and silver bullion, meaning half a pound (originally six ounces when the libra was still counted on the Roman measure), and finally it reappeared as a money of account, reckoned at two-thirds of a pound. Its inclusion in the Saxon treaty with the Danish leader Guthrum proves that Alfred's first coinage retained the Gothic system because the 2250 grains it represents is in rough correlation to the value of silver against gold traditionally used in Scandinavia. To the Saxons, though, the term mark originally meant simply 'a number of men or things', giving us the word 'market'.

It must have suited Alfred for a few years to go along with the Danish currency, but it seems he was determined that his Angelcynn should have a distinctive monetary system because he changed it twice more during his reign, moving further away from the Gothic valuations and towards the classical Roman system.

With this in mind, the silver content of the pennies in Alfred's second coinage, introduced about 878, was five grains more than in those of his first coin issue. Since the amount of base metal was reduced in proportion, this made no difference to the penny's value relative to monies of account. A shilling weight was still assessed at five pence and 150 pennies continued to be counted as a mark. What had changed, however, was the value of the penny against the gold coins then in circulation. The effect was to increase the weight of silver required in exchange for a gold coin, altering the ratio from about eight for one – as used in the Gothic system – to ten for one, or closer to the valuation of gold accepted in Rome, which continued to be twelve ounces of silver for one ounce of gold.

For those of us accustomed to taking money at face value, because the modern coinage in daily use contains no precious metals, these relative values are not easy to grasp. Perhaps the best way to put them into context is to take the Arabian gold mancus as the standard, which in the ninth century was accepted in England and most of the rest of Europe where few, if any, domestic gold coins were produced. The mancus contained sixty grains of fine gold and was valued at thirty silver pennies. King Alfred's first pennies each contained fifteen grains of fine silver, which meant that the silver weight of thirty of them would amount to 450 grains. Sixty grains of gold, therefore, was worth 450 of silver, giving a ratio of seven and a half for one, close to the accepted Gothic measure. When, in his second coinage, the king raised the penny's silver content to twenty grains, thirty pence added up to 600 grains: a ratio against the mancus of ten for one, or nearer to the Roman valuation of gold.

The effect of this increase in the silver weight of the penny was to uprate both the gold standard and the English coinage, the penny becoming more valuable because of its higher bullion content. The revaluation may suggest that there had been an increase in economic activity to improve the supply of bullion, but more likely it was a sign that as Arab influence waned in northern Europe in the face of spreading Christianity, the circulation of the gold mancus was coming to an end. Certainly by the time of Alfred's next recoinage, almost at the turn of the century, a lighter coin of fifty grains of fine gold had replaced the old mancus and this was reflected in the valuation determined by the king. The weight of the penny remained at twenty grains fine but the exchange rate against the lighter mancus was also retained at thirty pence: 600 grains of silver against fifty of gold, or twelve for one. The English currency was now on a par with that of the Frankish empire, which with the support of the pope was the most powerful economic force in Europe.

At this time, however, the shilling and the mark, rather than the pound, remained the most commonly used units of account. For example, in the laws agreed by Alfred and Guthrum for the purposes of the peace treaty, the following provision appears:

How a twelve-hynde man shall be paid for.
A twelve-hynde man's wer is twelve hundred shillings. A two-hynde man's wer is two hundred shillings. If any one be slain, let him be paid for according to his birth.

This law relates to the financial value ('wer') placed on a man in relation to his position in the community and the paying of 'wergild', or blood-money, by anyone who killed such a man. The term 'hynde' refers to a group of ten men, so someone who had twelve hyndes or 120 men at his disposal would have been a substantial figure, vital to the agricultural economy and therefore worth his weight in cash. The going rate was apparently a hundred shillings per hynde, which at five pence to the shilling adds up in the case of a twelve-hynde man to 6000 silver pennies. Even on the basis of Alfred's early coinage, at fifteen grains of silver to the penny, the total would have been the equivalent of about eighteen pounds, though the notion of that money of account was clearly not established.

However, what evidence there is shows that either in the wake of Alfred's third monetary system, shortly before his death in 899, or early in the following century the English pound began to make its appearance in the record books. At about the same time a single national currency was established by law. Both would be promoted by King Alfred's illegitimate grandson, Athelstan, who seems to have been something of a chip off the old block.

Alfred's immediate successor was his son Edward, known to history as The Elder, whose achievements have been rather overlooked alongside those of his father and his son. As one might expect, he had been well educated and thoroughly trained in the arts of kingship, from soldiering to diplomacy, and he had inherited Alfred's keen mind and inexhaustible patience. A methodical man, Edward planned meticulously but also displayed a good deal of dash and verve in his military campaigns. By the middle of his twenty-five-year reign he had retaken large swathes of territory from the by then fragmented Danish armies and in effect created the prototype kingdom of England.

What he could not accomplish by force, his acute political sense brought about through diplomacy. Alfred's overlordship of Mercia was converted by Edward into an unbreakable alliance and he also secured the allegiance of the Scots, the Welsh and even, finally, of the unruly Northumbrians. He continued his father's creation of a system of government and social organisation based on the rule of law and further developed the coinage, making his pennies even more like those of Rome. Interestingly, one success he chose to celebrate on his coins was the planning of more fortified burhs. On the reverse of a silver penny in the British Museum is the representation of a classically styled building that looks like a castle keep.

It was Edward The Elder's remarkable combination of abilities that helped to make Athelstan, his son by a mistress, the self-declared 'king of the English, elevated by the right hand of the Almighty, which is Christ, to the throne of the whole kingdom of Britain'. Not that it was quite so simple, of course. When Edward died in 924 the bold and prodigiously energetic Athelstan had to beat off rivals for the throne and later he had to replay many of his father's military campaigns in order to maintain the supremacy of the House of Wessex – a task in which he is notable for never having lost a battle. At the end of it his power was even greater than his father's had been and in addition he had placed England firmly in the main stream of European politics and society.

A builder rather than an innovator, King Athelstan also possessed the sort of vision that had motivated his grandfather and, like Alfred, he understood the relationship between a state and its currency. Accordingly, just four years into his reign, Athelstan held a council at Grateley in Hampshire where he promulgated a unique new law:

> ... that there be one money over all the king's dominion, and that no man mint except within port. And if the moneyer be guilty, let the hand be struck off that wrought the offence, and, be set up on the money-smithy but if it be an accusation, and he is willing to clear himself; then let him go to the hot-iron, and clear the hand therewith with which he is charged that fraud to have wrought. And if at the ordeal he should be guilty, let the like be done as here before ordained.
>
> In Canterbury seven moneyers; four the king's, and two the bishop's, one the abbot's.
>
> At Rochester three; two the king's, and one the bishop's.
>
> At London eight.
>
> At Winchester six.
>
> At Lewes two.
>
> At Hastings one.

Another at Chichester.

At Hampton two.

At Wareham two.

At Exeter two.

At Shaftesbury two.

Else, at the other burhs one.

So England became the first important European power since ancient Rome to have a single currency, fully six centuries before the same thing was achieved by its main rival, France, and some 900 years before Germany acquired its mark and Italy its lira. The concept of national unity was supported by monetary union and equally by central control of both the money supply and the state. There would be many diversions in the 1000-year history of the English pound, but its connection with a unified state would always remain and would ultimately always be respected. For that enduring idea we have King Athelstan to thank.

But establishing a single English currency was one thing – ensuring consistent standards for it was quite another. In spite of the reforms of Alfred, Edward The Elder and Athelstan, there had still been nothing to match the quality and beauty of the pennies produced during the reign of King Offa. The busts of the later monarchs were considerably cruder than on Offa's coins and the lettering was in general poorly executed. One reason was no doubt the vast increase in the amounts of coins minted in order to meet the costs of the Danish wars and their aftermath, and the consequent rise in the number of moneyers. Though the monetary law of Athelstan required minting to take place only 'in port' – that is inside the walls of a city where the royal or episcopal writ could run easily and strict regulations were in force – it was difficult to be sure that the appointed moneyers had the necessary skills. Probably they were chosen more for their technical abilities than for their artistic talents.

The techniques of metallurgy were presumably well known throughout the civilised world by the ninth and tenth centuries, so that the weighing and melting down of silver and the maintenance of its proper content in coinage were no longer particularly problematic. The English penny would not have been so rapidly and so widely accepted – as well as copied abroad – unless its weight–value ratio could be more or less guaranteed. What does seem to have caused trouble was the making of the steel dies in which the coins were cast. Perhaps that helps to support the theory that the proficiency shown in the coins of Offa came from Arab moneyers, or at least hands-on Arab training.

Eventually, signs of marked technical improvement did begin to appear. King Edgar The Peaceable, who came to the throne in 959, used the sixteen war-free years over which he presided to undertake a thoroughgoing reform of the coinage, the results of which would set the pattern for the next two centuries. Along with laws regulating weights and measures, and instituting a fixed price for the vital commodity of wool, he increased the number of mints in operation to forty and recalled all the coins currently in circulation for recycling in a new and completely uniform style. The moneyers were selected with care, the king controlled the issuing of dies and the quality of the coins produced was strictly monitored.

'And let one money pass throughout the king's dominion,' noted Edgar's law of about 973, 'and let no man refuse; and let one measure and one weight pass; such as is observed in London and Winchester.'

The new coins had a shape considerably more regular than that of most of their predecessors and the legend 'EDGAR REX ANGLORUM' was very skilfully executed. One might have reservations about the quality of the royal image, but even so it was better than the coined heads of either Alfred or Athelstan. This quality must reflect the care taken by either the king or his officials, because his son Edward The Martyr, who was murdered in the third year of his reign, had much less success when he tried to copy his father's design on his own brief coinage.

Edgar's other monetary innovation stemmed from his realisation that the standard of the currency could only be maintained through a regular cycle of recoinage. Not only were the soft silver pennies easily damaged but they were also subject to deliberate destruction or debasement. The lack of any small change meant that a halfpenny was literally that – a penny cut in two. Achieving equal halves cannot have been easy, while the condition of a farthing, or quarter-penny, can easily be imagined. And then, as now, there were the criminally minded who would seek to enrich themselves at the expense of others. The temptation to shave small amounts of almost pure silver off each coin that came into one's possession must have been hard to resist. There are records of pennies being skimmed to almost half their original weight, and of the perpetrators, when identified, being executed.

For reasons that are not known a coinage cycle of six years was established. That probably had less to do with the natural lifespan of a penny than with the king's belief that such a period would be acceptable to people who had to turn in their old coins and pay a commission to the mint – and therefore the king – to receive a new issue. Some of his mediaeval successors were less reasonable, imposing this early form of wealth tax as often as every three years or, when they were really desperate to raise revenue, even shorter terms.

Silver pennies of this sort had by now become very popular throughout the country, not only in the 'England' controlled by Edgar. Given the extremely crude nature of contemporary coins produced in, say, the Viking Northumbria of the aptly named King Eric Blood-Axe or the Wales of Hywel Dda, it is not hard to see why. Yet it is worth remembering that a great deal of trade, and even the collection of taxes, was carried on in kind. One of the earliest lists of tolls in England concerns what was, in the tenth century, the River Thames port of Billingsgate in London and it shows that when it came to payment, money was only one option. It also demonstrates that ancient financial terminology was still very much in evidence.

> If a small ship arrives at Billingsgate it will give one
> obole [halfpenny] as thelony [import or export duty];
> if a larger ship, and if it has a sail, one denarius. If it
> is a long ship, or a barge, and if it stays there, one
> denarius [penny] as thelony.
>
> From a ship full of timber, one log as thelony. A
> freight ship gives thelony on three days a week,
> namely, Sunday, Tuesday and Thursday. If anyone
> comes to the bridge with a boat full of fish, he will
> give one obole as thelony in order to sell the fish;
> from a larger ship he will pay one denarius.

The men of Rouen who come with wine or deep-sea fish will pay six solidi [shillings] for a large ship as a toll, and will give one twentieth of their large fish. The men of Flanders, Ponthieu, Normandy, and France showed their merchandise and were exempt from toll. Those of Houck, Liége, and Nivelles who went through our territories paid a toll for the right to display their goods, and thelony. The men of the Emperor who came in their own ships were held, like ourselves, worthy of good laws. Moreover they were permitted to buy and take on their ships uncarded wool, cut off pieces of fat, and three live hogs . . . And they must give thelony; and on Christmas Day two grey garments and one brown, ten pounds of pepper, gloves for five men, two leathern tuns of vinegar, and as much at Easter; from a basket of fowls, one hen as toll; and from a basket of eggs, five eggs as toll if they come to sell them. Dealers in fat, who sell cheese and butter, will pay one denarius fourteen days before Christmas and another denarius seven days after Christmas.

It may be that the burgesses of Billingsgate did not use the terms penny and shilling, or merely that the Latin words were preferred to the vernacular in official documents. At all events, the toll record shows how extensive foreign trade was and therefore how important a trustworthy monetary system. The kings Alfred, Athelstan and Edgar had founded and developed such a system, and brought it firmly under governmental control. They left to their successors and their emerging nation a structure that could help propel it towards prosperity and economic expansion that would be virtually unmatched until the latter half of the nineteenth century.

The immediate future, though, proved to be less than bright. By the last quarter of the tenth century a succession of three strong and visionary rulers had first fought for and later maintained peace and an extraordinary degree of national unity. But the Danes had not yet exhausted their attempts to dominate Britain and the years following the death of Edgar The Peaceable in 975 would threaten to overturn much of the progress that had been made under the late Saxon kings. Remarkably, through nearly a century of upheaval English money would survive rather better than the new English monarchy. It had to, because it faced pressure that would result in pennies being minted at a rate never seen before.

A policy of trying to buy off the new Danish invaders would at its height see some seventy-five mints producing a total of up to 40,000,000 pennies at a time. With such large amounts to be accounted for, the English pound was about to come into its own.

4

Danegeld to Domesday

*At Michaelmas he must pay ten pence tax, and at
Martinmas twenty-three sesters of barley and two
hens; at Easter one young sheep or twopence.*

Obligations of a villein under Anglo-Saxon law

He has left his name to history as King Ethelred The
Unready, though in reality his title is simply a mis-
reading of a pun on his name. The name Aethelraed
means 'noble counsel', to which some tenth-century wag added
'unraedy', meaning 'no counsel'. On the other hand, it might
well be argued that the younger son of Edgar The Peaceable
was far from well prepared to take the throne when his half-
brother Edward was killed in 978, even though his own
supporters are the chief suspects for the murder. Neither,
perhaps, was he quite ready for a new wave of Viking invasions
more violent and determined than any seen since the dark early

days of King Alfred. But the years have been less than kind to poor Aethelraed, who might rather have been dubbed 'The Unlucky'. In a troubled reign that ended in disaster, he probably did the best he could with the limited talents at his disposal and the personality flaws that marked him. And if nothing else he was a great survivor, ruling – if that is the right word – for no fewer than thirty-eight years.

For the purposes of this story, though, the lasting legacy of Aethelraed The Unraedy is Danegeld, the notorious levy raised in a vain attempt to buy off the Vikings who were trying to take over Britain. As was indicated earlier, local policies of appeasement had been tried by earlier generations with only limited success, so it is somewhat surprising to find the king pursuing a course that had not only failed previously but also tended to make his own situation worse. Any self-respecting brigand offered cash as a result of his depredations is likely to indulge in even more murder, rape and pillage on the ground that he will receive an even better deal next time and so it proved with Danegeld.

At the beginning it seemed the Danish raids were to be no more than a reprise of the piratical adventures that had been going on for a couple of hundred years and no doubt the sum of £10,000 recorded at Ipswich by the *Anglo-Saxon Chronicle* in 991 would have seemed a reasonable price to pay for the marauders to board their long ships and go back home. But of course the prospect of easy money tempted others to try their hand and the next payment made was more than double that given to the Ipswich raiders. As the scale of the bribes grew, Aethelraed was forced to press more mints into service, so that by the beginning of the new century he had something like ninety available to produce the increasing numbers of coins needed, although only about three-quarters of them appear to have been operating at any one time.

This critical need for sound money – the Danes, after all, wanted to be sure of what they were getting – and the resulting drain of coinage appears to have led to the appearance of what might be politely termed independent minting. Aethelraed reacted promptly by passing strict laws against counterfeiting:

> And we command, in order that no one shall speak ill of pure money of correct weight, that it shall be struck only in whatever port it may be struck in my kingdom, upon pain of my displeasure. And concerning merchants who bring false or chipped money to our port, we have said that they shall defend themselves if they are able; if they cannot, let them incur the penalty of their wer or of their life just as the king wishes . . .

The demand for coins also affected the monetary system as a whole. During the early part of his reign, Aethelraed had issued silver pennies weighing twenty grains, much as his predecessors had done. During the year before the first large payment to the Danes he had increased the weight of the penny to twenty-five grains, giving only four to the shilling as opposed to the earlier five and therefore just forty-eight shillings to the pound against the previous sixty. That may have been done for reasons of trade because its effect would have been to make imports cheaper, since the English penny would have been overvalued against continental coinage. But by 1016, when the tribute paid to Danish armies had reached the order of £50,000 or £60,000, Aethelraed's penny was down to just eighteen and a half grains of silver and there were twelve pence to the shilling – an equivalence that would later become familiar to generations of Britons, as would the following calculation of twenty shillings to the pound. They were the numbers finally attached to £.s.d.

Aethelraed's late coinage was by way of being a primitive form of the competitive devaluation of currency that would be practised by much later administrations in the constant battle for economic advantage. Whereas the twenty-five-grain penny had been overvalued against the European bullion standard, the lighter one was undervalued. English exports became much cheaper on the Continent while goods from the sort of regions we saw trading at Billingsgate in the last chapter would have risen sharply in price. In consequence, more of the newly minted money remained at home and there was a constant supply of recyclable silver coming in from overseas. Available records suggest that in spite of the scores of millions of pennies handed over to the Danes, the money supply remained fairly constant, though it was not evenly distributed throughout the country.

Part of the reason for the constancy of supply was a fiscal innovation introduced by the king. With money flooding out of his coffers into Viking hands during the early years of the eleventh century, Aethelraed decided that the burden must be shared by the whole country. His solution was to impose what was called 'heregeld', which is literally translated as 'army debt'. This tax seems to have raised something between £5000 and £6000 a year, and was intended sufficiently to replenish a treasury depleted by appeasement so that a mercenary army could be maintained to keep the Danes at bay. Unfortunately, it was no more successful than the bribes, 'for the Danish army went about as it pleased', according to a contemporary account, 'and the English levy caused the people of the country every sort of harm, so that they profited neither from the native army nor the foreign army'.

In fact, the English became so desperate that in 1013 they decided to acknowledge the reality of Viking occupation across most of the country and chose the Danish leader Sweyn Forkbeard as their king, forcing Aethelraed to flee to Normandy. When Sweyn died the following year and his son Cnut was proclaimed king, Aethelraed returned to lead another taxpayers' army against the invaders, but although he had some early success it did him little good in the long run. He died in 1016 and a Danish king again sat on the throne of England. Heregeld survived Aethelraed, however, and subsequently became Danegeld, a tax exploited by a series of rulers until a later and more lasting invasion swept it away.

Aethelraed had changed the currency no fewer than seven times during his long reign, more or less in line with the cycle established by Edgar The Peaceable, but with his passing it was about to change again. The new king, Cnut – whose name is normally rendered in modern English as Canute – came out of a tradition very different from the one that had spread through England from the reign of King Offa.

The English had gradually strengthened their links with Rome and the church had become very much a power in the land. Even the coinage had altered, with King Alfred, to reflect Roman precepts more closely. The Scandinavians, on the other hand, had remained essentially Gothic in character and clung to their old gods, though many of those who had settled in England had converted to Christianity and accepted the concepts of the emerging English law. Cnut was not one of the latter, having succeeded his father as King of Denmark and Norway, but somewhat eccentrically he had been baptised into Christianity and, like many converts, he wore his religion very obviously on his sleeve. Whether this was out of conviction or mere political expediency is open to question, since the king was also notable for his cruelty and ruthlessness. The chroniclers of the twelfth century would have us believe that it was Cnut's humility before God that gave rise to the episode on the beach when he attempted to prove that not even a ruler of his stature could stem the oncoming sea, but the plain fact is that the great European power of the time was the Holy Roman Empire and it did an ambitious leader no harm to espouse the faith. What is equally true, though, is that his Christianity did him little good among his Scandinavian subjects, even if it helped to gain him support among the Saxon and Anglo-Norse aristocracy of England.

His accession to the English throne in 1016 brought few fundamental changes to the way the country was governed. Many of the courtly personnel remained the same as during the reign of Aethelraed – and Cnut even went so far as to marry the widow of his predecessor. What did alter, however, was the coinage as the new king officially recognised the division between the Anglo-Saxon parts of the country and the so-called Danelaw, and also incorporated his other kingdom to the north. For that reason the sheer variety of coins dating from Cnut's reign is remarkably wide.

In regions such as Viking Northumbria Gothic coinage had survived since the days of the early invasions, but it had been minted by rulers such as Eric Blood-Axe rather than the Saxon kings. With the entire country at his command, Cnut maintained the different identities but institutionalised what had always been the free exchange among the different types of currency.

The Gothic or Danish coins consisted of the old sceattas, oras and mancusses, following a silver-to-gold ratio of nine for one, slightly above the original Gothic value. The Roman-style or Christian coinage followed the £.s.d. pattern of previous reigns, although the penny went to a rate of about 300 to the pound and the silver–gold equivalence was again nine for one rather than the Roman twelve for one. That made it possible for coins from both traditions to be exchanged at thirty pence to the Arabian mancus.

Where there was no change, though, was in the heregeld – save for the amount and the fact that on this occasion it was levied in the first place not to raise an army but to send one back to Denmark. The chroniclers note that in 1018 'was the payment of the tribute over all England; that was, altogether, two and seventy thousand pounds, besides that which the citizens of London paid; and that was ten thousand five hundred pounds'. How much of that enormous sum, the equivalent of some 25,000,000 pennies, was paid in Gothic coins and how much in English is not recorded, but it may help to explain why the weight of the penny fell from its usual eighteen or twenty grains to as little as sixteen or even twelve grains. And the taxes went on. With two kingdoms to run and a sea between them, Cnut was often out of England and fell into the habit of leaving behind him a force of élite soldiery known as 'housecarls' which had to be paid for by a less than grateful citizenry.

Yet it was far from being all bad news. Though a hard man, Cnut was no brutal foreign dictator and in some ways he made Britain more united and influential than it had ever been, which is why he was accorded the accolade of 'The Great', even if it did not long survive him in the way it has done with Alfred. His was an Anglo-Scandinavian empire that encompassed Scotland and the Norwegian communities on the east coast of Ireland. Some of the rather regressive coinage of his reign, which had little technical or artistic merit, was minted in Dublin. He also had strong connections with the Continent, particularly what would ultimately prove to be the fateful one with Normandy. England lay in the midst of a putative European common market, so that it was not only taxes that greatly increased the demand for coinage but also a dramatic expansion of trade.

It was therefore a relatively peaceful and prosperous realm that Cnut left behind him when he died in 1035, a country with a highly developed system of government, a sophisticated legal process and an efficient monetary system – all of which would be of enormous benefit to England as it stood on the brink of a new world.

There was something of a dramatic pause before the new age arrived, marked only by the reign of the pious but ineffectual Edward The Confessor, founder of Westminster Abbey. He looked every inch a king, judging by the bearded image we have of him on the Bayeux Tapestry, but he was naïve and lacking in judgement to the extent that he even managed to mess up a successful currency, both debasing it and adding confusion to what had been a fairly standard system of values.

The weight of some of Edward's pennies varied between sixteen and a half and eighteen and a half grains of fine silver and at one stage they were contaminated with an amalgam of copper and zinc. There is reason to suspect that at least part of the excuse for this debasement was the continuing demand for Danegeld, some of which could have been paid in these lower-value coins.

The cycle of recoinage was reduced from six to three years, no doubt to increase profits from the seventy or so mints in operation, with the result that the reign produced ten different types of coin. Not only that, but there were at least two systems of valuation, though each was allegedly based on the £.s.d. standard and lacked the rationale of Cnut's Roman-Gothic formula. In the first scheme there were forty-eight shillings to the pound, against sixty in the second structure. The penny could be four or five to the shilling if it was a heavy coin of twenty to twenty-five grains, or more if it was one of the lighter variety. The zinc and copper mixture of the debased pennies reduced their silver content to just eight and a half grains, giving at least twelve to the shilling, but it is not clear whether these were used mostly for Danegeld or were in general circulation. In any case, the situation must have been extremely confusing for traders, especially if they were importing or exporting, and made worse by the fact that the silver–gold ratio was constantly changing, too.

Yet if the results were less than satisfactory, the system that produced the coins was impressively efficient, as was demonstrated after Edward The Confessor died on 5 January 1066. The very next day, the unroyal Earl of Wessex had himself crowned as Harold II and he must have started to issue coinage almost immediately because nearly a hundred different moneyers turned out pennies during his violent nine-month reign.

Harold certainly needed money, facing as he did military threats from William of Normandy, King Harald Hardraade of Norway and his own brother Tostig, Earl of Northumbria. Taxes were hardly an option, since collecting them would have taken more time than Harold had available in which to raise an army, but there were quick returns to be made from minting, since the controlling authority received a commission of up to ten per cent of the silver that went into the coins. It is likely that in order to increase the money supply, Harold allowed some of his supporters in the aristocracy and the Church to mint on his behalf, and probably to keep the commission for themselves. He needed friends, too.

This orgy of minting, though, was to little avail. Early success against his enemies in the north left Harold in command of a depleted and battle-weary force with which to face Duke William near Hastings, and 14 October 1066 became a date that every English schoolchild remembers.

We may imagine that William The Conqueror and his invasion force were rather surprised by the speed and completeness of their victory. Within six weeks or so of the Battle of Hastings, the duke was being crowned King William I of England at Westminster Abbey, a ceremony occasioning such celebration that the Norman troops on duty thought it was a riot and, in their habitual way, burned down the surrounding houses. Among those vociferously greeting the new king were undoubtedly members of the Saxon ruling élite, or more probably Anglo-Danes, since the Normans were descended from Scandinavians, too. But the great mass of the population remained hostile and, with just a few thousand armed men at his back, William sought conciliation rather than confrontation. When that did not work – and there were organised rebellions in each of the next three years, as well as guerrilla warfare for much longer – he resorted to brute force and what we now know as ethnic cleansing.

During the next two decades at least 4000 English landowners would be dispossessed, their holdings divided among no more than a couple of hundred barons from Normandy and neighbouring regions. A good deal of other land, mainly in the north, had been laid waste by rampaging troops and both Scotland and Wales had been bent to the Conqueror's will.

Curiously, however, there was little change in the methods of government. The House of Wessex, in particular, had done a thorough job in creating an administrative and legal structure and, like Cnut before him, William appreciated its efficacy. All it needed was the application of a little Norman practicality, together with the imposition of a new official language, and the unitary state to which the early Saxon kings had pretended became a reality. Most likely it would have happened anyway; the whole of Europe was undergoing sweeping social change as the complex legalistic precepts of the feudal system took hold with its network of rights, responsibilities and obligations. Under the Normans, though, the change was more rapid than it might otherwise have been and as a result England became stronger than might have been the case if the invasion had not happened.

Another thing that survived the Norman conquest intact was the English currency, which was equally strange given the fact that William had shown a proclivity for debasing the coinage in Normandy, a practice that had helped him to pay for his invasion force. Perhaps the fact that English coins had long been admired on the Continent for their quality persuaded him to maintain the standard, although in order to do so he did import moneyers from Normandy. Harold II had already raised the silver content of the penny above the level found during Edward The Confessor's debasement and William added to it again, operating nearly sixty mints in various parts of the country and producing eight different coins during his reign, which indicates that he kept to Edward's three-year cycle.

He needed a steady supply of cash to maintain his army, which was constantly in action against the resentful English, and minting was a good way of acquiring it. Rather than taking a slice of the silver used, the king seems to have levied a flat fee on the moneyers of one pound a year, with an additional pound for every change of design. Each of his fifty-seven mints had at least three moneyers, with some employing as many as ten, so the annual income would have been worth having and would have delivered a tidy bonus every third year as recoinages were ordered.

But that regular flow into the royal treasury was as nothing compared with the money raised from taxation and here William had a sound basis to work on. The Danegeld had, at its peak, raised tens of thousands of pounds a year and although it had been abolished by Edward The Confessor, the template it provided was extremely useful. It had been based on land-holding, at the rate of a certain number of pence per hide, an ancient measure equivalent to about 120 acres. The threat of a renewed invasion by the Vikings had not entirely disappeared, but William saw no need to reimpose the tax, although he did take advantage of its familiarity. In 1083, according to the chroniclers, 'after mid-winter the king ordained a large and heavy contribution all over England; that was, upon each hide of land, two and seventy pence'.

This was an excellent tactic, but it also served to create a doubt in William's methodical Norman mind. There was no entirely reliable record of the hidage on which the Danegeld had been based, other than reports from local officials, and they were almost certainly out of date. Most land had changed owners in the aftermath of the conquest, with many farms and estates consolidated into larger units. How carefully had all that been noted? In addition, urbanisation had proceeded apace since the first imposition of heregeld, which meant that merchants, traders and craftsmen had multiplied – and who had kept track of whether they were all paying the tolls and duties they should be? The expansion of trade domestically and overseas had also promoted a general rise in economic output, so it followed that many people might be paying less than their fair due.

What followed from such reflections was the most remarkable document of the mediaeval world, the Domesday Book, the first ever statistical record of the wealth of a nation. At first it was known as The Great Survey or The Inquisition and it did not acquire its now accepted name until a century later. Domesday was the English word for what a Norman observer, writing in old French, described as 'to us The Book of the Day of Judgement' because 'its verdicts are just and unanswerable'.

William ordered the survey in 1085 and it is a tribute to Norman organisational ability that his commissioners and sheriffs had completed their work within a year. And nothing was omitted. The Domesday Book is one case in which it is possible to say almost literally that no stone was left unturned, as the introduction to the book explains:

> Here is subscribed the inquisition of lands as the barons of the king have made inquiry into them; that is to say by the oath of the sheriff of the shire, and of all the barons and their Frenchmen, and the whole hundred, the priests, reeves, and six villeins of each manor; then, what the manor is called, who held it in the time of king Edward, who holds now; how many hides, how many ploughs in demesne, how many belonging to the men, how many villeins, how many cottars, how many serfs, how many free men, how many socmen, how much woods, how much meadow, how many pastures, how many mills, how many fish-ponds, how much has been added or taken away, how much it was worth altogether at that time, and how much now, how much each free man or socman had or has. All this threefold, that is to say in the time of king Edward, and when king William gave it, and as it is now; and whether more can be had than is had.

The number of place names featured in the record was 13,400 and nearly 300,000 people were identified as the owners of land, property, livestock, mills, bakeries, breweries, smithies and all kinds of material possession or businesses.

In the county of Norfolk, for instance, we find the property of one Robert Malet – a Norman, judging by his name – at what had obviously been Danish settlements called Fredrebruge and Glorestorp. Another Viking name, Godwin, appears as the tenant and the extent of the holding is described not in hides but in the Danish equivalent as 'two carucates'. There have been changes since King Edward's time: 'Then and afterwards 8 villeins [main sub-tenants]; now 3. Then and afterwards 3 bordars [smallholders]; now 5. At all times 3 serfs, and 30 acres of meadow. Woods for 8 swine, and 2 mills. Here are located 13 socmen [free peasants], of 40 acres of land. At all times 8 swine, then 20 sheep, and it is worth 60 shillings.'

The catalogue of my lord Malet's land goes on. One carucate at the manor of Heuseda, with meadowland, woods and a salt pond, altogether worth thirty shillings and taxed at twenty, of which the tenant pays twelve pence; two carucates at Scerpham Hundred, Culverstestun, of which a socman claims forty acres as a gift from the king and the tenant in chief is Walter of Caen. We even learn that in King Edward's time the landowner was a man named Edric, no doubt dispossessed after the invasion, though he is simply described euphemistically as Malet's 'predecessor'.

This astonishing detail was recorded throughout England, with the exception of the counties of Cumberland, Westmorland, Northumberland and Durham, which had been so badly ravaged by Norman troops that there was little surviving that was worth taxing. London was also left out of the book, presumably because its tax potential as the country's main commercial centre was already well documented, and likewise Winchester, the ancient Wessex capital. Elsewhere, 'not a single hide, not one virgate [about thirty acres] of land, not even one ox, nor one cow, not one pig escaped notice,' says the *Anglo-Saxon Chronicle*.

As all this information was collected, it was painstakingly transcribed – apparently by an English rather than a Norman hand – and stored in the royal treasury at Winchester. And what a treasure it proved to be. William now had, perhaps for the first time in history, the basis of an honest, just and unchallengeable tax system upon which he could draw for resources whenever the need arose. Like all taxation it caused widespread resentment, but no one could argue about the care with which it had been established. Of equal importance, though, was the fact that this obligation to the crown was to be paid not in service or commodities, as much of feudal law prescribed, but in cash.

The quid pro quo, so far as the reluctant taxpayers were concerned, was the maintenance by the crown or its agents of a stable and trustworthy currency, and this William The Conqueror both promised and delivered. How much it all meant at the time to the various classes of poor peasant, obliged to render to their lords so many days' work or military service, or so much wood or grain, milk or livestock, is debatable. But, just as the emergence of increasing numbers of legal documents covering most aspects of life had little immediate impact on the great mass of the population who could not read, the development of the cash economy promoted a change in the habits of thought from the highest to the lowest in the social order. The seal of a king's official on a piece of parchment now had value for a socman who had previously determined his tenure on a handshake and similarly the acquisition of money was becoming something to be desired.

Some idea of the nature and magnitude of everyday transactions may be gained from one of the laws of King William:

> Let no one buy anything living or dead to the value of four pence without four witnesses either from the city or the country vill. But if anyone afterward make charges against the exchange and he have no witnesses or warranty, let him return the property and pay a fine to whom the property by right belongs. But if he have witnesses, let them see the property three times, and on the fourth time let him vindicate his claim or lose it.

Clearly four pence was a not inconsiderable sum of money, at least worth the trouble of gathering witnesses to its exchange. The conclusion must be that most everyday transactions were likely to be in fractions of a penny, something no monarch or moneyer had yet come to grips with, and that fact would have serious implications for the development and the quality of the coinage for a long time to come. Chances are that when the peasantry actually got their hands on cash, they would rather save it than spend it and still rely on barter exchange for their everyday needs.

Meanwhile, at least so far as those who made use of money were concerned, the Conqueror had rescued the coinage from the doldrums of Edward The Confessor's reign and the confusion of Harold's. His favourite son, William Rufus, continued in much the same way when he succeeded to the throne in 1087, recycling coins every three years or so and maintaining the silver standard set by his father. The only significant change was one of style: whereas the image of William I on his coins was full-frontal, that of his son faced to the left. Perhaps, given the relatively poor state of the moneyer's art at the time, it was merely emphasising difference. It was pretty difficult to distinguish one head from another on a penny.

William Rufus moved the administrative capital of England from Winchester to Westminster, but the treasury remained where it was and the Domesday Book with it. No doubt it was consulted regularly, because the new king certainly had need of income. His reign was punctuated by a series of expensive rebellions at home and a number of military excursions across the Channel to press his claim to Normandy, where his elder brother Robert Curthose had inherited the dukedom. On top of that, he was famous for his grand and extravagant way of life. The tax impositions did not please the cloistered chroniclers, who disliked Rufus in any case on account of his tight control over the activities of their church: '. . . because of the counsels of wicked men, which were always agreeable to him, and because of his avarice, he was always harassing the nation with military service and excessive taxes . . .'

Whether or not that was unfair, Rufus used his gains to good effect from his kingdom's point of view. In 1096 Duke Robert suffered a fit of religious fervour after a European tour by Pope Urban II and joined the movement to wrest Jerusalem from Muslim control. So that he might safely go crusading, Robert effectively left his dukedom in pawn to his brother for an advance of 10,000 marks, the equivalent of more than 1,000,000 pennies. The taxpayers might have been less than happy, but William Rufus's bargain helped to lay the foundation for the first English empire.

Not that Rufus would live to see it. He died four years later from an arrow fired by one of his party during a hunt in the New Forest and the crown passed, not without difficulty, to his younger brother, Henry. Claimants to the throne had to move quickly in those days and Henry's first move was to take possession of the treasury even before he had had himself anointed as king. It was something of an omen. During the long reign that ensued, and the civil war that raged after it, the English penny would be reduced to the sorriest state it had seen for centuries.

Taken in the broader sweep of history, however, something much more important would happen to the currency while Henry I was king. It appears to have been noted first by an Anglo-French historian, Ordericus Vitalis, who early in the twelfth century toured England gathering material for a voluminous book entitled *Historia Ecclesiastica*. Buried among the facts, anecdotes, gossip and observations of this work is the phrase *XVlibr sterilensium* – Latin for 'fifteen pounds of sterling'. It appears to be the first recorded use of the word that would help to make the English pound a worldwide monetary phenomenon.

5

Hard Currency

*Between Christmas and Candlemas men sold the
acre-seed of wheat for six shillings; and the barley
for six shillings; and the acre-seed of oats for four
shillings.*

Anglo-Saxon Chronicle, 1124

Today the word sterling is recognised all over the world as
representing the British currency. In the leading
financial markets from New York to Tokyo the sterling
exchange rate is one of the main measures of value for
currencies. To be sure, it is not as important as it once was. For
some years now it has been eclipsed by the American dollar
and forced to share the spotlight with the Japanese yen. Even
more recently, the controversial euro has begun to figure in
foreign exchange dealings. Yet the pound sterling remains one
of the vital ingredients of the global economic system.

In a narrower sense, sterling is also a symbol of reliable value, denoting silver of 92.5 per cent purity. The acceptance of that standard dates back to the guarantee of quality found in the best of the early English silver pennies. And the term has been extended to imply more generally an idea of soundness, worth or distinction – as in the phrase 'sterling work', for instance, or 'a sterling fellow'. We use it knowing precisely what it means but, for the most part, ignorant of why or where it came from.

Readers who have followed the plot so far will not be surprised to learn that the origins of sterling are by no means clear. When the monk Ordericus Vitalis referred in abbreviated form to *librae sterilensium* in his twelfth-century history, he was obviously sure that the meaning would be clear, but that does not necessarily give us a clue as to the extent and duration of the use of the word. The book would have been primarily intended for an audience of well-educated ecclesiastics, along with a few members of the still relatively small group in secular society who could read not only their own languages but also Latin – the likes of kings and princes, great noblemen and high government officials, of which many of the latter were clerics anyway. Such people would have been aware not only of the latest intellectual trends but also the newest terminology. Was *librae sterilensium*, then, just a highfalutin Latin term, or did it have its equivalent in the vernacular? Or was it a Latin translation, for the purposes of the book, of a phrase from English or Norman French?

Ordericus was born in Shrewsbury a decade or so after the Norman conquest, of an English mother and a French father, and educated at the abbey of Saint Evroul in Normandy, where he subsequently spent most of his life. Norman French would probably have been his first language, but he would almost certainly have spoken English, too. In both tongues he would have come across words related to 'sterling'. Where he would not have found anything similar was in classical Latin, for *sterlingus, sterlingorum* and *sterilensium* do not appear in texts before the Middle Ages. We can be fairly sure, then, that while libra dated back to antiquity, the rest of the phrase was a Latinisation of a word from another language.

In Norman French the nearest equivalent to sterling is *esterlin*, which has been identified as current in the eleventh century. The word might have meant 'little star' because it seems to have been applied to a whole series of early Norman pennies bearing a star device, the reason for which is obscure. Thus it might be assumed that *esterlin* travelled across the Channel with the Conqueror and was absorbed into the native speech along with many other French words that survive in modern English. Yet the coinage of William I closely follows the Anglo-Saxon tradition in design, rather than the Norman, and there is no evidence of little stars on surviving coins of the reign. Perhaps, then, it was just Norman usage to rechristen the penny 'esterlin'.

Or maybe not. The Domesday Book sticks to the classical denarius in referring to the penny and rather than using *sterlingorum* or *sterilensius*, it prefers *libra arsa* to denote a pound of fine silver. Of course, that may simply mean the unknown English writer was rather more pedantic than Ordericus Vitalis and stuck to classical Latin as closely as he could.

There is an Old English word, 'steorra', which also means

'star' and when given the suffix meaning 'small' would have produced 'steorling'. Early historians – including the Elizabethan writer Raphael Holinshed, upon whose work Shakespeare based most of his historical plays – traced the use of steorling in reference to coinage to the ninth-century kingdom of Northumbria before it was occupied by the Vikings. But why did the Northumbrians, who under Viking rule were to call their pennies stycas or sceattas long after most others had abandoned the term, hit upon little-star coins well before the Normans?

Well, there is a possible explanation for that, too – and, as with Offa's penny, it involves the Arabs, at least indirectly.

During the eighth century the Gothic tribes of northern Europe had spread far to the east, reaching the borders of Mongolia and establishing new settlements as they went. One of these was the now almost mythical kingdom of Iestia, completely obliterated by waves of later invaders. Archaeological research has discovered that the coinage used in Iestia – of which one of the main centres was the now Russian city of Novgorod – was Arabian dirhems and half-dirhems, no doubt introduced as a result of trade but possibly minted in the region itself at some stage, again with Arab help. In the laws of the Ripuarian Franks, an ancient tribe living along the Rhine, there is a reference to 'Iesterling' money: could that be the real derivation of sterling? As a descriptive term the word might well have spread back westwards through the various Gothic peoples and found its way into both Old French and Old English. Perhaps, in the end, the theories about esterlin and steorling are mistaken and stars have nothing to do with sterling at all. Either that or the English misheard the word 'Iesterling' and saw stars instead.

Whatever the truth of the matter, the pound of sterlings began to make its presence felt during the reigns of the Norman kings of England, although the final word was frequently rendered in vernacular documents as 'starlings', which might tend to support any or all of the above suggestions concerning its origins. At that time, however, the sterling penny did not indicate the high standard and reliability it would come to represent later. The main reason was the cavalier attitude to the coinage of King Henry I, who when it came to money much preferred quantity to quality.

It could hardly have been otherwise. He had seized the English crown in a lightning coup and was concerned to establish in perpetuity the temporary hold William Rufus had gained over Normandy for the trifling sum of 10,000 marks. But Duke Robert of Normandy was on his way back from crusading both to reclaim his duchy and to press his perceived right to the English crown. Henry knew the duke was likely to be supported by large numbers of the nobility on both sides of the Channel, which left the king with the options of bribing potential enemies or preparing for war. Either course would require substantial amounts of cash.

At first Henry tried to buy off the putative supporters of Robert. The duke landed in England in 1101 to press his claim to the throne, but Ordericus Vitalis observes that Henry treated his barons 'with honour and generosity, adding to their wealth and estates, and by placating them in this way, he won their loyalty'. He also managed to placate Robert with the promise of a pension of £2000 a year in return for his relinquishing any rights of inheritance in England, while he would of course keep Normandy. Once the duke had returned home, though, he thought better of the arrangement and began to raise an invasion force. Henry spent huge sums on strengthening England's defences, then even more in assembling his own army to invade Normandy, where he eventually routed Robert's forces in 1106, took his brother prisoner and claimed the duchy for himself.

That settled the Norman question for the time being, but the rest of Henry's reign was to be a continual struggle to hold on to the realm he had thus created. So far as England was concerned, much could be achieved through diplomacy. The Welsh warlords were subdued and merely had to be kept in that condition, while the Scots were brought onside through Henry's marriage to Matilda, the daughter of King Malcolm Canmore. Normandy, however, was to be a source of trouble, surrounded by neighbouring warlords only too anxious to expand their territories.

'Though he seemed to be the most fortunate of kings,' wrote the archdeacon of Huntingdon, also called Henry, 'he was in truth the most miserable. Each of his triumphs only made him worry lest he lose what he had gained.'

Perhaps it was understandable in a man who, as the youngest of three brothers, had grown up without land of his own either in England, where he was born, or in Normandy. A cheerful, highly intelligent man – well-built but tending to fatness in later life, like his father – Henry appears to have suffered from something approaching an obsession about holding on to what he regarded as his by right. It was an anxiety that turned out to be costly, as the chroniclers noted for the year 1118: 'King Henry spent the whole of this year in Normandy on account of the war with the king of France, count of Anjou and count of Flanders. England paid dearly for this in numerous taxes from which there was no relief all year.'

But high taxes were not the only financial problem associated with the king's other realm across the Channel. Since the conquest that had first united England and Normandy, trade between the two had naturally grown quickly, with the result that their currencies had become more or less interchangeable. The trouble was that the silver content of the Norman coinage was much less reliable than the English penny had traditionally been, which is why it is to the credit of William I that he decided not to debase the penny in the way that he had reduced the Norman denier in order to finance his invasion. William Rufus had maintained much the same policy, but Henry I showed no such scruples. He needed as much money as he could lay his hands on and if English coinage could not adequately supply him, there was the debased Norman currency to fall back on.

In addition, the king's military activities across the Channel meant that mercenary troops were paid as often in deniers as they were in pennies and they were not fussy which they spent when they returned to England. The flood of Norman coins offered an excellent opportunity to English moneyers. If people were happy to accept debased deniers as readily as they did pennies, then there was no reason why silver should not be skimmed from the English coins that were being produced. The mints either kept the silver they saved in this way or used it to make even greater numbers of sub-standard pennies.

At first Henry did try to follow the lead of his father and brother, and in rather drastic fashion. In 1108 he decreed: 'False and bad money should be amended [i.e. subject to penalty], so that he who was caught passing bad denarii should not escape by redeeming himself but should lose his eyes and members.'

The king also did his best to make sure that all the taxes he was owed would be properly collected. Every six months or so a committee headed by Bishop Roger of Salisbury would meet to review the accounts of the shires and to determine that royal revenues had been fully subscribed. The meetings took place at a table covered with a chequered cloth upon which piles of tokens were laid out to represent sums of money and moved from square to square as appropriate – an early form of calculator on which the results would be clear even to people who could not read. Each sheriff was summoned to appear before the committee to have his accounts audited and to explain any discrepancies that might emerge as the tokens were placed on the squares denoting various types of income and expenditure. The committee was known, because of the cloth, as the 'exchequer' and that is the reason why even today the British government's chief financial officer is given the title of Chancellor of the Exchequer.

Yet this attention to detail was not reflected in the supervision of the coinage. The idea of complete royal control over the currency was by then well established and the laws against unauthorised moneying were draconian. The system, however, depended on the wisdom of the monarch and the amount of time he was prepared or able to devote to it. William I, who had also been much preoccupied with Norman affairs, had delegated some of his responsibility to a man who in his day was the foremost moneyer of Europe, one Otto the Goldsmith, who had also been employed by William Rufus.

Otto made sure the fifty-odd mints across England operated precisely as his master decided they should, but the celebrated mint-master's death left Henry to fend for himself and he appears either to have failed to appoint a qualified successor to Otto or to have relied on officials who were not up to the job.

Not that the king showed any lack of interest in the coinage – far from it. His constant need of cash produced no fewer than fifteen changes of currency during his reign, which means that the already shortened recoinage cycle was further reduced from about three years to barely more than two. But, whether as a result of deliberate policy or because of insufficient supervision, each new penny seems to have turned out to be less pure than its predecessors, while counterfeiting was able to flourish because of the generally poor state of the currency.

The decree of 1108 proved to be a complete failure. People took to making small cuts in their pennies in order to try to ascertain whether their cores were made of a base metal such as copper and, as the number of bad pennies increased, so the cuts became larger. Of course, the practice of cutting pennies into halves or quarters to produce small change had been going on for centuries, as had skimming their edges for the purpose of building up a stock of silver that could be coined later. Each cut inevitably removed silver and that caused problems not only with exchange but also when the coin fragments were collected for recycling. Henry's decree had insisted that half-pennies should only be round or at least retain part of the circular form, but this was widely ignored and a plan to produce proper halfpenny coins was dropped because of the expense of making them.

By 1112 the great mass of pennies were so battered, chopped about and thoroughly unreliable that the king ordered a nick to be cut across half the length of each new coin as it was minted as evidence of its soundness. This panic measure was a gift to the unscrupulous, who simply cut their own nicks into coins, rendering the mark of quality useless. The practice was subsequently discontinued, having merely increased suspicion of the coinage and added to uncertainty of its value.

The decree of 1108 had also sought to regulate the activities of the moneyers, but again it was largely ineffective. Mint-masters were banned from transacting exchange – that is accepting silver for coining – outside their own shires and, even where they were permitted to operate, could only carry out the transaction in the presence of two witnesses. The regulation was intended to ensure that only full-weight pennies with a proper silver content were issued and that individual moneyers who produced debased coins could easily be identified. But of course 'witnesses' were as susceptible to the lure of profit as anyone else and, in an extraordinary oversight, there was no law preventing moneyers from making dies bearing the name of another mint. It was almost a forger's charter and thousands, if not millions of pennies appeared on which the name was illegible and the inscriptions incomprehensible.

Within twenty years or so of Henry's coronation the money supply was completely out of control. An entry in the *Anglo-Saxon Chronicle* for the year 1124 notes sourly: 'The penny was so adulterated, that a man who had a pound at a market could not exchange twelve pence thereof for anything.' It was a particularly bad time to be worrying about the worth of your penny. Foul weather had devastated the cereal and fruit crops, leading to a severe shortage of seed for new planting and a consequent sharp rise in prices.

Henry, of course, was in Normandy as the crisis developed, but shortly before Christmas he sent an edict to London that laid the blame squarely on the moneyers: 'He bade that all the mint-men that were in England should be mutilated in their limbs . . . because the man that had a pound could not lay out a penny at market,' according to the *Anglo-Saxon Chronicle*.

That entry overstates the case, if another writer in the *Chronicle* is to be believed. Roger of Salisbury, who was placed in charge of the inquiry, was apparently not the sort of man to set aside the idea of a fair trial. He summoned every moneyer to Winchester at Christmas and each was examined before a tribunal. Where evidence of misdeeds was found, 'then were they taken one by one, and deprived each of the right hand and the testicles beneath'. By Twelfth Night, when the trials had ended, about half the total number of moneyers in England – or nearly a hundred men, by some accounts – had suffered the punishment. It might have concentrated the minds of the remainder and perhaps it reassured the public for a time, but the main effect of Henry's desperate measure was significantly to reduce the capacity of the mints and make good money, or indeed any money, scarcer than it had been before.

Once the envy of Europe for its consistent quality and imaginative design, the English silver penny had now slipped back into something approaching the crudest coinage of the Dark Ages – and even in those days its weight had in general been more reliable. While William I and Rufus had not exactly produced coins of beauty, they had at least ensured an even weight by exercising firm control over the supply. Henry I, able and successful king though he was, had squandered that advantage and come close to breaking the established link between crown and currency. And things would get considerably worse before they got better.

England was about to be plunged into its first real civil war since becoming a more or less united kingdom. The cause, as so often during the days of feudal monarchy, was the royal succession. Henry I had seized the throne from his elder brother, who had a legitimate claim to it, and it was almost a foregone conclusion that there would be rival claimants when he himself died, mainly because of the royal habit of political marriages. In the case of a successor to Henry, matters were more complicated on account of the fact that his only legitimate son had died in 1120 along with many other younger members of his family as the *White Ship* bringing them across the Channel foundered in a storm. Henry had attempted to settle the succession question by 'rather compelling than inviting' an oath from his barons that they would recognise his daughter Matilda – widow of the German Emperor Henry V – as ruler of England and Normandy when he died.

Naturally the Norman branches of the family of William The Conqueror were not entirely in accord with this solution. Already the son of Duke Robert, William Clito, was pressing his claim to Normandy, and who could know where that might lead? Then there was the other remaining child of William I, his daughter Adela. She had married the Count of Blois, with which Normandy shared a border, and had three sons with potential claims to their grandfather's realms.

The king died on 1 December 1135, but even before then

his barons had decided not to abide by their oath to him. There were several reasons why they did not want Matilda as their queen. The main one was that in the whole of Norman history there had never been a female ruler but, even if that could have been overcome, there were also problems with the personality and background of the woman in question.

Few of the barons knew Matilda and those who did were less than enamoured, although she was regarded as a great beauty. Sent away from home at the age of eight as the future bride of the emperor, she spoke German rather than Norman French and behaved with a stiff formality that was abhorrent to her own countrymen. Some idea of her interpersonal approach might be gleaned from the fact that she was always known as 'the Empress'.

So as the old king lay dying, it was not to his only surviving legitimate child that his courtiers turned but to his nephew, Stephen of Blois, grandson of the Conqueror through his daughter Adela. Stephen had been a familiar figure at the English and Norman courts of his uncle Henry while his elder brother had controlled the family province of Blois. He had even been given English lands, at Lancaster and at Eye, in Suffolk. When it came to marriage, Henry had secured a suitable match with the only daughter of the Count of Boulogne, to which title Stephen had succeeded upon the death of his father-in-law. To the barons it seemed that he was an ideal successor to the Anglo-Norman crown.

The nature and speed of Stephen's accession closely followed that of his uncle. The moment the news of King Henry's death reached him in Boulogne he took ship to England and, in a frantic few days, visited London to gain the support of the citizens, travelled to Winchester for the purpose of securing the treasury – his uncle happened to be the local bishop – and ended up in Canterbury to arrange his coronation. A large group of barons supported him and by 22 December 1135 the new king had been crowned.

England settled down to one of the most peaceful transfers of power it had ever known. Stephen was cultivated and charming, and seemed ready to listen to the advice of his confidants and counsellors, which gave the barons who had supported him reason to think they had made a choice that would be very much to their benefit. Even to those who were suspicious, because of the manner of his arrival or because they feared for their own futures under his rule, the king seemed anxious to please and to reassure. Then, of course, he had the respected Bishop of Winchester at his side and he appeared to show good sense by retaining the services of his uncle's chief civil servant, Roger of Salisbury.

To ordinary people it really made little difference who was king, provided they could get on with their daily existence in some security. They had become accustomed to the whims of their haughty and often cruel Norman overlords and were grimly prepared for the sudden descent of armed men to harry them, steal their goods and burn their poor cottages. Mediaeval life generally was, to quote the famous phrase of the seventeenth-century philosopher Thomas Hobbes, 'poor, nasty, brutish and short' and among the downtrodden masses there was a high degree of fatalism mixed with sullen resentment and the comforting certainty of a better world in the hereafter.

For the increasingly important merchant classes, however, Stephen's accession may have been seen as something of a bonus, which could help to explain the ease with which he had won over the people of London. As Count of Boulogne Stephen had been in control of one of the most significant Channel ports, Wissant, and in consequence had become seriously interested in trade, upon which he depended for much of his revenue. The burghers of England's trading capital, therefore, might look forward to a new age of expansion and possibly some special treatment to encourage their endeavours.

Unfortunately, such hopes were soon disappointed. King Stephen's easy and generous manner disguised a mind of only moderate intelligence, with little capacity for analysis, allied to a certain low cunning and – as is often the case with people of limited abilities – a dogged and destructive kind of determination. One contemporary commentator, admittedly hostile to the new king, described him as 'adept at the martial arts but in other respects little more than a simpleton'. That was an unduly harsh verdict, but Stephen's record does show a man given to vacillation followed by snap decisions that were wrong more often than they were right.

The king also had a talent for alienating the very people who could be of most help to him while at the same time favouring those who only wanted to use him for their own ends. The indispensable Roger of Salisbury was falsely accused and imprisoned, along with two other bishops, and the administration was largely taken over by placemen of the Beaumont family, who had become royal advisers as they sought to build on their already considerable power. Within three years of Stephen's coronation, England was thrown into chaos as the consensus that had brought him to the throne collapsed and the barons sought to capitalise on the king's weakness by splitting the country into their own heavily armed power blocks.

First, Empress Matilda, by then married to the Count of Anjou, attacked Normandy as a precursor to pressing her claim to the English throne. Stephen, fearing imminent invasion of England, lost control of the country by creating a series of military governors who immediately set about establishing themselves rather than the king as the rulers of their earldoms and any others they could take by conquest. Crucially, the king also lost control of the currency.

Given the state in which the coinage had been left by Henry I, the last thing it needed was a civil war. Even less was it able to survive in any meaningful form the almost complete rupture of royal links with the mints. But that is precisely what happened. Between 1138 and 1153, almost continuous guerrilla fighting, interspersed with a few pitched battles, spread across England. As gangs of men-at-arms roamed the countryside, no one ever quite knowing whose side they were on until it was too late, supplies of silver to the mints were disrupted along with everything else. The moneyers had to rely on local mines, which were of course controlled by the newly appointed provincial warlords. These men – whether they nominally supported the king and were losing confidence in him, or whether they had taken Matilda's side – were principally interested in enriching themselves. One quick way to do that was to coin their own money.

There was no attempt to maintain even the poor standards of the previous king's coinage and it is impossible to gauge the levels to which the silver content of the pennies fell. There was also the problem of whose money to accept in any transaction:

as well as not knowing what it was worth, you ran the risk of being murdered if you attempted to pass coins issued by one earl to somebody from a rival faction that also had its own mint. Nor could you be sure of whose coinage it really was. Inscriptions and moneyers' names were deliberately obscured and a lot of coins had no 'official' imprimatur at all.

Far from being a symbol of national pride and fair dealing, the penny was now treated with contempt. Many coins from the remaining royal mints were defaced by people opposed to the king gouging deep scores across his image.

But in 1142 the man who would make England greater than it had ever been before, and save the penny in the process, first set foot on English shores at Wareham in Dorset. His name was Henry Plantagenet and he was the son of Empress Matilda and Count Geoffrey of Anjou, which of course made him the grandson of Henry I. He was just nine years old when Angevin soldiers lifted him from his ship, having fought their way into the little south-coast port in the first stage of Matilda's invasion. By the time he was twenty he would be King of England and ready to prove himself one of the country's greatest monarchs.

6

Taxing Times

The scarcity of good money was so great, from its being counterfeited, that sometimes out of ten or more shillings, hardly a dozen pence would be received.

William of Malmesbury, *Historia Novella*, 1142

It could have been sheer exasperation that prompted King David I to issue the first ever royal coinage in Scotland towards the middle of the twelfth century. Certainly, like everyone else in the British Isles at the time, the Scots placed little faith in English pennies and in any case it looked as if England was falling apart as Stephen, Matilda and later Henry Plantagenet battled for the crown. So the 'gentle, just, chaste and humble' Scottish ruler appointed moneyers to produce a native silver coin, based on the best English design and bearing on its face an artistically stylised image of the king.

Of course, there might also have been a degree of opportunism about David's decision. He certainly took advantage of the shambolic state of England to occupy its northern counties in 1141, though his ambitions were to be thwarted by accession of his great-nephew, King Henry II, in 1154.

Henry Plantagenet had finally triumphed in the civil war, forcing Stephen to make peace and to recognise him as the legitimate successor. In return, Stephen was to remain king for his lifetime. He was already a sick man, however, and broken by the death of his wife and son within two years of each other. He died at Dover castle on 25 October 1154 and for almost two months England was without a monarch as Henry first quelled a rebellion in Normandy and then found himself unable to cross the Channel because of south-westerly gales. Almost unbelievably, no pretenders to the throne emerged in the interregnum and the country quietly went about its business – 'for love or fear of the king to come', according to a contemporary account.

They were emotions upon which the new king would have to rely heavily and he inspired plenty of both, though fear was undoubtedly dominant. He was a big man with 'a large round head, grey eyes which glowed fiercely and grew bloodshot in anger, a fiery countenance and a harsh, cracked voice'. Not someone, then, you would want to cross too often. At the same time, however, he displayed a keen and inquisitive intelligence, an impressive range of learning and a highly developed imagination. He was also a firm believer in justice and the rule of law, but perhaps his most striking characteristic was his apparently inexhaustible energy. From a tribe despised in Normandy as barbarians, this remarkable Angevin would expose the myth of Norman superiority and build a modern, efficient and stable nation from the ruins that his predecessors' greed and violence had left behind them.

Henry II would also place England firmly at the forefront of European nations. As well as ruling over Normandy and Anjou, he had acquired through his marriage to Eleanor of Aquitaine the great province that ran from Poitiers down to the borders of Spain along the Bay of Biscay. Before long he had added Brittany, the Auvergne and the Cahorsin to his dominions and only just failed to annexe the important southern region of Toulouse. England was therefore, through its king, at the heart of an empire stretching from the Scottish border in the north and Ireland in the west to the Pyrenees in the south and almost to the Ile de France in the east. Not that Henry saw it quite that way. To him England would always be just another province, albeit a very important one, and he spent only thirteen years there during his thirty-four-year reign. His was essentially a European power.

That did not mean England was ignored. It was, after all, Henry's only royal seat and its dominance in the wool and cloth trades made it an extremely valuable asset. With so much else to occupy him, though, it was essential that England remained as peaceful as it could be in those days and that its government was firm, fair, well-financed and efficient.

His first move was to restore the royal power Stephen had let slip from his grasp and, in the words of the contemporary historian Gervase of Canterbury, 'to root out all causes for renewal of warfare and to clear away all inducements to distrust'. He sent packing the Flemish mercenary troops Stephen had employed and ordered that all castles formerly held by the crown should be returned to it. Then he set about demolishing so-called 'adulterine castles', from which the private armies of the local warlords operated. Finally he decreed that the royal demesne and the general pattern of landholding among the aristocracy should return to what it had been during the reign of Henry I.

Another echo of the previous Henry's reign was the restoration of the administrative system that had served him so well. Again, the new king played his hand astutely, appointing a former official of Stephen to fill the role once taken by Roger of Salisbury and ensuring the support of the English church by making the Archbishop of Canterbury's clerk the royal chancellor, or chief of the secretariat. The second, as it happened, was a decision from which fateful consequences would flow, for the talented and ambitious young man was destined to be a future archbishop himself. His name was Thomas Becket.

One crucial appointment, given the battered condition of royal finances and of the economy as a whole, was that of treasurer. Henry had suffered direct experience of this very early in his reign when, needing money to pay troops for an expedition to France, he reimposed the old Danegeld tax but found that he received almost as many bad and counterfeit pennies as good ones. His first response was again to hark back to the days of his grandfather and recall from retirement Bishop Nigel of Ely, who had kept the books for Henry I. That done, and with the continental dispute settled, the king could turn his attention to the coinage problem so that any further embarrassment would be avoided and his realm would have the currency it deserved as one of Europe's main trading centres.

Having dispossessed overbearing barons of their illegal

castles, Henry II made sure they would not undermine him financially as they had done Stephen and closed down their private mints. That more or less put a stop to counterfeiting. The next step was to rebuild confidence in the legal currency and this he began to do in 1158 with the issue of entirely new coinage from just thirty officially designated mints.

These *esterlins*, starlings or sterlings – or to many just pennies – restored the silver content to about twenty-two and a half grains fine and were made to a design intended to last. They bore a three-quarter-face image of the king and the legend 'HENRI(cus) REXANGL(orum)', while on the reverse were a cross with four smaller crosses between its arms, the name of the moneyer and the place of minting. Such was their quality and so tightly was their issue controlled – with no more than half a dozen mints producing them once they had been established – that it would be twenty years before a second wholesale recoinage became necessary.

Having regained control of the currency and assured himself of its reliability, Henry next set about acquiring a regular income. Royal revenues tended to be the driving force for the progress of the currency during the Middle Ages. The restoration of royal demesne lands previously granted to others provided a firm foundation, but rents and receipts still amounted to only £8000 a year. Meanwhile, the increasingly complex nature of government was bound to lead to greater emphasis on taxation. The Domesday Book notwithstanding, many taxes had been imposed on an ad hoc basis. Some feudal duties and obligations had already been replaced by cash equivalents in earlier reigns, but Henry II foresaw the growing importance of a money economy and undertook a series of reforms that would eventually bring about the end of the feudal system and replace it with a primitive version of the tax structure so familiar to us today.

Perhaps the most significant new tax was scutage, so called from the Latin word for a shield. Under feudal law, different ranks of the aristocracy were obliged to supply the king with varying numbers of soldiers in the event of a military emergency. This was a highly undesirable system from two points of view: it robbed the land of large numbers of workers and it produced at best a poorly trained, if not an incompetent and often resentful army. For the sake of both numbers and effectiveness, kings had always relied on mercenary troops and Henry merely took that concept to its logical conclusion. Instead of supplying men, knights and barons would pay a mark of sterlings or a pound with which trained troops could be hired. It was not by any means a standing army, but it was a professional one and, as one of Henry's officials noted, 'the prince prefers to expose mercenaries, rather than natives, to the fortunes of war'. It is probably from this period that the word 'soldier' itself dates, based on the solidus or shilling the men-at-arms were paid.

Henry's second main tax innovation was *taillage* – literally meaning 'taking a cut' – or tallage in English. Previously, levels of taxation had been based on landholding, but tallage took account of a man's revenues (an early form of income tax) and of his movable property, along with the numbers of people owing him feudal service. The money from this tax was used first to support spreading towns and cities, and alleviate the undesirable side effects of urbanisation many of us still recognise, such as crime, traffic congestion and rubbish disposal. In many places access and weight restrictions had to be introduced in order to deal with the numbers of merchants' carts jamming narrow streets and also the public health risks of growing piles of horse dung on the roads. Other hazardous pollutants came from early industrial processes such as brickmaking and tanning, while crime was an ever present threat. Twelfth-century Lincoln, for example, suffered about 144 unlawful killings a year, along with forty-five rapes and nearly 300 other recorded criminal acts. Such problems could only be tackled if funds were readily available.

Later, tallage would be used to raise money for the Christian armies in the Holy Land and for various other purposes until it was abolished in the fourteenth century. It was not an annual tax and its rate could vary from a thirteenth to a quarter of a man's assessed wealth, depending on the sums required by the crown and the urgency of their purpose.

Crucial to the maintenance of the English coinage and the increasingly sophisticated ways of using it was the royal treasury. Nigel of Ely had restored the book-keeping to the exemplary state in which it had been kept under Henry I, but he was an old man and some time before 1160 it all became too much for him. The king replaced him with his son, Richard, who if anything was more learned and punctilious than his father, and who went on to run the treasury for forty years.

Richard FitzNigel has left us a unique treatise illuminating the way the treasury worked and describing the origins of practices that would last for centuries. His *Dialogus de Scaccario*, or *Dialogue Concerning the Exchequer*, became a textbook throughout Europe, used to initiate apprentices into the mysteries of what was known – as it still is in France – as the 'fisc'. The term, from which of course 'fiscal' derives as applied to public revenues, was first used by the Romans to mean treasury and comes from the Latin word for a basket or purse, *fiscus*.

According to Richard, the word exchequer refers not only to the cloth on the treasury table but also to the fact that 'just as, in a game of chess, there are certain grades of combatants and they proceed or stand still by certain laws or limitations, some presiding and others advancing: so, in this, some preside, some assist by reason of their office, and no one is free to exceed the fixed laws. Moreover, as in chess the battle is fought between kings, so in this it is chiefly between two that the conflict takes place and the war is waged – the treasurer, namely, and the sheriff who sits there to render account; the others sitting by as judges.' The exchequer met twice a year and was divided into two parts, the Receipt or lower exchequer – where sums due were collected – and the upper exchequer where the unfortunate sheriff had to deliver and justify his accounts, a process described by Richard FitzNigel as 'the conflict'.

Twice a year was more than enough, since the process was a lengthy, complicated and expensive one, particularly when it came to the Receipt. The clerk to the treasurer presided over a team consisting of five knights, four tellers to count the money, two scribes, an usher and a watchman. Richard goes into great detail about their jobs and their remuneration.

The clerk to the treasurer, for instance, 'when the money has been counted and put in boxes by the hundred pounds, affixes his seal and puts down in writing how much he has received, and from whom, and for what cause; he registers also the tallies . . . concerning that receipt. Not only, moreover, does he place his seal on the sacks of money, but also, if he wishes, on the chests and on the separate boxes in which the rolls and tallies are placed, and he diligently supervises all the offices which are under him, and nothing is hidden from him.' For this responsibility the clerk was paid five pence a day.

Tallies were controlled by two knights known as exchequer chamberlains. They were pieces of wood – hazel was the most favoured type – into which notches were cut in differing sizes signifying different sums of money: 'At the top they cut £1000 in such a way that its notch has the thickness of the palm; £100 of the thumb; £20 of the ear; the notch of one pound, about of a swelling grain of barley; but that of a shilling, less; in such wise, nevertheless, that, a space being cleared out by cutting, a moderate furrow shall be made there; the penny is marked by the incision being made, but no wood being cut away.' Large amounts were apparently noted on one side of the tally, smaller sums on the opposite side, and there were different marks for amounts in gold and in silver.

The tally was normally about nine inches long and when the notches had been cut in accordance with the sum paid, it was split lengthwise through the notches, one half being given to the payer as a receipt and the other retained by the exchequer as evidence of payment. Later, as literacy advanced, the name of the taxpayer was inscribed on each side of the notch, so that both incision and name would match up in the case of any dispute.

Such is the English love of tradition – or perhaps suspicion of things written on paper, which can always be altered – that the system of wooden exchequer tallies survived almost into the nineteenth century. The old tallies themselves were preserved until 1834, when the manner of their demise turned out to be disastrous. They were burned in the heating stove at the House of Lords, where the intensity of the flames caused a conflagration that destroyed the parliament buildings.

The exchequer chamberlains each received fees of eight pence a day. As well as supervising the keeping of the tallies, 'it is their duty to weigh the money which has been counted and placed by the hundred shillings in wooden receptacles, so that there be no error in the amount; and then, at length, to put them in boxes by the hundred pounds'.

One of the interesting facts that emerge from the *Dialogue*, which seems to have been written some time during the 1180s, is that in spite of the recoinage ordered by Henry II there was still a great variety of coins in circulation. Some counties, such as Cumberland and Northumberland, were allowed to pay in whatever silver currency they could lay their hands on, since they did not have their own mints. But Richard also mentions marks of gold (no doubt weight rather than coins), which were the equivalent of a pound of silver, and of 'gold obols'. Since the silver penny was the only English-minted coin, the gold pieces must have come from other places.

Equally, there remained serious difficulties with the weights and silver contents of the coins that were offered. When the money was presented to the tellers, for example, the pennies would be in heaps representing pounds, marks and shillings. The tellers 'diligently mixed the whole together, so that the better pieces may not be by themselves and the worse by themselves, but mixed, in order that they may correspond in weight; this being done, the chamberlain weighs in a scale as much as is necessary to make a pound of the exchequer. But if the number shall exceed twenty shillings by more than six pence in a pound, it is considered unfit to be received; but if it shall restrict itself to six pence or less, it is received, and is counted diligently by the tellers by the hundred shillings.'

Of course, that test only verified the weight of the coins. There was still the question of the quantity of silver they contained. To save time, rent and tax collectors would often accept whatever coins were offered at their face value, but require an additional payment of a shilling in the pound to allow for bad money. Some sheriffs, however, would bring to the treasury payments in what were said to be 'blanched' coins, which meant that samples had been tested locally for their purity. Bitter experience had shown this to be less than reliable, so blanched money was set aside during the accounting process in order for the exchequer to carry out its own random verification process.

For this, two other knights were employed. One, known as the knight silverer, counted out from what was claimed to be blanched money forty-four shillings, of which twenty were set aside for testing. These twenty were passed to the melter, who counted them again, then placed them 'on a vessel of burning embers which is in the furnace. Then, therefore, obeying the law of the art of inciting, he reduces them to a mass, blowing upon, and cleansing, the silver. But he must take care lest it stand longer than necessary, or lest by excessive boilings he trouble and consume it; the former on account of the risk of loss to the king; the latter, to the sheriff; but he shall in every way, with all the industry possible, provide and procure that it be not troubled, but that it be boiled only so as to be pure.'

Assuming the weight of silver thus produced was

equivalent to twenty shillings, or a pound, that amount was credited to the sheriff who had brought the money. The remaining twenty-four shillings, incidentally, was available for a further test if the sheriff objected to an unfavourable result. The outcome was crucial because it was assumed that 'for as much as, through the purging fire, falls off from this pound, so much the sheriff knows is to be subtracted from each other pound of his sum: so that if he pays a hundred pounds and twelve pence be fallen off the test pound, only ninety-five are computed to him'.

If this testing process seems rather destructive, it is worth bearing in mind that, according to Richard FitzNigel, the melted-down silver could be set aside 'so that, if the king wishes silver vessels to be made for the uses of the house of God, or for the service of his own palace, or perchance money for beyond the seas, it may be made from this'. Otherwise it could simply go to make new coins. Such are the virtues of money that it is literally worth its weight in precious metal.

An idea of the amounts of money generally in use towards the end of the twelfth century, and what they would buy, is given in some of the surviving treasury records: 'For 100 bacons supplied to the castle of Caerleon, 100 shillings authorised by the king's writ. And for 100 axes sent to Ireland, 22s. 11d. And for two horses sent to Ireland, 60s.' Thirty cartloads of lead used in the construction of Dover Castle cost the king twenty-one pounds seventeen shillings and sixpence, with an additional twenty-seven shillings and sixpence carriage from King's Lynn in Norfolk, while a certain Ralph of Haverhill received a payment of twenty pounds for looking after the king's hawks. On the revenue side, the treasurer made a note to 'speak to the lord king about the £145.10s.8d. arrears of rent on the silver mines at Carlisle, outstanding for many years, which have not been rendered because of defects in the mines – so the sheriff says'. And then there were the profitable wheels of justice: 'Ralph of Lund and Alice his wife owe seven marks for the favour of having their plea . . . heard in the king's court.'

The cash economy was developing well, then, but twenty-five years or so into Henry's reign some of the difficulties with the cash itself had still to be overcome. As Richard FitzNigel pointed out, in addition to the depredations of 'forgers and clippers or cutters of coin . . . the money of England can be found false in three ways: false, namely, in weight, false in quality, false in the stamping'. It remained common practice to cut pennies into halves or quarters, though the resulting fragments were by this time usually less hacked about than they had been in the days of Henry I and Stephen, and in spite of more efficient supervision at the mints, underweight and debased coins were still much in evidence.

It was customary for the king to hold a council at Christmas and in 1179 it took place at his castle in Oxford. Though by that year the royal revenues had been more than double the amounts received in the early part of the reign, Henry told his advisers he was still dissatisfied with the state of the currency and he had decided on a second, once-and-for-all recoinage to put the standard of the penny beyond doubt. It was clear that English moneyers were not really up to the job, so continental methods would be employed and, to reduce the opportunities for forgery, the processes of money changing and money producing would be separated, with the profits from the former going directly to the crown instead of being shared with the moneyer. The king wanted the whole process to be complete by next Martinmas.

Naturally, Richard FitzNigel was put in charge of the project. He well knew how to please his master and he called in a leading artist, architect and builder, Philip Aymer, from the city of Tours, in Henry's native Anjou. Aymer designed an impressive coin, at eighteen millimetres in diameter slightly smaller than that of the previous recoinage, and weighing what would become the sterling standard of twenty-two and a half grains. On the face was a flattering portrait of the king, bearded and wearing a diadem on his head, with a sceptre shown on his right. With Henry's imperial status in mind, the word 'Anglorum' was dropped from the legend, which read simply 'HENRICUS REX'. On the reverse, Aymer kept to the style of Henry's existing coin, but the cross became smaller and more elaborate, and the crosslets between its arms were replaced by quatrefoils, a popular decorative device in contemporary architecture.

With the design approved by the king, the moneyers who would produce the coins were hand picked by FitzNigel and his team, no doubt with Aymer's advice. Only eleven mints were designated and we know that one of the chosen mint-masters was Isaac of York, a Jew who was to be immortalised by Sir Walter Scott in his mediaeval romance *Ivanhoe*.

The moneyers worked on the basis of fixed fees rather than a percentage of the silver coined, so there was no incentive for them to skim the coins, especially since FitzNigel's scrupulous record keeping would rapidly have revealed any differences between the weights of silver received and coins issued. In fact, the moneyers were not allowed to take in old coins for recycling. That was how things were done in Anjou and Normandy, and in the spring of 1180 the supervisors of official coin exchanges in Tours, Le Mans and Rouen were brought to England by one of the king's closest advisers, Richard of Ilchester, Bishop of Winchester and Archdeacon of Tours. These *cambitores*, as they were known in the Latin of official documents, described the requirements of the system to Philip Aymer, who designed new buildings specifically for the purpose. Nine 'royal exchanges' were built at a cost of about fifty pounds each and they more than paid for themselves in a very short time since all the profits went directly to the king.

There must have been a good deal of feverish activity among the counsellors and exchequer officials that year. The king was not noted for his patience and if he set a deadline of Martinmas, none would have relished the prosect of going to him with news of any delay. So on the feast of St Martin, 11 November 1180, England had its first official, truly national currency, which was to serve it well for more than a century with nothing more than changes in the heads of the successive kings – and not even that, in some cases.

Moreover, as the Dean of St Paul's at the time, Ralph of Diceto, sardonically remarked in his journal, they had actually managed to make the pennies round for once.

It would not be until the reign of Edward I – like Henry II, a monarch in many ways ahead of his time – that the next important development in the cash economy, and the story of the pound, would take place.

7

Coining It

About this time, the English coin was so intolerably
debased by money-clippers and forgers, that neither
natives nor foreigners could look upon it with other
than angry eyes and disturbed feelings.

Matthew Paris (1220–59)

He was known as 'The Lion-Heart' and he is the subject of more gallant legends than perhaps any other English king, but the simple truth is that the heart of Richard I was closer to almost anywhere than England, where he spent barely two years of his ten-year reign. Henry II had designated Richard his successor, but it was towards his duchy of Aquitaine rather than his new kingdom that Richard's fancy really turned. At the same time, as a restless man of action, he was attracted by the idea of crusading against the great Muslim leader Saladin to save the Holy Land for Christendom, so between his continental dominions and his eastern adventures there was little time left for the offshore island he had inherited.

Henry II, who himself spent little more than a third of his reign in England, had nevertheless left the royal finances, the national economy and the currency in a pretty reasonable state. His coinage had been copied on the Continent and his fiscal system worked extremely well – there was even an early form of self-assessment to make tax collection more efficient and less costly. The tallies used so successfully by the exchequer had spread into the private sector as a primitive kind of credit guarantee and the king had even opened a sort of offshore bank account, depositing some £20,000 of silver, raised from taxation, with the Knights Templar and Knights Hospitaller in the Holy Land to be used when necessary to finance the war against Saladin. The general prosperity of England and the expansion of the money supply encouraged by Henry's careful recoinages may be judged by the fact that during the final ten years or so of the reign there was moderate but steady inflation, especially in the prices of grain and livestock, no doubt prompted equally by increasing demand and the availability of cash.

In this context, Richard's more or less permanent absence was probably more of a blessing than anything else. So marginal was his interest in England that he did not even bother to place his own head on any new coins, content to leave the image and the 'HENRICUS REX' of his father. As the bureaucracy created by Henry continued to function smoothly there was even a slight deflation, which helped to maintain economic stability, and the idea promoted by later balladeers that there was rampant extortion and exploitation of the poor by wicked nobles taking advantage of the king's lack of attention is hard to sustain on the basis of historical fact.

This, of course, was the period most commonly associated with the stories of Robin Hood, supposedly an unfairly dispossessed aristocrat who turned outlaw and, with the help of his Merry Men in Sherwood Forest, robbed the rich to help the poor. Although the character crops up at various times from the beginning of the Norman Conquest to the reign of Edward II in the early fourteenth century, Robin of Locksley is mainly portrayed as a supporter of good King Richard and an enemy of bad Prince John, the king's brother, who takes the opportunity to grind the peasantry under his heel while the brave and noble monarch is fighting for God in the Holy Land. There is precious little evidence to suggest that Robin ever existed and if he did, it would have been more than a century later than the most popular legends suggest, but clearly he is linked to very powerful folk memory, rather in the manner of King Arthur.

If the Arthurian legend is related, as some authorities suggest, to the loss of English independence as a result of the Norman invasion, that of Robin Hood might well have arisen from the rapid and widespread urbanisation of the eleventh and twelfth centuries — with the accompanying flow of wealth away from the countryside. It could also reflect the growth of the cash economy, in which ordinary working people were the last to share. Curiously, there is nothing to suggest that people were any worse off or particularly badly treated during the reign of Richard The Lion-Heart, yet there is no doubt that the increasing formalisation of a cash-based tax system caused great resentment, even when attempts were made to improve its fairness.

In 1198 the Abbot of Bury St Edmunds, in Suffolk, provoked outrage when he tried to respond to complaints from the poor of his town about the way taxes were collected and how the wealthier citizens seemed able to avoid paying their due. The abbey chronicler, Jocelin de Brakelond, recorded what happened:

> Afterwards, all the burgesses sought . . . an agreement with the lord abbot . . . offering an annual tax in place of [the customary] exaction; and the abbot, thinking of how the cellarer [rent and tax collector] went shamefully through the town for the collection of rep-silver [payment based on the harvest], and of how he caused pledges to be taken in the houses of the poor, sometimes stools, sometimes the doors, and sometimes other useful things, and how the old women drove him away with their distaffs, threatening and cursing the cellarer and his men, decreed that twenty solidi [shillings] should be given annually to the cellarer . . . by those burgesses who undertook to pay a tax for this. And thus it was done . . . and another quittance of the same kind was given to them called sor-penny [payment for use of pasture land], to be paid by four solidi at the same time. The cellarer was accustomed to receive one denarius a year for every cow belonging to the men of the town for exit and pasture . . . But . . . when the abbot had spoken about it in chapter, the monks were angry and thought it unseemly on his part . . .

Obviously there was resistance among conservative elements to the idea of yearly tax payments in the place of seasonal feudal levies – the word 'unseemly' is something of a clue. The problem with annual bills is that they bear no relation to the purpose for which they are collected. If you pay a penny a year to graze your cow on the abbot's land there is a distinct cost–benefit ratio, whereas when the community hands over four shillings for that collective right the link is broken: it is easy to forget what the money is for. In the modern world there is a trend in political thought that goes back to the old idea of breaking down fiscal revenues into specific purposes, so that people can see precisely what their money is being spent on just as if they were buying something from a trader.

The Bury St Edmunds story illustrates another element of the Robin Hood myth, in which many of the villains are senior clergymen. Bishops, abbots and the like were closely associated with the regime, both as officials and as rent and tax collectors in their own right, and the impression of their collusion with the temporal power was reinforced in 1199 by papal permission to make payments to civil authorities. The original intention was to help finance the crusades but church wealth was later used merely to prop up impecunious monarchs whose religious faith made them worthy causes.

That money came from taxes and rents the church increasingly demanded in cash rather than kind, and it seems likely that the invention of the anti-establishment Robin Hood, who lived freely in the forest, was a popular response to the accelerating displacement of traditional systems of payment through barter and personal service.

Certainly, the connection between the saint of Sherwood

Forest and financial developments is familiar to modern economists through what is known as the Robin Hood Paradox. This theory, first expressed by the economic historian Peter Lindert, suggests that 'redistribution toward the poor is least given when most needed' and is used to test the relationship between capitalism and inequality at various periods of history. Though it has many detractors, the Robin Hood Paradox could explain why the stories of Britain's most famous outlaw are placed at a variety of times throughout the Middle Ages.

Richard's successor, the unpopular King John, reverted to the old practice of imposing one-off taxes in order to finance his generally unsuccessful military campaigns. In 1207, for instance, he used the tallage to raise no less than £60,000, which helped to finance an expeditionary force for a doomed attempt to recover lands on the Continent he had previously lost in battle.

Having grown accustomed to a king across the water, the English now found themselves with a monarch who had no choice but to stay at home and to burden them not only with his constant demands for money but also his peripatetic presence, such was his suspicion of his own subjects and the necessity to quell frequent rebellions among them. It was during his last excursion that he lost part of his military baggage train while crossing the Wash, but people who down the years have believed quantities of treasure went into the quicksands, too, have so far failed to find it. The chances are that by 1216 any treasure had been squandered.

John is reputed to have been assiduous in his attention to matters of government, but there seems little doubt that such petty activity was intended to take his mind off the much weightier and more difficult affairs of state. He certainly paid little attention to the currency, apart from the amounts of it he had in his coffers and, like his elder brother, left his father's distinguished head on the coinage – except in Ireland, of which John had been overlord during his brother's reign, where pennies, halfpennies and farthings were issued bearing the new king's image.

An idea of the way cash had come into general use, and of the value of things in the early years of the thirteenth century, comes from the accounts of the bishopric of Winchester, the ancient English capital, for the year 1208:

Downton: William FitzGilbert, and Joselyn the reeve [foreman of the manor], and Aylward the cellarer render account of £7.12s.11d. for arrears of the previous year. They paid and are quit. And of £3.2s.2d. for landgafol [land rental]. And of 12d. by increment of tax for a park which William of Witherington held for nothing. And of 2s.6d. by increment of tax for half a virgate of land which James Oisel held without service. And of 19s. for 19 assize pleas in the new market. And of 10s. by increment of tax for 10 other assize pleas in the market this year. Sum of the whole tax £36.14s.8d.

Expenses: For ironwork of 8 carts for the year and one cart for half the year, 32s.10d. For shoeing of 2 plough-horses for the year, 2s.8d. For wheels for carts, 2s.9d. For 6 carts made over, 12d. before the arrival of the carpenter. For wages of the smith for the year, 8s.6d. For one cart bound in iron bought new, 5s.7d. For wheels purchased for one cart to haul dung, 12d. For leather harness and trappings, iron links, plates, halters, 14d. For purchase of 2 ropes, 3d. For purchase of 2 sacks, 8d. For wages of one carpenter for the year, 6s.8d. For wages of one dairy woman, 2s.6d. For payment of mowers of the meadow at Nunton, 6d.

The same fascinating document, in accounting for payments that were still made in kind from land owned by the Church, gives an insight into the way the privileged classes lived and of the importance of religious festivals:

In expenses of the lord bishop at the feast of St. Martin, 8 sides of bacon. In expenses of the same at the feast of St. Leonard, 17 sides of bacon, the meat of 5 oxen, and 1 quarter of an ox. In expenses of the same on the morrow of the feast of the Holy Cross, delivered to Nicolas the cook, 27 sides of bacon. In expenses of the lord bishop delivered to the same cook at Knoyle on the Saturday before the feast of St. Michael, 15 sides of bacon. In expenses of the same and of the lord king on the feast of the Apostles Peter and Paul, 50 sides of bacon. In allowance of food to Master Robert Basset on the feast of All Saints, half a side of bacon. In allowance of food to the same on Wednesday and Thursday before Pentecost, 1 side of bacon. In those sent to Knoyle for autumnal work, 6 sides of bacon. In three autumnal festivals at Downton, 9 and a half sides of bacon. Sum: 134 sides of bacon. And there remain 74 sides of bacon.

As for the currency, King John did have to do something about it, though little enough, in 1205 when some foreign traders began to refuse English coins because of the systematic clipping that had damaged them. John's response was to ban the exchange of coins at less than seven-eighths of the legal weight and to decree that underweight pennies should be seized and collected in the royal treasury, where of course they could be melted down and the remaining silver extracted for recycling. The system of 'royal exchanges' seems to have collapsed because the king restricted moneyers' fees to sixpence when they exchanged old coinage for new. This was of little benefit however, when the condition of coins in circulation meant that most people received no more than the bullion weight if they did try to exchange them.

All this made little difference. By the end of the reign, clipping and forgery had reached epidemic proportions. Even when contemporary commentators were trying to be fair to John – 'he was indeed a great prince' – they had to add 'but less than successful'.

For the next king there was no need to change the legend on the coins because 'HENRICUS REX' naturally applied equally to John's son, Henry III. Only the image needed to be altered, though it never was. The only improvement that was made concerned the reverse, which was changed in 1247 from a short cross to a longer one, extended to the edge of the coin in an attempt to prevent clipping. Sixty-seven years had gone by since the second currency reform of Henry II and the constant wars and insurrections of John's reign had had their usual ill effects on the money supply, a situation made worse by the reappearance of an inflationary trend much more significant and steeper than the previous one.

In addition to the demand for cash prompted by sharply rising prices and the difficulties with a flood of bad and forged coins, the money supply was affected by the activities of Henry III himself. Feckless is a word one might think of in attempting to describe him. Crowned at the age of nine, he grew up to be capricious, wilful, demanding and inordinately fond of pomp and ceremony.

By no means uncultivated, he was a munificent patron of the arts and where his family was concerned his generosity was unstinting. Such proclivities made him a high-maintenance monarch and he was almost permanently in debt. This was obviously not a king who could be trusted to control government finances or manage the economy. The situation became ridiculous in 1254 when he assumed a papal debt of 150,000 marks and agreed to finance the invasion of Sicily in return for the pope's ultimately fruitless offer to recognise Henry's second son as king of the island. It was all too much for the barons, who decided on the revolutionary step of electing a council of their own to run the country, effectively taking government out of the hands of the king and his foreign advisers. It was a step towards the legislative assemblies that, later in the century, would become known as parliaments, but of course it was bound to cause trouble and in 1264 civil war broke out.

The leader of the anti-royal faction was the king's own brother-in-law, Simon de Montfort, Earl of Leicester, who defeated Henry's army at Lewes in Sussex and captured the king and his sons. Flushed with success, the earl summoned a meeting of the new assembly in London, supported by leading nobles, courtiers, royal officials and citizens. His experience of government was to be short-lived, however. Henry's heir,

Edward, bought his way out of captivity and faced the revolutionaries in battle at Evesham, Worcestershire. Simon de Montfort was killed along with some of his most powerful supporters, many others of whom were captured, and royal authority was restored.

Afterwards, according to the report of a monk named Matthew,

> the king and the nobles of the kingdom assembled at Winchester, and ordered that the richer citizens of the city of London should be thrust into prison, that the citizens should be deprived of their ancient liberties, and that the palisades and chains with which the city was fortified should be removed, because the citizens had boldly adhered to Simon de Montfort, earl of Leicester, in contempt of the king and also to the injury of the kingdom; all which was done, for the more powerful citizens were thrown into prison at the castle of Windsor, and were afterwards punished with a pecuniary fine of no inconsiderable amount. All liberty was forbidden to the citizens, and the Tower of London was made stronger by the palisades and chains which had belonged to the city.

Henry was back in control, but de Montfort's rebellion had been a salutary lesson and the king was obliged to accede to some of the barons' demands for better government. Nor was the experience wasted on his successor, Edward I, who would do more than might have been expected of an arrogant, self-willed Plantagenet to establish a fair system of laws and government in England. He also earned himself a place in monetary history through his successful reform of the currency.

When Henry III died in 1272, England was awash with foreign coins, partly the effect of increasing trade but also because of the shortage of native currency resulting from widespread clipping. Continuing price inflation had greatly raised the demand for fractions of a penny and the introduction of the 'long-cross' coin had done little to prevent the butchery. Foreign coinage was useful, but it was always a matter of haggling when people came to exchange it. Official records show, for example, that when silver coins minted in Brussels were weighed, they fell short of an English pound by as much as three shillings on face value and that was also the case with coinage from Cologne. Italian coins were more reliable, with a difference of only a few pence and in some cases just a penny, but overall the use of foreign money was bad news not just for consumers but also for moneyers, since they had to pay their fixed fees to the king even if the coins they bought turned out to be sub-standard. Since weighing was unreliable and blanching the coins laborious, it was common for moneyers to discount on face value, often by amounts considerably greater than the actual loss of silver.

Before tackling the coinage, however, Edward had to stabilise the royal finances. After the consolidation of the demesne by Henry II, which produced along with judicial fees more than three-quarters of annual treasury revenues, the absenteeism of Richard and the necessity of buying favours that had marked the reigns of John and Henry III had seriously depleted this income and other sources had to be found urgently. Edward started as his father had by borrowing from

Italian bankers and by 1290 his debt would be something of the order of £400,000. To finance it he reintroduced the customs duty first imposed by Richard and John but allowed to lapse when the exigencies of war receded. Wool was England's principal export and duty was imposed in 1275 at half a mark per sack, which produced a yield of up to £13,000 a year.

Then there was the tallage, the value of which had been greatly increased by inflation. Assessed at one-fifteenth of every pound, the tax was bringing well over £100,000 into the exchequer by 1290. That did not stop the king applying for 100,000 marks from the famous 'crusading tax' of the papacy, which he received in 1291. He had already unilaterally declared a tax on the English church in return for his agreement at least to consider any complaints the senior clerics might have about their rights and privileges.

To begin with he kept the old coinage of Henry III, but in 1279 he began to issue his own pennies, as well as halfpennies, farthings and the fourpenny groat – so called, from the French word *gros,* because it was the largest coin in circulation. The appearance of fractions of a penny was the best way to prevent clipping but previous attempts to produce small change had failed on grounds of cost. Edward was the first king to overcome this difficulty. He reduced the fee paid by the moneyers to the crown, thereby allowing the mints to maintain a satisfactory margin when making lower-value coins. In the case of the farthing, which cost as much as the penny coin to produce, the king ordered that the silver content of the coin should be slightly below what it should have been at a quarter of the weight of a penny, again helping the moneyers' margins.

Of course, the other requirement was to maintain the

standard of the penny at twenty-two and a half grains and this Edward did in two ways. First, he confirmed London as the benchmark for coinage by taking the Royal Mint into the Tower of London, where it was to remain for centuries. Second, he called on the Goldsmiths' Company of the City of London to take responsibility for the quality of the coinage. This the goldsmiths did by bringing into public view the sort of tests that had been carried out by the exchequer on coins presented by the sheriffs in their tax payments.

In 1282 Edward issued a writ convening a public trial in which a jury of twelve 'discreet and lawful citizens of London' would join with twelve members of the Goldsmiths' Company in order to establish the purity of newly minted coins. It was the first sitting of what became known as the Trial of the Pyx, named after the container in which the coin samples were kept. The word pyx comes from the Greek for a casket and it was the name given to the vessel in which consecrated bread was kept for the purposes of Holy Communion. Presumably the goldsmiths' box was meant to be sacred in its own way, signifying that the coins had not been tampered with and were the true products of the mint. All aspects of the samples were verified, from their diameter to their weight, and some were melted down as in the old blanching process so that their silver content could be determined.

It was a procedure that helped everyone. The king could be certain that his revenues really were worth their face value, while merchants and traders had less to fear when coins were handed over by their customers. Even the moneyers were satisfied, since the expert goldsmiths could advise them on the most efficient techniques of minting. As for the goldsmiths themselves, it was the beginning of an association with the national currency that would give them a considerable advantage when the use of money entered a new phase four centuries later. The Trial of the Pyx would survive to celebrate its seven-hundredth anniversary in the presence of Queen Elizabeth II in 1982 and it continues to this day as an annual test of coins issued by the Royal Mint.

These monetary reforms of Edward I placed the pound of sterlings in something of a class of its own among European currencies. The quality of continental coins was variable at best, execrable at worst, whereas anyone receiving English money could be reasonably sure that 240 pence really did add up to a pound. That is, of course, so long as the bullion content was never altered by royal command.

Regrettably, the improvement in the coinage did little to help the king's finances in the long run. He might be sure of what he was receiving from the range of new taxes he had imposed, but somehow it was never enough. Edward's invasion of Wales, his long war in the north that earned him the title 'Hammer of the Scots' and his disputes with the King of France were expensive undertakings. Exchequer accounts indicate that between the years 1294 and 1298 the king's military budget amounted to £730,000 against a basic income of just £150,000. Small wonder that a crippling tax burden led the barons to issue what they called 'Remonstrances' criticising the king's overambitious and ultimately unfulfilled policies.

On the other hand, the king's desperate need of money did contribute to the development of a parliamentary system. If he was to raise taxes without provoking rebellion, Edward had to extract some measure of consent and the successor to the barons' assembly of the previous reign was the best means of doing it. By 1295 the king was summoning archbishops, bishops, abbots, seven earls, forty-one barons and two representatives each from all the shires, cities and towns to Westminster to consider 'provision for remedies against the dangers which in these days are threatening our whole kingdom'. These men had to be convinced that ends justified means, while the king needed to be sure that he was carrying the country with him. Since the money supply was influenced more than anything by the need to raise government funds, the parliament gained some control over the currency.

It would not be an idea that appealed to all Edward's successors and for many of them in dire financial circumstances there would remain the only too tempting option of simply decreasing the bullion content of the coinage.

8

Toil and Trouble

*To Petir Herton cordewaner for a paire of shoon
double soled of blac leder not lyned price 5d; two pair
shoon of Spanish leder double soled and not lyned
price the paire 15d.*

From the Wardrobe Accounts of King Edward IV, 1480

By the last quarter of the thirteenth century England was on its way to becoming what Napoleon would later famously describe, somewhat loosely, as a nation of shopkeepers. Although agriculture remained the most important single industry, the engines of economic development were predominantly manufacturing and mercantilism, but it must be said that the pace of growth was slow. English wool from the country's estimated 18,000,000 sheep dominated the European textile trade, while tin from the mines in Cornwall had gained an international reputation for its quality. Coal, iron and lead were also starting to contribute both to national wealth and the beginnings of a primitive industrial revolution. In purely domestic terms the market had become the centre of trade, with about 1000 royal licences granted to hold regular markets and fairs in small towns throughout England and Wales. Underlying all these activities was the rapidly developing cash economy, as recognised by the new coinage introduced by King Edward I.

But the supply of coins could not keep pace with the demands of an expanding mercantile economy, with the result that many transactions were carried out on the basis of credit. This was a haphazard business, with promises made on a handshake that could later be denied or on some document that might or might not be accepted in a court of law. Disputes often led to violence, as contemporary records from the Manor Court in Wakefield illustrate:

> William Proudfot, against Philip de Mora and William his brother in a plea of assault, says that on the Sunday before the Assumption of Blessed Mary [15 August], before the ninth hour, as he was coming in God's peace from church towards the inn between the town of Wakefield and Thornes, they wounded him in the head and badly beat him on account of a debt; he claims 20s. damages, and 100s. for the affront.

Such unregulated credit arrangements would inhibit the economic growth necessary to sustain a rising population, which had probably trebled since the compilation of the Domesday

Book to a figure somewhere between 5,000,000 and 7,000,000. If mercantilism was to prosper, providing jobs, income and revenues for the increasingly sophisticated needs of government, some means of regulating transactions was required.

A statute of 1283 provided for the official recording of credit arrangements at one of the main commercial centres – London, Bristol, York, Winchester, Shrewsbury or Lincoln – so that if the debtor failed to honour his obligation by the due date the creditor could appeal directly to the mayor to have the offender's property seized and sold. If there was nothing saleable the debtor would be sent to prison until some settlement could be reached.

However, local loyalties continued to make it difficult for a merchant from a different district to collect on his debts, so in 1285 a new statute was drawn up making prison the first recourse and allowing credit records to be established in any city or 'good town'. This new law proved to be highly effective and in some ways too successful. The ease of access to enrolment resulted in a rush to have debts officially recognised, even when the creditors were not merchants and when the amounts involved were no more than a few pence. So a further refinement of the law in 1311 restricted the debt provisions to transactions 'between Merchants and Merchants, and of Merchandises made between them'.

With this official recognition of commercial credit, the English economy was coming of age. But the beginnings of financial regulation and the stabilisation of the coin production undertaken by Edward I, together with the introduction of a more useful range of coins, were not destined to have a lasting effect on the quality of the English currency. War and pestilence made sure of that. Edward's ceaseless military activity – not only in England but also in Wales, Scotland, Ireland and France – helped to ensure that the country remained at war with somebody, including itself, throughout the fourteenth century. And it was an expensive business. At a time when a highly skilled craftsman was earning rather less than two shillings a week, and a labourer about a penny a day, the king was spending upwards of £3000 a year on building castles to underpin his authority in Wales. A year's campaign against Welsh rebels in 1294 left the treasury with a bill of £55,000. And as the disastrous fourteenth century got into its baleful stride, the strain on the money supply increased.

Matters were not improved by the fact that Edward III, who came to the throne in 1327, preferred the old mediaeval virtues of chivalry and honour to the more prosaic challenges of mercantilism that arose as England groped its way unsteadily to what we now call the early modern period of history. His response to a coinage crisis in the 1330s, when the output of the mints was limited to money made from base metal, was typically grandiose – a gold coin known as a florin, because of the flower featured on its reverse, worth six shillings of silver. That lasted just a few months before it was replaced by a larger gold piece called the noble, valued at eight pence more than the florin and containing 136.7 grains of fine gold.

The noble was a splendid piece of work, its face showing the gallant king with sword and shield aboard a great warship, while the reverse featured a complicated and highly artistic design incorporating the cross of Christianity, the crown above an English lion and French fleur-de-lis. Sadly, its glorious ambition bore no relation to economic reality and within a few years the gold had been significantly reduced in both weight and fineness, while even the reintroduced silver penny had failed to retain its purity.

By that time the Black Death was making its presence felt and the mortality rate was seriously affecting economic activity, especially in agriculture. As whole communities were wiped out, the shortage of labour led to what was for the times serious inflation in wage rates. Between the turn of the century and its mid point, day rates for labourers more than doubled, to about threepence farthing, and in the case of craftsmen such as carpenters the rate reached fourpence by 1351. The landlords upon whom the fundamentals of the economy still depended, in spite of the increasing importance of merchants, began to panic and as early as 1349, the first full year of plague deaths, the king came under pressure to stop further wage rises. It is an indication of how rapidly the plague took its toll.

The Ordinance of Labourers, drawn up in council at Westminster, notes that although 'a great part of the people, and especially of workmen and servants, [have] late died of the pestilence, many seeing the necessity of masters, and great scarcity of servants, will not serve unless they may receive excessive wages, and some rather willing to beg in idleness, than by labour to get their living'. There was, it seems, a particular shortage of ploughmen and other farmworkers, so the ordinance directed that any able-bodied man or woman under the age of sixty and living on the land, 'free or bond not living in merchandise, nor exercising any craft, nor having of his own whereof he may live, nor proper land, about whose tillage he may himself occupy, and not serving any other, if he in convenient service, his estate considered, be required to serve, he shall be bounden to serve him which so shall him require; and take only the wages, livery, meed, or salary, which were accustomed to be given in the places where he oweth to serve'. The penalty for unjustified failure or refusal to respond to the landowner's call was prison, as was the punishment for leaving a job without good cause.

As for the landowners, they were forbidden to meet their need for labour by paying more than the customary wages for their region, on pain of a fine of three times any amount they paid above the average. The law was retrospective in that employers who had already hired labour at inflated rates were instructed not to keep to the bargains they had made.

The ordinance also attempted to freeze the prices of everyday necessities:

> Butchers, fishmongers, hostelers, breweres, bakers, and all other sellers of all manner of victual, shall be bound to sell the same victual for a reasonable price, having respect to the price that such victual be sold at in the places adjoining, so that the same sellers have moderate gains, and not excessive, reasonably to be required according to the distance of the place from whence the said victuals be carried; and if any sell such victuals in any other manner, and thereof be convict in the manner and form aforesaid, he shall pay the double of the same that he so received, to the party damnified, or, in default of him, to any other that will pursue in this behalf.

Finally, it directed that no one 'under the colour of pity or alms' should give money to beggars who appeared to be fit for work 'so that thereby they may be compelled to labour for their necessary living'.

Of course, the main effect of this ill-considered piece of legislation was to make matters worse, much as the wage-restraint policies of governments in our own times have tended to do. The restriction on the movement of workers meant that employers in districts devastated by the Black Death found it even more difficult to find people to work the land and had no choice but to risk the penalty for paying over the odds if crops were to be planted and harvests gathered in. Food shortages arising from the lack of labour inevitably forced up prices, which meant that traders either could not buy because they would be selling at a loss or were obliged to risk fines for charging more than the arbitrary going rate. Most serious, however, was the resentment the ordinance fostered among the labouring classes, which would boil over into violent rebellion within a generation.

Bad law, however, does not prevent authorities from trying to enforce it and in 1351 the Statute of Labourers was designed to make the regulations even tighter because of 'the malice of servants, which were idle, and not willing to serve after the pestilence, without taking excessive wages'. Attempting to maintain the level of pay at that customary in 1347, or the twentieth year of the reign, the statute spelt out what the rates should be:

First, that carters, ploughmen, drivers of the plough, shepherds, swineherds, deies [dairy maids], and all other servants, shall take liveries and wages, accustomed the said twentieth year, or four years before; so that in the country where wheat was wont to be given, they shall take for the bushel ten pence, or wheat at the will of the giver, till it be otherwise ordained. And that they be allowed to serve by a whole year, or by other usual terms, and not by the day; and that none pay in the time of sarcling [hoeing] or hay-making but a penny the day; and a mower of meadows for the acre five pence, or by the day five pence; and reapers of corn in the first week of August two pence, and the second three pence, and so till the end of August, and less in the country where less was wont to be given, without meat or drink, or other courtesy to be demanded, given, or taken; and that such workmen bring openly in their hands to the merchant-towns their instruments, and there shall be hired in a common place and not privy.

Item, that carpenters, masons, and tilers, and other workmen of houses, shall not take by the day for their work, but in manner as they were wont, that is to say: a master carpenter 3d. and another 2d.; and master free-stone mason 4d. and other masons 3d. and their servants 1d.; tilers 3d. and their knaves 1d.; and other coverers of fern and straw 3d. and their knaves 1d.; plasterers and other workers of mudwalls, and their knaves, by the same manner, without meat or drink, 1s. from Easter to Saint Michael; and from that time less, according to the rate and discretion of the justices.

Item, that cordwainers and shoemakers shall

not sell boots nor shoes, nor none other thing touch-
ing their mystery, in any other manner than they
were wont the said twentieth year: item, that goldsmiths, saddlers, horsesmiths, spurriers, tanners,
curriers, tawers of leather, tailors, and other workmen, artificers, and labourers, and all other servants
here not specified, shall be sworn before the justices,
to do and use their crafts and offices in the manner
they were wont to do the said twentieth year, and in
time before, without refusing the same because of
this ordinance; and if any of the said servants,
labourers, workmen, or artificers, after such oath
made, come against this ordinance, he shall be
punished by fine and ransom, and imprisonment
after the discretion of the justices.

Edward III and his counsellors might as well have taken a
lesson from King Cnut. They could not turn the tide any more
than he could and by the 1360s, when the worst ravages of the
plague had abated, wages had reached record levels and the
scarcity of labour remained acute. Many parts of England were
devastated: the village of Tusmore in Oxfordshire reported that
it could not pay taxes because there were no taxpayers left
alive; Seaford in Sussex described its remaining inhabitants as
so few and so poor that they could neither meet their tax
commitments nor defend themselves in the event of expected
raids by the French. The war with Scotland also continued and
the largest numbers of abandoned settlements were to be found
in the northern English border counties, not only as a result of
the plague but also because of the regularity of Scottish attacks.

Landowners had seen their incomes fall by ten per cent or so and the nation was simmering with discontent as the harsh labour laws and war taxation further depressed an already damaged economy.

When the king died – alone, senile and largely unloved – in 1377 the unhappy realm, plunged even further into misery by three more epidemics of deadly disease that followed the Black Death, passed to his ten-year-old grandson, Richard II, and within four years a full-scale revolution was under way. The immediate cause was the imposition of flat-rate taxes on all adults as a means of restoring a treasury that had virtually bankrupted itself through war. No direct taxes had been levied for twelve years in the wake of the plagues, but from 1371 onwards the familiar levies on land, property and movable goods progressively returned and became ever more pressing in their demands. Nor was the burden fairly shared, because the assessments took no account of the uneven falls in population caused by the epidemics, so that the sheriffs in the worst-hit areas were still expected to produce their tenths or fifteenths of assessed wealth even though there were far fewer people left to participate. To redress this imbalance and also to increase revenues for the war effort, Richard's advisers, no doubt with the best of intentions, came up with the idea of the poll tax.

So called from the word meaning a human head, the poll tax was first imposed in 1377 at a rate of fourpence, or a groat, for every inhabitant over the age of fourteen. The theory was that with the rise in wages and the decline in serfdom occasioned by the plague-induced labour shortage, most ordinary people were better off than they had been in previous generations and were therefore able to take full responsibility for a contribution to government revenues. To the logical, educated minds of the royal functionaries it seemed perfectly reasonable and just. But, as the British Conservative administration of Margaret Thatcher would rediscover 600 years later when it also tried to impose a poll tax, logic, reason and justice count for little against the real, everyday perceptions of people's ability to pay. Doubtless there were peasants who could afford to meet the tax bill, but many more could not.

The problem with flat-rate, per capita taxes is that while they may seem fair in theory, in fact they throw up a whole range of anomalies. Why, for instance, should a family of five living in a hovel face a higher bill than a couple with a mansion? Logic suggests that the more you are in number, the more you should pay but the reality is that numbers alone form a deeply flawed assessment. Larger households, for example, may contain a greater proportion of non-contributing members, such as old people or invalids who are being supported entirely by the others, and that has a serious effect on ability to pay. And taxes are only workable when people are both able and willing to pay them.

The council ruling on behalf of the boy king, led by John of Gaunt, got away with it in 1377 and the poll tax netted more than £22,000 for the exchequer, based on contributions from about 1,500,000 people. Thus encouraged, they tried again two years later at fourpence a head, though the revenue was somewhat lower because exceptions were made on the basis of anomalies that had been identified first time round. There was some resentment because the poll tax was collected in addition to the usual land and tallage impositions, but it was not until the third attempt to collect it in 1381 that open rebellion broke out.

By that time it was clear that the war with France was going badly and John of Gaunt, as the real power in the land, was blamed for mismanagement and waste of money. In an attempt to recover the situation, John and the council proclaimed that the rate of the poll tax would treble to three groats per head – equivalent to a shilling – and that virtually everyone would be obliged to pay the full amount. Most of the exceptions granted in 1379 would no longer be allowed. The shock of the announcement quickly turned to anger and a great many people simply refused to pay, often with the connivance of their sheriffs and local tax collectors, who were equally dismayed and saw at close quarters the risk the government was taking. In some areas tax officials were attacked by mobs and, when troops were sent in to punish offenders, more than half the nation rose up against them.

The heart of the rebellion was in Kent where, according to the contemporary French writer Jean Froissart, passions had been excited by the preachings of an inflammatory priest named John Ball, who railed against the nobility: 'They are clothed in velvet and camlet [expensive Eastern cloth] furred with grise, and we be vestured with poor cloth; they have their wines, spices and good bread, and we have the drawing out of the chaff and drink water; they dwell in fair houses, and we have the pain and travail, rain and wind in the fields; and by that that cometh of our labours they keep and maintain their estates.' But the country people of Sussex, Essex, Bedfordshire, East Anglia, Staffordshire and Warwickshire also joined the unrest, encouraged by disaffected citizens of London who urged them to march on the capital.

Led by Wat Tyler – 'and he was indeed a tiler of houses, an ungracious patron,' reported Froissart – some 60,000 rebels converged on London, where they pillaged the Savoy, home of John of Gaunt. Moving on to the Tower of London, they demanded that the king give an account of why it was necessary to raise the hated poll tax. When a confrontation with the young monarch took place, an overconfident Tyler became abusive and was killed by the mayor of London, Sir Nicholas Walworth. The rebellion collapsed and King Richard went on to become a vicious tyrant, but the Peasants' Revolt was to serve as an early signal that when it came to manipulation of the economy the condition of those who benefited least from it would have to be taken into account. As the use of cash increased, it would not be just the rich who had a stake in the pound of sterlings.

Most of the following century turned out to be a story of political turmoil and economic stagnation. A series of short reigns, interspered with coups and counter-coups, murders and conspiracies, left England without stable leadership as the aristocratic houses of Lancaster and York and their partisans battled for supremacy and the throne. The spoils of war, both at home and abroad, allowed the rich to live more splendidly than ever, while the working people enjoyed only modest improvements in their standard of living but at least benefited from years of minimal price inflation.

In trade and industry, it was a period of slow, gradual change as landowners moved towards a more intensified system of agriculture based less on serfdom and feudal tenancy and more on the enclosure of croplands and pasture to maximise production and profits. The wool business entered its early industrial phase, with the focus on the manufacture and export of cloth rather than the sale of fleeces and yarns. The centre of the trade began to move from East Anglia to the north and the west as new milling techniques exploited the energy source of rapdily flowing highland waterways, enabling the development of towns such as Leeds and Bristol.

None of this was particularly dramatic, however – in contrast to the continuing crises of the currency. We saw earlier that the Black Death and a series of political upheavals throughout Europe had seriously affected the supply of bullion for coinage, while the dominant economic treatise of the age – by Nicholas Oresme, an adviser to the French king – had postulated that the value of currencies was dictated by the total quantity of gold and silver in circulation. Acceptance of this theory ruled out the use of base metal in coinage, which had been tried during the fourteenth century, and led to the adoption of gold in England in order to make up for a lack of silver sufficient to meet rising demand.

In 1412 Henry IV reissued the gold noble at 108 grains fine, a long way short of the grandiose coin of Edward III, and at the same time reduced the penny to fifteen grains of silver. This relieved the pressure on bullion supplies, so that for about twenty years the mints were able more or less to keep pace with demand for coinage. By the 1430s, however, there was clearly a problem with gold and the production of nobles almost ceased, forcing the face value of the coin up to eight shillings and four-pence, a rise of some twenty per cent. To fill the resulting gap with silver coinage, the weight of the penny was further reduced to twelve grains, but currency remained in short supply and it became common to use foreign coins generated in abundance by the growth of cloth exports to the Continent.

The Yorkist Edward IV – notorious for his riotous living and the murder of his brother, the Duke of Clarence – introduced, in 1465, a gold ten-shilling piece, known as the ryal, or rose noble from the design on its reverse, and another gold coin, called an angel, to replace the original noble at six shillings and eightpence but containing just eighty grains fine. During the second part of his reign, from 1471 to 1483 (he alternated with the Lancastrian Henry VI, whom he finally executed), the angel became the coin of choice, when it could be obtained, and the rose noble fell into disuse, probably because its weight of 120 grains had caused it either to be hoarded or melted down into less easily exchanged treasure, such as golden goblets and plates. With the debased penny still at twelve grains, there remained a good case for using the currencies of continental states in daily transactions and holding on to whatever English gold was available.

The only really significant development in the coinage of the British Isles during this period occurred in Scotland, when the self-regarding but undoubtedly cultured James III issued a silver groat bearing a portrait of himself fine enough to rival anything that came out of the mints of the Italian Renaissance. Little good it did him, since he was murdered by rebels a couple of years later – and in 1489 the artistic quality of his fourpenny piece would be completely overshadowed by the dazzling gold pound of Henry VII.

9

The Good, The Bad
and The Ugly

That realm cannot be rich whose coin is poor or base.
Lord Burghley, Lord High Treasurer, *c*.1599

The stabilisation of bullion supplies and the reform of the coinage undertaken by Henry VII – not least the reduction in mint charges by two-thirds in the case of gold and one-third for silver – ensured a dramatic increase in the money supply. At the same time the introduction of the gold sovereign in 1489 and the shilling, also known as a testoon, in 1504 made money easier to use, as did improvements across the whole range of coinage, from the groat, half-groat and penny to the six-and-eightpenny silver angel and the ten-shilling ryal, which had replaced the rose noble issued in gold by Edward IV.

It is no exaggeration to describe Henry VII as the father of modern English coinage and perhaps he might equally be identified as the prophet of strong currency, which was to play such an important part in economic life a few centuries later. His pound – designed, as was the shilling, by a German named Alexander de Bruchsal – has been described as the greatest coin ever to be minted in England and by the time of his death in 1509 the English currency was the envy of Europe for its value, quality and appearance.

Unfortunately, such was not the case at the end of the following reign, that of Henry VIII. Just as the handsome, vigorous and self-assured young king would decline into obesity, suspicion and indulgence, so the 'finest, best executed and most handsome coinage in Europe' would turn into 'the most disreputable money that had been seen since the days of Stephen – the gold heavily alloyed, the so-called silver ill-struck and turning black and brown as the base metal came to the surface', according to the historian Charles Oman in his book *Coinage of England*, published in 1931.

Modern psychologists have suggested that Henry VIII, the second son who succeeded to the throne after the death of his elder brother, suffered from an inferiority complex which, combined with a brain less acute and disciplined than his father's, drove him into an obsession with self-aggrandisement. His reign, his power, his country were to be more glorious than anything that had gone before; his military exploits were to surpass those of the heroic Henry V; his realm was to become an empire again, rivalling those of the Continent. It was an approach that was ambitious, certainly popular – and economically disastrous.

During the early years, under the arrogant and sometimes brutal but always efficient Lord Chancellorship of Cardinal Wolsey, matters seemed to be firmly under control. Like the sons of Henry II, the new king even left his father's superb portrait on the coinage, contenting himself with merely changing the VII to VIII. He was in any case much more interested in sport, music and love than in the boring details of administration and accounting. After Wolsey's fall in 1529, however, Henry's ambition was unrestrained and its costs mounted alarmingly.

The king was unlucky in that his grandiose and expensive policies coincided with a new wave of economic change as England, far behind the rest of Europe, began finally to recover from the effects of the Black Death and its successors, and to adjust to the changes brought about by the plagues. Between 1525 and 1541 the population rose by 500,000 and during the following decade would top 3,000,000 for the first time since the early fourteenth century. The immediate result was that the conditions which had produced stability and even stagnation were reversed. In the place of high wages and low prices there was price inflation provoked by rising demand and a general reduction of wages caused by the expanding labour market. It has been calculated that between 1490 and 1530 the price index of consumables rose by nearly seventy percentage points while the wage index – based on the pay of craftsmen – almost halved. And as the century went on the imbalance would grow worse, with the price index recording growth of just under 500 per cent by 1600.

This placed enormous strain on the money supply, in spite of the presence of silver on the newly discovered American continent and its subsequent importation into Europe, and the burden was increased by Henry's demands for cash to finance the expansion of the navy and military excursions to France, Scotland and Ireland. The king's first recourse was to lay hands on the enormous resources of the Church, which owned lands producing revenues that were perhaps greater than those of the crown itself. Official assessments put the gross income of the 800 or so monasteries, nunneries and friaries in England and Wales at just under £140,000 a year, but the likelihood is that it was nearer £200,000.

Properly used, these would have been of enormous benefit to the royal treasury, but prudence was not one of the virtues of Henry VIII and he squandered all the revenues he had raised from the suppression of the monasteries by selling off not only the bulk of the valuables contained in the religious houses – those put on the market in London alone fetched some £75,000 – but also their lands. Thus long-term wealth was sacrificed for the sake of short-term gain. The king's profit from the dissolution of the monasteries is thought to have been more than £1,000,000, yet even that failed to assuage his appetite for cash.

With his room for financial manoeuvre now limited and an ever increasing outflow of money from his coffers, Henry had no choice but either to reduce his spending or to increase the supply of money in circulation. Given the demands of his ego, it is no surprise that he opted for the latter. So began what is known in English numismatic history as the Great Debasement.

The first sign is noticeable in 1536 when a series of new coins appeared, minted in Ireland and with a silver content ten per cent lower than their English-produced equivalents. At first these 'harps' were used to pay the king's toops in Ireland but it was not long before they were circulating freely in England. No one appeared to notice and in 1540 a further reduction in the silver content of Irish coins took place, followed two years later by a similar debasement of coinage minted in London and elsewhere.

Almost in parallel, the face value of existing higher-denomination coins was increased, effectively reducing their true value by breaking the accepted relationship between coinage and the bullion from which it was made. Already in 1526 the gold sovereign had been 'cried up' from twenty shillings to twenty-two, with a further sixpence added a few months later. The angel went from six shillings and eightpence to seven and sixpence, its previous value now embodied in a new coin called the george noble. At that time their content of fine gold had been maintained, but this was subsequently reduced from just over twenty-three carats to twenty-two.

A similar process occurred with the silver coinage. The testoon, now officially renamed to reflect its supposed value of a shilling weight, began to be made from adulterated metal and the venerable penny fell to its lowest ever bullion content of just ten and two-thirds grains, or less than half of its traditional pure silver value.

Then, in 1544, the king unveiled the third strand of his money supply policy by announcing significant increases in the premiums paid by the mints for recoinage, an inducement made possible by the continuing reduction in the silver content of new issues. What this meant was that anyone presenting old coins for recycling would now receive in exchange new pieces with a face value some twenty-five per cent higher than what had been melted down. Since people had by this time become accustomed to accepting money at its face value, as we do today, the recoinage premium proved to be by far the most successful element of Henry's dubious monetary approach. So great was the rush to make 'profits' that the long-suppressed ecclesiastical mints in Canterbury and York were brought into service again and new civil mints had to be opened in London and Bristol.

For Henry there was a double bonus. As well as augmenting the supply of coins, the new premiums increased the activity of the mints so substantially that the exchequer's share of the fees exceeded £1,000,000 over an eight-year period – considerably more than the amount raised by taxation.

For the public, on the other hand, the results of the debasement were dire, mainly because its full effect was seen in the silver coinage most people used while the gold coins of the rich remained closer to their bullion value. Though new outbreaks of disease and a falling birth rate contained population pressures during the 1550s, with the result that wages actually rose slightly, everyday prices almost doubled in the years between the death of Henry VIII in 1547 and the turn of the century. There were also serious implications for trade, because although English exports were cheaper as a result of the undervalued currency, many foreign merchants refused to accept English money in the state to which it had fallen. Within fifty years all the literally sterling work of Henry VII in establishing the pound as Europe's finest currency had been carelessly undone.

The short and unhappy reign of the boy king Edward VI – the son of the third wife of Henry VIII, Jane Seymour, he died of tuberculosis at the age of fifteen – saw the coinage and the economy sink even more deeply into difficulty as attempts to raise the bullion standards failed because of the chaotic royal finances the new monarch had inherited. The largely copper coins that Edward's father had attempted to disguise with a thin coating of silver had peeled to reveal their true character and the debased shilling was now only accepted as sixpence.

Some attempts were made to restore stability after the Duke of Somerset was toppled as Edward's effective regent in 1550 and the Earl of Warwick became Lord President of the Council. Warwick closed down all the mints save for those in London and Dublin, and issued orders that new coinage should be struck at pre-debasement bullion standards, though the poor Irish were left with their sadly corrupted currency. He also made a further raid on the churches, stripping parishes of a total of £20,000 worth of gold and silver. The effects were minimal, however. Reduction of activity at the mints meant that most of the coins in circulation remained of the base-metal type and the profligacy of Henry VIII had left the crown still dependent on what had become an established unsound money policy.

Queen Mary I, the second of Henry's children, who would become known as Bloody Mary because of the mass of executions carried out on her behalf, actually tried hard to rescue the currency during her five years on the throne, although all she had time to achieve in practice was the restoration of the fine gold standard in the higher denominations. In coinage terms she is notable only for her introduction of Spanish-style shillings and sixpenny pieces bearing portraits of herself and her husband, the hated Philip of Spain, but she did begin the process by which her successor, Elizabeth I, was finally able to repair the damage done by Henry VIII.

Crucial to this recovery was Thomas Gresham, a Norfolk merchant's son who went on to found England's first financial institution, the Royal Exchange, where currency and other forms of transaction could be bought and sold, and to become by far the richest man in the country for his time. In a career devoted to finance, he formulated what has become known to economists as Gresham's Law which, simply stated, is that bad money drives out good. Gresham argued that if two coins of differing intrinsic value were worth the same amount as legal tender, the one with the lower content of precious metal would inevitably push the more valuable one out of circulation. Even to those for whom economics remains what Thomas Carlyle described as 'the dismal science', the truth of Gresham's Law must be evident. If you have a coin made of pure gold worth a pound and another made partly of alloy but still worth a pound on face value, which do you hand over to someone else as payment? The intrinsic worth of the purer coin will tempt you to hoard it – as a store of value – while the debased one offers the same return as a medium of exchange.

The Great Debasement saw Gresham's dictum proved beyond doubt. The post-Henry VIII attempts to return to accepted gold standards failed because people were reluctant to pass on the coins when they could obtain goods with the corrupted variety. Gresham tried to redress the balance during Mary's reign by purchasing gold coins in Spain for reminting in England, but it was not until Queen Elizabeth took advantage of her predecessor's plans for currency reform that the bad money was eventually supplanted – and Gresham received a well-deserved knighthood.

If Henry VIII had taken a step backwards from the modern world with his manipulation of the coinage to meet royal needs, Elizabeth reached even deeper into the mediaeval past by taking personal charge of the recoinage project. With Gresham's advice she decided on a complete recall of the debased currency and its replacement by coins of standard gold and silver content, so that their value in terms of both exchange and bullion would be unarguable. With perhaps more than £1,000,000 worth of corrupted coins in circulation it was a formidable task, requiring skill, speed and, most of all, the confidence and participation of the public.

To prepare the way the queen issued a series of proclamations that revalued existing coins by between a quarter and a half, depending upon their degree of debasement. Some shillings, for instance, were now given special marks that reduced their acceptable face value from the already diminished sixpence to fourpence-halfpenny. It was further proclaimed that debased coins would cease to be legal tender in April 1561 but that, as an incentive for them to be handed over, a premium of threepence in the pound would be paid for their surrender by certain dates. Finally, people were reminded that there were heavy penalties for melting down coins or exporting them in exchange for purer foreign currency.

With the demand side of this remarkable financial operation thus primed, the queen turned her attention to the supply side. Gresham scoured the British Isles and Europe for coinage, and bullion experts and craftsmen imported the latest pressing technology to maximise output and assure standardisation, greatly extended the Royal Mint at the Tower of London and borrowed 200,000 gold crowns on the Antwerp exchange for a ready supply of bullion to augment that extracted from the recalled coins. The extraction process on which the whole plan depended was carried out mainly by a German company, which had developed the most advanced and efficient techniques, with help from a London firm and the Royal Mint. Gresham's arrangements proved to be excellent. The recoinage programme was completed in less than a year – and a delighted queen made a profit of £50,000 from it.

This was to be the first of six coin issues as Elizabeth tried to restore confidence in the currency and overturn the effects of Gresham's Law. The gold standard was maintained in coins worth a pound, ten shillings, five shillings and two shillings and sixpence, while the fine silver content of pennies, groats and other pieces of smaller denomination rose from the 0.25 per cent of Mary's reign to 0.81 per cent. But with coin production still relatively crude – and the refusal of Royal Mint workers to accept new presses that would increase output and reduce labour costs – there remained the problem of providing enough small change for everyday use, particularly as inflation began to rise sharply again after a lull during the middle years of the century.

The fourpenny groat was joined by pieces worth sixpence and threepence, but even with inflation there were still many daily transactions involving sums of less than a penny and it continued to be unprofitable to produce halfpennies and farthings. Elizabeth solved this difficulty, no doubt with advice from Gresham, by authorising the issue of coins with face values of three-halfpennies and three-farthings, making them the same size as the standard silver pieces and distinguishing them by the addition of a rose design that appeared behind the royal portrait. This meant that people could give a penny for goods worth a halfpenny or farthing and receive change easily in coins that were large enough not to be lost.

The new range and variety of coins meant that the groat and the farthing fell into disuse and eventually, about the middle of the seventeenth century, the silver halfpenny also disappeared. Even so, the demand for coins in small denominations always seemed to outstrip supply and in some regions merchants introduced tokens made of lead or tin to provide a sort of credit arrangement until bills could be settled in real money. In 1601 there was an attempt to ease the situation by producing copper pennies, but with bitter memories of the use of that metal during the Great Debasement still fresh in the public mind, the whole issue was dumped on the unfortunate Irish. Though the cash economy was now firmly established, the means to make it work to its full potential had still not been fully developed. By the end of the reign the national money supply in good coinage was thirty per cent higher than it had been in bad coins during the worst years of the debasement, but in the meantime prices had nearly doubled and more than 1,000,000 people had been added to the English population. The monetary system could barely keep pace with economic and social change.

Elizabeth, like her grandfather Henry VII, well knew the value of money and was meticulous with her accounts. Her long war with Spain and the serious Irish rebellion that broke out during her reign meant a constant drain on her resources, yet she imposed no new taxes and, in fact, the exchequer's tax burden overall on both the rich and working people tended to decline. Prudent herself almost to the point of parsimony – she spent just £9000 a year on her wardrobe – the queen resisted all suggestions from her counsellors and parliament for new ways of raising national revenue. On the other hand, she did reduce government expenditure by devolving some responsibilities to the shires and towns, which meant a rise in local taxation that was often substantial.

Local authorities had to bear the costs of building and repairing roads, and also of recruiting, training and equipping militias, especially during the years of war with Spain, when invasion was expected imminently. Records from the county of Kent show that during the years surrounding the arrival of the Spanish Armada in 1588, military expenditure in that county alone was running at more than £1000 per annum, which had to be raised almost entirely from local taxpayers. That and the imposition of 'ship money' to equip and maintain the navy caused a great deal of discontent, especially among the residents of inland areas, which had previously been exempt from naval levies.

To replenish the royal coffers the queen borrowed heavily – £500,000 to finance the campaign against the Spanish, for example – and also took to selling off crown lands. Between 1550 and her death in 1603, she raised almost £900,000 from land sales, a short-term strategy that would damage future royal revenues yet ensured that her successor, James Stuart, inherited a 'national' debt of just £365,000, barely more than that left by Queen Mary nearly half an inflation-ridden century earlier.

Loans and land sales were not the exchequer's only sources of cash revenue, however. During the last half of the sixteenth century England had embarked upon what the modern economist John Maynard Keynes would describe as its first forays into overseas investment — although perhaps 'investment' is not the most appropriate word, as the following report makes clear:

When we were at sea our General rifled the ship, and found in her good store of the wine of Chili, and 25,000 pesos of very pure and fine gold of Valdivia, amounting in value to 37,000 ducats of Spanish money, and above . . . From hence we went to a certain port called Tarapaca; where, being landed, we found by the sea side a Spaniard lying asleep, who had lying by him thirteen bars of silver, which weighed 4,000 ducats Spanish. We took the silver and left the man . . .

Not far from hence, going on land for fresh water, we met with a Spaniard and an Indian boy driving eight llamas or sheep of Peru, which are as big as asses; every of which sheep had on his back two bags of leather, each bag containing 50 lb. weight of fine silver. So that, bringing both the sheep and their burthen to the ships, we found in all the bags eight hundredweight of silver . . .

Herehence we sailed to a place called Arica; and, being entered the port, we found there three small barks, which we rifled, and found in one of them fifty-seven wedges of silver, each of them weighing

> about 20 lb. weight, and every of these wedges were of
> the fashion and bigness of a brickbat . . .

The extracts come from a book entitled *The Famous Voyage of Sir Francis Drake into the South Sea, and therehence about the whole Globe of the Earth, begun in the year of our Lord 1577*. It was written by Francis Petty, one of Drake's gentlemen-at-arms, and it tells a story of not only brave exploration but also naked piracy. Wherever the treasure of the hated Spaniards could be found, Drake and his men seized as much as they could, so that when they docked at Deptford on the Thames in September 1580, at the end of their historic journey, they brought with them some £600,000 worth of gold and silver bullion and perhaps as much as £1,000,000 more in jewels, objects in precious metals, fine cloths and other goods. Small wonder that, in spite of official protests from Spain about this ugly face of capitalism, the queen visited Drake on his ship and knighted him.

Apart from swelling the royal coffers, though, Drake's exploits and the accounts of the exotic virgin lands he had visited set in train another policy initiative that would have profound implications for Britain and the rest of the world. In 1584 Elizabeth signed a charter that laid the early foundations upon which the first great international economic power of the modern era would eventually be built.

> Knowe yee that of our especial grace, certaine
> science, and meere motion, we have given and
> graunted, and by these presents for us, our heires and
> successors, we give and graunt to our trustie and

welbeloved servant Walter. Ralegh, Esquire, and to his heires and asignees for ever, free libertie and licence from time to time, and at all times for ever hereafter, to discover, search, finde out, and view such remote, heathen and barbarous lands, countries, and territories, not actually possessed of any Christian Prince, nor inhabited by Christian People, as to him, his heires and assignees, and to every or any of them shall seeme good, and the same to have, horde, occupie and enjoy to him, his heires and assignee for ever, with all prerogatives, commodities, jurisdictions, royalties, privileges, franchises, and preheminences, thereto or thereabouts both by sea and land, whatsoever we by our letters patents may graunt . . .

Armed with this exhortation to go forth and multiply the dominions, and therefore the income, of the English crown, Ralegh fitted out a fleet later the same year to found a colony on the eastern seaboard of North America. The adventurers finally landed near the Spanish outpost of Florida, in a region to which the queen gave the name of Virginia. There was a long, hard road ahead, but the English pound had taken its first step towards world domination.

10

Money Makes the
World Go Round

*Depreciating the Value of nummary Denominations,
to defraud the Creditors of the Publick and of private
Persons; by Proclamations of Sovereigns, by
Recoinages, and by a late Contrivance of a
depreciating Paper-Credit-Currency; were never
practised but in notoriously bad Administrations.*
William Douglass, *A Discourse concerning the Currencies
of the British Plantations In America*, 1740

Queen Elizabeth had successfully reformed and stabilised the coinage, but she and her ministers were powerless to halt a growing economic malaise which, by the end of her reign in 1603, was developing into a serious crisis. Part of the problem was that throughout the sixteenth century the population of the British Isles had been steadily increasing and, in its closing years, was beginning dangerously to exceed the capacity of the nation to feed and provide work for it. The situation was not helped by a series of bad harvests throughout the 1590s as a fundamental change in the European climate brought about what has been described as a mini ice age. Food prices became so inflated that many people were reduced to eating grass, moss and tree bark, while the demand for more cultivable areas sent land prices soaring. At the same time agricultural production had become seriously unbalanced because England's domination of the cloth trade meant there was considerably more profit in grazing sheep than in raising crops. Wool was probably more plentiful than food.

At least the queen had been modest in her revenue demands, but unfortunately she was succeeded by a monarch who lacked her prudence and saw no virtue in keeping his expenses under control. James I had come from a different tradition as James VI of Scotland, where the coinage had been routinely debased to the extent that a loaf of bread costing a penny in England sold for twelve Scottish pence in Edinburgh. It is no surprise, then, that one of the new king's first acts so far as the currency was concerned was to reduce the weight of the gold pound coin, which he also tried unsuccessfully to replace with a piece known as the Unite, symbolising the coming together of the two kingdoms. Later the value of all the gold coinage was 'cried up' by ten per cent, but in 1619 lighter pieces were issued reflecting the original worth of gold coins at twenty shillings, fifteen shillings and ten shillings – the laurel, the spur-ryal and a new angel.

There was also some fusion of the English and Scottish

coinage. By royal proclamation the Scottish mark – known in the vernacular as the 'thistle-merk' – became legal tender in England, but it was less than popular because of its awkward exchange rate of thirteen shillings and fourpence. Scottish sixpenny pieces circulated, too, with a nominal value of a halfpenny, and a so-called thistle crown in gold was also produced, although somewhat confusingly it was worth four shillings against an English crown of five shillings.

Since the first Stuart king saw himself as monarch of a united Britain – it was James who started the policy of transplanting large numbers of Scottish and English farmers in Ireland – Irish coins were also circulated in England, but not, for once, as nominal substitutes for the native variety. An Irish shilling, for example, would fetch ninepence in English coinage and a groat threepence rather than fourpence.

These changes were intended to ensure the stability of the money supply but, as in the reign of Elizabeth, economic forces were at work that negated many of the supposed benefits. Inflation continued apace and, as usual, the greatest pressure was on the lower denomination silver coinage. In many districts tokens reappeared, usually made of lead, and by 1613 so many were in use that the king officially banned them. Like some of his predecessors he experimented with copper coins, again foisting them on the Irish, but their introduction into England proved to be uneconomic because of the vastly greater numbers required, so James privatised the activity on the basis that half the profits would accrue to the exchequer. The private sector fared no better than the Royal Mint, however, though at least there was a supply of copper farthings for those who needed them.

Not that quarters of a penny were of great use as price rises accelerated and trade slumped right across Europe. Textiles, one of the mainstays of Britain's agricultural and industrial sectors alike, entered a fifty-year decline after 1620, with catastrophic consequences for many of the 200,000 or so workers in the industry and severe knock-on effects for the pastoralists who supported them. So great was the distress that the Poor Laws had to be strengthened in 1626, with the result that children as young as six were forcibly apprenticed to crafts such as lace-making, at which they would spend ten or more hours a day for a payment of as little as fourpence a yard.

Market records from the 1620s show the price of wheat running at thirty-six shillings a quarter (twenty-eight pounds) for the best quality, butter at threepence-halfpenny a pound, cheese at twopence-halfpenny, chickens at fourpence each, a goose at a shilling, and peas and beans at nearly eightpence a pound. With the best wages at perhaps ninepence or a shilling a day and many people employed only part-time because of the recession – as well as being unable to find land on which to grow their own food, or in some cases forbidden by law to do so – the standard of living for most families was low, to say the least. A day's pay would not buy a pound of flour for bread and for many people would hardly stretch to a pound of peas.

For the desperate there were two options – emigration or revolution. Both came to pass, with the second and its aftermath serving to speed up the process of the first.

Even before Sir Francis Drake had returned from his piratical and highly profitable voyage round the world, England was seriously considering the economic potential of the new territories discovered with thrilling regularity as the age of exploration got into its stride. Spain, as the dominant European power of the time, had already staked claims in the southern part of the Americas and the French were active in the far north, or what is now Canada, while – as one intrepid English navigator, Edward Haies, commented – 'many voyages have been pretended, yet hitherto never any thoroughly accomplished by our nation, of exact discovery into the bowels of those main, ample, and vast countries'.

This was particularly irritating to men such as Haies in view of the fact that 'the first discovery of these coasts, never heard of before, was well begun by John Cabot the father and Sebastian his son, an Englishman born, who were the first finders out of all that great tract of land stretching from the Cape of Florida unto those islands which we now call the Newfoundland'. It was clear, therefore, to all right-thinking people that 'God hath reserved the same to be reduced unto Christian civility by the English nation'.

In 1579, a former hero of Queen Elizabeth's Irish campaigns, Sir Humphrey Gilbert, had lost his entire fortune in attempting to fulfil what was clearly divine destiny by founding an English colony in Newfoundland. The euphoria that followed Drake's triumphant return, however, encouraged Gilbert to try again and with the help of Edward Haies he set off in 1583 in a little fleet of five vessels with the aim of exploiting such secrets as might be found in North America, which was 'esteemed fertile and rich in minerals'.

The Gilbert expedition ended in disaster, with only Haies's ship surviving, and it was not until 1607 that a permanent English colony in the Americas was established. This was in Virginia and it was appropriately named Jamestown. It was followed by settlements in Massachusetts, Connecticut and Maryland, so that by the 1630s – when there were as many as 5000 English colonists in Virginia alone – transatlantic traffic was becoming almost routine and guides were being published to advise would-be emigrants what they needed to take with them. The recommendations give an idea of what a pound would buy in the mid-seventeenth century.

It was recommended, for instance, that colonists should equip themselves with a cart, a pair of wheels and an axletree; a plough and a wheelbarrow; a pair of bellows, a scoop, a 'great pail', a short oak ladder, two shovels and a lantern. The cost of this equipment was estimated at forty-two shillings and sixpence. Household items should include a large iron pot, three pans of various sizes, a large frying pan and two skillets, a spit and a gridiron: total cost about three pounds seventeen shillings and eightpence.

How these brave adventurers raised the money to furnish themselves with their necessities is not clear – and no doubt many did not – but the fact is that in the course of the seventeenth century more than 300,000 people, mainly young single men, left the British Isles to settle on the other side of the Atlantic. That figure represents more than five per cent of the total population of England and Wales in the seventeenth century.

Emigration reached its peak in the wake of the civil war that brought the execution of King Charles I and the dictatorship of Oliver Cromwell. The touchstone for the conflict was the king's tussle with Parliament over his right to raise taxes, but it had its roots in the economic dislocation that had begun to destabilise the English social structure as far back as the last years of Elizabeth I. Discontent took many forms, sometimes translated into religious conviction and bigotry, and in other cases focused on the vast gulf between not merely the rich and the poor but between what we would now think of as the employers and the workers. In a curious way the colonists also had their part to play in fomenting dissatisfaction with the established order. Stories filtered back of great achievements in the New World based on participation, community spirit, social justice and shared religious zeal. Englishmen looked about them and saw exploitation, division, injustice and corruption in both a religious and a secular sense. The civil war had no particular identifiable cause – it just happened as a result of pressures that had been building for half a century, punctuated by sporadic uprisings in Scotland, the West Country, the Midlands, East Anglia, Ireland and London.

Naturally, the war itself did nothing to improve the economic condition of Britain. Soldiers have to be armed, supplied, supported, fed and paid, and the ebb and flow of the fighting played havoc with the money supply, even though regular bullion stocks had been ensured by means of a treaty with Spain. On the outbreak of war in February 1642, Parliament took control of the Royal Mint, obliging the king to strike his own emergency coinage in provincial mints, which subsequently changed hands depending on which side held them at the time. Oxford, York, Bristol, Shrewsbury, Aberystwyth, Truro and Wellington, Shropshire, all produced coins at various times, ranging from one-pound and ten-shilling pieces in silver to a new version of King James's Unite made from the Oxford college plate and farthings in brass or copper. Some places where mints could not be established – among them Chester, Newark, Scarborough and Carlisle – produced crude coins while under siege simply by cutting them out of gold or silver objects.

It is often said that war promotes technical advances, and in this case it served to hasten the introduction of the faster and more efficient screw-presses that Elizabeth I had failed to persuade the Royal Mint to use. From now on it would be possible to issue coinage in greater volume, more variety and at lower cost. With the cash economy set to make a further leap forward, this was a crucial advance.

Meanwhile, in the new colonies far away from the troubles at home, the supply of money was also becoming a problem. Founding settlements and cultivating land was one thing, but to survive the settlers had to have access to some means of exchange enabling them to trade and make the sort of profits dangled before them by the likes of Edward Haies. Given that England itself had long suffered problems in obtaining bullion, the new English territories had little hope of being able to produce coinage in a form comparable to the limited supplies the colonists had taken with them, which rapidly degraded anyway to the point where they had to be replaced.

Spain and Portugal had vastly enriched themselves through their South American settlements, having discovered huge quantities of gold and silver almost sitting there for the taking. The British colonists were not so lucky. Newfoundland yielded little more than fish and forestry, while would-be miners in Virginia had to content themselves with iron, copper and allum, the double phosphate of aluminium and potassium used principally in dyeing and papermaking. These were still valuable commodities, but whereas the Spanish and Portuguese could quickly transform their natural resources into coinage, the British had to resort to the slow, costly and uncertain processes of trade. Either they had to find the cash to finance ships for their exports, or they had to manage without adequate supplies of currency until their goods had been sold back in Europe.

One solution was to use the traditional standard of value among the American Indians, the strings of white or black beads known as wampum – short for 'wampumpeag', which literally means white beads. These were made from the shells of clams and other molluscs, often fashioned into belts that might be between eighteen inches and six feet long, and some native American tribes specialised in their manufacture. Whether they were actually used as currency among the tribes is unknown, but they were certainly highly regarded and by the mid-1630s they had become recognised as legal tender in the Massachusetts colony. The white wampum had a value of six beads to a penny, while the rarer black variety were regarded as being worth three to the penny. At first their use was restricted to sums of up to a shilling, but within a few years it was legal to exchange wampum in amounts up to two pounds. So popular did the beads become, and so pressing the need for money, that the settlers began to set up factories producing wampum belts by industrial processes.

Other colonies returned to the barter system, exchanging crops such as rice and maize for goods and services, but as with wampum these were mainly of use for internal transactions. Funds and supplies from the home country could hardly be paid for indefinitely in native beads or hundredweights of maize and in any case an important part of the purpose of the new territories was eventually to contribute to the cash economy in Britain. An unofficial mint was set up in Massachusetts in 1652 and for more than thirty years it produced shillings, sixpenny pieces and threepenny coins by limiting them to about seventy-five per cent of the silver content they would have had in Britain. Inevitably, though, the output of the mint was relatively small and the coins were not legal tender elsewhere.

Of more use were the high-quality Spanish pesos, minted in Mexico or Peru from local silver, and the Portuguese eight-real silver coin, which became something of an international currency during the seventeeth and eighteenth centuries, and was immortalised in the 'pieces of eight' of pirate lore and legend. Both these coins became legal tender in Britain, worth between four shillings and sixpence and six shillings, which made it easier for the colonists to deal with trading houses there. They also helped to ensure that the pound sterling would never establish itself in the New World.

It was the peso, in fact, that would later give America its now all-powerful dollar. The large Spanish coin was based on a venerable central-European silver piece produced in Bohemia and known as the Joachimstaler after the town in which it was minted. The name was later abbreviated to 'taler' and the coins circulated widely in the British Isles, partly as a result of trade but also to fill the gaps left by the frequent shortfalls in the domestic money supply. The name taler therefore became common in reference to money and the Scots in particular adopted it to distinguish their currency from that of the English while, in the manner of borrowed words, the pronunciation was corrupted to dollar. Since the peso resembled the taler and because many later American colonists were Scottish, the term dollar was widely used for coinage in the New World.

Of equal significance to the arrival of the peso-dollar was another development arising from the chronic shortage of currency in the American colonies. The settlers in Virginia had been encouraged to plant tobacco, imported from the West Indies, as a cash crop, but of course their problem was actually obtaining cash for it to finance new planting. Smoking was gaining popularity in Europe and the leaves had a ready export market, but the risks of shipping meant it might often be months before the tobacco farmers and merchants could collect the money earned from the trade and in the meantime they had little to meet immediate needs or service debts. The Virginians voted to accept as legal tender handwritten credit notes based on the value of tobacco stored in warehouses awaiting sale – the forerunners of the banknotes that in succeeding centuries would separate the money supply from the amounts of bullion currently available.

Within less than fifty years these 'tobacco notes' would be copied in other colonies in a way that caused great consternation back in Britain and a violent debate would break out over the legitimacy of 'paper money' that would not be settled finally until well into the nineteenth century.

Such difficulties apart, by the time of the restoration of the English monarchy under Charles II in 1660, the economic structure of international trade had begun to be built and – inspired partly by the settlers in the New World – at last the British were seriously looking outward, following the example of the Spanish, Portuguese and Dutch. The aggressive traders of the Netherlands, in particular, had shown the way towards the end of the sixteenth century when they had attempted to monopolise the trade in pepper, a commodity highly prized to the extent that it was sometimes literally worth its weight in gold. In response, James I had issued a charter for the formation of the London East India Company in an attempt to break the hold of the Dutch, but Charles I had severely compromised its operations by forcing the company to sell him on credit its entire pepper stock, which he then disposed of at a substantial loss on the open market. The years of civil war and the Protectorate under Cromwell had done nothing to improve Britain's position as an international trader, but the growing success of the colonies meant that by the time of the Restoration it was becoming clear that foreign investment now involved something more than scouring the seas for rivals' ships and emptying them of their cargoes.

In 1664 a merchant named Thomas Mun, who was involved in the East India Company, published a seminal book setting out the case for large-scale mercantilism and arguing that only through a favourable balance of trade could a modern nation hope to meet its needs. It was no longer the available supply of bullion that dictated the exchange value of currency and therefore the health of the economy, according to Mun's thoughts in *England's Treasure by Forraign Trade*:

> Although a Kingdom may be enriched by gifts received, or by purchase taken from some other Nations, yet these are things uncertain and of small consideration when they happen.
> The ordinary means therefore to increase our

wealth and treasure is by Forraign Trade, wherein wee must ever observe this rule; to sell more to strangers yearly than wee consume of theirs in value. For suppose that when this Kingdom is plentifully served with the Cloth, Lead, Tin, Iron, Fish and other native commodities, we doe yearly export the over-plus to forraign Countreys to the value of twenty-two hundred thousand pounds; by which means we are enabled beyond the Seas to buy and bring in forraign wares for our use and Consumptions, to the value of twenty hundred thousand pounds: By this order duly kept in our trading, we may rest assured that the kingdom shall be enriched yearly two hundred thousand pounds, which must be brought to us in so much Treasure; because that part of our stock which is not returned to us in wares must necessarily be brought home in treasure. . . .

Only through a healthy balance of overseas trade, Mun argued, and the 'Noble profession of the Merchant', could Britain achieve 'The supply of our wants, The employment of our poor, The improvement of our Lands, The means of our Treasure' and 'The honour of the Kingdom'.

The focus of attention had so far always been on the bullion value of the currency, Mun wrote, with the result that trade and the economy in general had been judged on the basis of whether the gold or silver content of the coinage had been greater or lesser than of currencies elsewhere. That, however, was not the point.

It is a certain rule in our forraign trade, in those places where our commodities exported are over-ballanced in value by forraign wares brought into this Realm, there our mony is undervalued in exchange; and where the contrary of this is performed, there our mony is overvalued. But let the Merchants exchange be at a high rate, or at a low rate, or at the Par pro pari, or put down altogether; Let Forraign Princes enhance their coins, or debase their standards, and let His Majesty do the like, or keep them constant as they now stand; Let forraign coins pass current here in all payments at higher rates than they are worth at the Mint; Let the Statutes for employments by Strangers stand in force or be repealed; Let the meer Exchanger do his worst; Let Princes oppress, Lawyers extort, Usurers bite, Prodigals waste, and lastly let Merchants carry out what mony they shall have occasion to use in traffique. Yet all these actions can work no other effects in the course of trade than is declared in this discourse. For so much Treasure only will be brought in or carried out of a Commonwealth, as the Forraign Trade doth over or under ballance in value.

This was the beginning of what was to become one of the great economic disputes of history, a debate that influenced the American Civil War and has perhaps reached its zenith in the creation of the European single currency. Is it the money supply and the exchange rate that matters most in determining a nation's economic health, or is it the balance of trade? It was an absolutely vital question in the closing years of the seventeenth century and one equally critical for the history of the pound sterling.

All the alarums and excursions that had attended the development of the cash economy throughout the Middle Ages and even into the early modern period – the supply of coinage, its weight, its purity, the availability of bullion – were now mere bagatelles as the use of money entered an epoch that would be shaped by the technical and scientific advances that had allowed ships to circumnavigate the globe with relative certainty and the people they carried to discover new resources perhaps ultimately more valuable than the precious metals upon which sophisticated economic activity had been based for 1000 years.

As Britain made its choice between the traditional integrity of currency and the potentially glittering prizes of mercantilism, the pound was poised to transform itself from a simple piece of gold into the symbol of a power the like of which the world had never seen before. It might have failed its American colonists, but there were plenty of other places to be explored and exploited.

11

Bankers' Hours

I do find upon my monthly ballance that I am worth
£650, the greatest sum that ever I was yet master of.
I pray God give me a thankful spirit, and care to
improve and increase it.

Samuel Pepys, Diary entry for 29 May 1662

Britain appeared to take a step backwards in 1660 when the republic created by Oliver Cromwell was replaced by a restored monarchy under King Charles II. In some ways it was almost as if the Civil War had never happened. All the acts of the Cromwellian Parliaments were declared null and void, while those passed during the reign of the executed Charles I were revived. Yet in the intervening twenty years or so the country and the world had been transformed. In political terms the absolutist view of monarchy had been replaced by the idea of consent: the acceptance of the divine right of kings might have survived, but in Britain they now ruled on the basis of power-sharing at both national and local level. It would be many years before the concept of the constitutional monarchy was fully developed, but by the time of the Restoration it had become inevitable.

To be sure, the powers of Parliament in governmental terms remained very limited, but in the crucial area of finance it had secured for itself the final say on exchequer revenues. Charles could in theory follow any policy he wished, but if it required funds he had to seek parliamentary support to raise them. No longer could the king impose sudden taxes on an unwilling population. Parliament voted him an annual income at a sum that would have made the mouths of his predecessors water – £1,200,000, raised mainly from indirect taxation – and if he required any more he had to convince the parliamentarians that the purpose was both necessary and wise.

The king had also, in a sense, lost control of the money supply. Though the Royal Mint remained the sole legitimate source of coinage, and was producing it at a rate of as much as £20,000 a week, the effects of inflation, growing trade and colonisation overseas and the disruption of the Civil War followed by the republic had effectively broken the link between commercial activity and the royal prerogative to determine the amount of currency in circulation. People had found other ways of doing business and from this point on it would be the balance of trade rather than royal needs that governed the demand for and the supply of money. At the same time, while the availability of bullion remained important in the sense that it formed the basis for the valuation of currency, the notion was spreading that in everyday terms money was worth only what it could be exchanged for, so it began to take forms other than coins made from a certain weight of precious metals. From now on the money supply would no longer depend on the numbers of coins in circulation.

An early example of the new representation of pounds, shillings and pence was the goldsmith's note. We have already seen how in the late thirteenth century the Goldsmiths' Company of the City of London was forming part of the monetary system through its validation of the standards of the coinage in the Trial of the Pyx. By the early seventeenth century, however, goldsmiths had become issuers of a sort of money themselves. To begin with, their notes were merely receipts for valuables deposited with them but as such they fulfilled one of the purposes of money, which is to symbolise a store of value. Among the uncertainties of the late-Elizabethan and early-Stuart periods, the practice of leaving deposits with goldsmiths became increasingly common – especially so during the Civil War, when either side might suddenly descend in search of treasure to confiscate with a view to financing their continuing military operations. As well as plate and precious objects, people began to hoard good coinage in goldsmiths' safes at a time when much bad money was circulating.

Soon it was obvious that if the goldsmiths' receipts represented a store of value then they also served as confirmation of the financial standing of their holders: someone who possessed a note relating to the deposit of a certain amount of items in gold or silver was clearly going to be in a position to make payments at least up to the value of his deposit. This was particularly useful to merchants, who could thus obtain on credit the goods they dealt in by presenting to the supplier a goldsmith's note affirming their personal worth. It was no longer necessary to hand over bags of cash in order to begin trading, so that ever more expansive deals could be made on the basis that the debt incurred would be repaid either when the profits arrived or by the redemption of the articles deposited with the goldsmith.

The provision of credit had become widespread since the church-inspired ban on usury had been lifted in 1545, when Henry VIII had issued a law permitting interest to be charged on loans up to a maximum of ten per cent per annum. The lack of such a facility had previously held back the development of financial institutions in Britain and had contributed to economic stagnation by limiting the country's ability to trade overseas. Without Henry's liberalisation of credit arrangements it is doubtful whether the likes of Drake and Ralegh, and the merchant adventurers who followed them, would have been able to pursue their ambitions and give Britain a stake in the new international trading system that was opening up. Goldsmiths' notes – of which the first known example was issued even before the Civil War in 1633 – helped to reduce the risks involved in lending money and therefore made credit even easier to obtain.

Before long, the notes themselves became a medium of exchange, endorsed for payment to a third party as what we would now call a cheque. The first such note ever recorded dates from 1659 and instructs a London firm of goldsmiths called Morris and Clayton to pay £400 to a certain Mr Delboe. In effect, the goldsmiths had turned into bankers.

The great diarist Samuel Pepys, who died in 1703, frequently refers to the primitive banking system operated by the goldsmiths. In 1666, for instance, he records a visit to one Sir Robert Viner, an alderman of the City of London who was knighted in 1665 and made a baronet the following year. Pepys had money 'lodged in Lumbard [Lombard] Street in Viner's hands' and had 'no mind to have it lie there longer'.

It was not only in private accounts that the goldsmiths acted. Pepys was an official at the Admiralty, where he rose to the position of secretary, and he notes several visits to Viner on account of financial arrangements entered into in his capacity as a civil servant – 'my main business was about settling the business of Debusty's £5,000 tallies, which I did for the present . . .' and, on another occasion, 'he and I into his garden to discourse of money, but none is to be had . . . he tells me how the taxes of the last assessment, which should have been in good part gathered, are not yet laid, and that even in part of the City of London . . . I parted, my mind not eased by any money, but only that I had done my part to the King's service.'

Sir Robert was not Pepys's only banker, either. In 1668 he records sending a 'banknote' for £600 to his father, drawn on his account with John Colvill, another goldsmith in Lombard Street. The goldsmith-banker's note had now turned into a genuine substitute for coinage, the forerunner of paper money.

What is really remarkable about this emergence of financial services in Britain is that it had taken so long. The explanation may have something to do with the fact that the retreat into primitivism after the fall of the Roman Empire had been more complete in most regions of the British Isles – Ireland being the exception, mainly because of its early adherence to Christianity – than in other parts of Europe. As we have noted, it took two centuries for the use of money to re-emerge in Britain after the overthrow of Rome and when that did happen the successive invasions and the consequent lack of central authority meant that the focus was always on the currency itself rather than on the opportunities money offered. It remains a curious fact, however, that even when trade began rapidly to expand, when the Norman and Angevin kings controlled a substantial empire on the Continent, and when English wool and cloth had turned into very marketable commodities overseas, the British relied mainly on foreigners to provide the financial expertise necessary for sophisticated economic development.

The basic functions of banking, which are deposit and transfer, had been in place for 2000 years before they became common in Britain. The temples of ancient Babylon had undertaken services exactly the same as those offered by the goldsmiths of London in the seventeenth century, storing valuables and authenticating depositors' ability to meet obligations. Archaeologists have found cuneiform tablets indicating that credit, interest charges and even mortgages on property were known to the Mesopotamian civilisation long before coinage had been introduced – depositors used grain, livestock and precious metals as a basis for their transactions. The appearance of coins in Asia Minor in about 600 BC led to the creation of commercial banks, mainly in the Greek city states, and the system was further refined later throughout the Roman Empire, with laws covering banking operations that would presumably have been present in Britain.

During the Dark Ages banking continued in the more easterly part of the former empire, but it was not until the eleventh century that such practices were revived in western

Europe. Records from the Italian city of Genoa suggest that the primary function of bankers at that time was merely to change money, which they did sitting at a table known as a *bancum*. By the next century, though, they were accepting deposits, offering loans and making investments in commercial ventures, and banking had spread to Florence and other cities, from where it would move on mainly to Spain and the Netherlands. Business was often transacted at the many large fairs that were a feature of international trade during the thirteenth and fourteenth centuries, and both the kings and the merchants of Britain were accustomed to arranging credit through representatives of the mainly Italian banking houses that attended them. Yet while in Spain, for example, perhaps more than a third of the population was operating private bank accounts by 1500, the inhabitants of Britain were still for the most part handing over bags of pounds in carrying out their transactions. Henry VII might have produced the most handsome currency in Europe, but it had not greatly encouraged the development of the sophisticated financial support systems that allowed Spain and Portugal to create their early overseas trading empires.

Even as Britain began to notice that it was falling behind its continental neighbours in the expansion of trade, and bills of exchange and other forms of credit were being routinely used by merchant adventurers and the growing class of manufacturers, it was to the bankers of Antwerp that Thomas Gresham was obliged to turn in order to help finance the recoinage of Elizabeth I. For a country that now depends on the financial services industry for the bulk of its national income, Britain was a very slow starter.

When it did begin to move, however, the British banking

system – at least insofar as its support for trade was concerned – soon made its presence felt, backed by international respect for the pound sterling, which after the Great Debasement of Henry VIII, the recoinage of Elizabeth and the vicissitudes of the Civil War, re-established itself as the premier currency of Europe under Charles II. Less of a dreamer than most of his Stuart relations, Charles adopted a pragmatic approach to both the money supply and the economy in general. His parliamentary grant, while insufficient for what he believed were his needs, at least gave him a reliable income, which meant that he had no cause to manipulate the coinage as so many impecunious kings of the past had done, even if he could have achieved it without the consent of Parliament. Equally, the king had an interest in promoting business for the simple reason that he would have recourse to the emerging financial markets to make good any shortfall in his official revenues.

One of his first acts so far as the currency was concerned was to insist on greater mechanisation at the Royal Mint, an improvement denied to Elizabeth I because of the vested interests of the craftsmen, who had continued to produce hand-hammered coins. In 1661 Charles imported a French engineer, Pierre Blondeau, to oversee the installation of new horse-powered equipment that prepared the metal at the proper thickness, cut the coin blanks in a continuous process, stamped the engraving so that it was identical on each coin and finally milled the edges in order to make clipping impossible. Blondeau's main job was to perfect the milling operation, which not only ingrained the edges of the coins but also added lettering, while the engraving and manufacture were placed under the control of three brothers called Roettier, who were mint-masters from Flanders.

The first production of this new minting regime, in 1663, was a gold pound coin, known as the guinea because it was made from bullion discovered in West Africa by a London company formed expressly to explore, exploit and trade from the continent. The insignia of this Royal Africa Company, an elephant, was featured under the portrait of the king on the face of the guinea, a splendid coin that would continue to be minted for 150 years and would survive long after that as the amount – one pound and one shilling – in which the prices of horses, paintings and antiques were calculated, and the fees of lawyers, doctors and other professional people were paid.

So fine was the guinea, which bore the motto 'An Ornament and Safeguard', that it rapidly became a victim of its own success, with people tending not to spend it but to hoard it and even to invest in its future, as Samuel Pepys explained in 1666: '29 October. [Sir Robert Viner] tells me that Ginnys, which I bought 2000 of not long ago, and cost me but 18½d change, will now cost me 22d, and but very few to be had at any price. However, some more I will have, for they are very convenient – and of easy disposal.'

By 1694 the coin with a face value of one pound, or twenty shillings, was changing hands at thirty shillings and its actual value continued to fluctuate until 1717, when its worth as legal tender was officially fixed at twenty-one shillings, the amount that continued to be associated with it both as a coin and as a notional amount until it fell into disuse after the decimalisation of the British currency in 1971.

Other reforms undertaken by Charles II served further to weaken the link between coinage and bullion, to prepare the way for the symbolic forms of currency that would rapidly follow and to promote the spread of banking and other financial services. As the guinea appeared for the first time, an Act for the Encouragement of Trade lifted the prohibition on the export of bullion and foreign coinage, provided its overseas origin could be established. Three years later the Act for the Encouragement of Coinage put an end to mint charges with the intention of persuading more people to have their gold and silver converted and to make recycling easier. The cost of minting and profits received by the monarch from it had been a critical factor in both the quality and quantity of the money supply, leading among other things to the chronic shortage of smaller denomination coins. Now, mechanisation had reduced the overheads and the Act provided for them to be met by customs duties on alcohol, including vinegar, so there was no bar to matching currency supply with demand.

An early sign of this was the issue in 1672 of the first ever government-approved English copper coins from the Royal Mint. These halfpennies and farthings were milled as carefully as their gold and silver relatives and in their own way were just as attractive, bearing the female figure representing Britannia that would grace British coins for three centuries afterwards and which still appears on banknotes today. The image, according to contemporary rumour repeated by Pepys and others, was based on the Duchess of Richmond, one of the queen's maids of honour, whose charms had captivated the king. 'As well done as ever I saw anything in my whole life I think,' said Pepys, 'and a pretty thing it is that he should choose her face to represent Britannia by.'

The new coinage of Charles II, like that of several

monarchs before him, represented a period of great confidence in the British economy and as such it was an important indicator. It would be many years before notional monetary reserves could compete with stocks of gold and silver, in the form of either coins or bullion – indeed, the furore in 1999 over the decision of the British and Swiss governments to sell off large amounts of their gold reserves and replace them with foreign currency might suggest that the argument has still not been settled. However, what had changed by the second half of the seventeenth century was the way in which the demand for large sums of money was being met. In the developing mercantile-industrial economy, cash was not the appropriate or the most convenient medium of exchange and by 1698 it was estimated that the London money market – which had grown rapidly to rival the then leading financial centre of Amsterdam – provided more currency in the form of bills, notes and other paper instruments than the sum total of the existing coinage.

One indication of the way the economy was moving is provided by an essay published in 1650 by Abraham Cowley, an official in the household of Charles I's queen who, after the Restoration, became a doctor in London. It is among the first of what would become a never-ending series of heartfelt cries of pain from the farming lobby as its traditional economic importance declined in favour of industry and commerce. Citing agriculture as the oldest art, Cowley complained:

> The utility (I mean plainly the lucre of it) is not so
> great, now in our nation, as arises from merchandise
> and the trading of the city, from whence many of the
> best estates and chief honours of the kingdom are

derived: we have no men now fetcht from the plow to
be made lords, as they were in Rome to be made
consuls and dictators; the reason of which I conceive
to be from an evil custom, now grown as strong
among us as if it were a law, which is, that no men put
their children to be bred up apprentices in agriculture, as in other trades, but such who are so poor,
that, when they come to be men, they have not
wherewithal to set up in it, and so can only farm some
small parcel of ground, the rent of which devours all
but the bare subsistence of the tenant: whilst they
who are proprietors of the land are either too proud,
or, for want of that kind of education, too ignorant, to
improve their estates, though the means of doing it
be as easy and certain in this, as in any other track of
commerce.

Land prices and rents were falling in the second half of the
seventeenth century and the price of most agricultural commodities remained more or less static well into the eighteenth.
Wage rates for farmworkers had hardly risen for years, at less
than a shilling a day, which explains why 'no men put their
children to be bred up apprentices in agriculture' unless there
was nothing else they could do. More and more young people
moved from the countryside to the growing towns and cities,
where they could find jobs in manufacturing, shopkeeping or
domestic service, while others emigrated to the colonies and
increasing numbers took to the roads to become carters and
packmen, transporting or selling the goods turned out in urban
workshops.

Though there had as yet been little technical innovation in manufacturing processes, goods had largely replaced domestic commodities and trading had superseded the tilling of land on the scale of economic activity. Above all, the notion that the balance of trade with foreign countries was the prescription for maintaining the health of the economy had now become the conventional wisdom. Because of this, the most lucrative parts of the agricultural market had moved overseas, with tobacco and sugar arriving in London to be exported elsewhere, spices from India and minerals from Africa all contributing to national wealth. Economic power was shifting from the landowning gentry and the yeoman farmer to a new class of merchants and traders whose horizons sat far beyond their native shores.

The financial requirements of the new rich were very different from those of previous generations. They needed access to large sums quickly, they wanted to make many transactions since their wealth depended on investment rather than property or savings, and most of all they demanded flexibility to cover the time lag between investing in and receiving returns from ventures that were essentially speculative. In short, they required a monetary system that was both more portable and more adaptable than coinage. The goldsmith-bankers, whose assets were generally stable because of their bullion dealing, met the challenge by means of the marketable bill, a refinement of the 'banknote' sent by Samuel Pepys to his father, which was based purely on the value of his deposit with the goldsmith. The new notes, usually denominated in pounds, were in fact bills of exchange, which could be used as a substitute for cash, passing through many hands before they were presented for redemption.

For example, a seller of goods could accept a promissory note from a buyer to be honoured at some future date for a certain amount of money and drawn on a 'bank' account with a goldsmith, or sometimes a lawyer or another merchant. The creditor could then pass on the note to settle debts of his own, perhaps with suppliers who in turn could use the same bill to pay for raw materials. Alternatively, the creditor might exchange the note for cash or credit from his own banker, who would take his profit by buying the note at a discount on its face value. Using the bill as capital, the banker could equally advance money to a third party, receiving in return a further negotiable note. At each stage, the bill had to be endorsed with the word 'accepted' and the names of both the deliverer and the recipient. In this way many deals could be done over a period of time without a single coin changing hands.

Limited at first to domestic transactions, the use of such notes had expanded by the end of the seventeenth century to cover business arrangements involving foreign exchange and 'London bills' endorsed by reputable companies had become a standard feature of overseas trading, as widely acceptable as notes issued in previously dominant Amsterdam. Underpinned by the integrity of the pound sterling, London's rise towards becoming the world's leading financial centre had begun.

What was principally a merchant banking system worked well except for one thing: it depended on its depositors meeting their commitments at some stage. Unfortunately, this did not always happen, especially when the depositors were companies involved in risky overseas ventures – or when they were governments and monarchs. Charles II was himself guilty in this respect, defaulting in 1672 on his debts of nearly

£1,500,000, stopping most payments from the exchequer and sending a dozen of his most exposed creditors into bankruptcy. Most of them were goldsmith-bankers, including Sir Robert Viner, whose business finally collapsed in 1684. Naturally, the failure of the banks had a disastrous effect on their other depositors and on those who dealt with them. For some years goldsmiths' notes ceased to be acceptable as payment. Even so, while 'hard money' traditionalists appeared to have been vindicated by the banking crisis, forward-thinking economists and businessmen continued to argue for the advantages of banking and the availability of a convenient means of non-cash exchange. The principle had been firmly established: it remained only to regulate it properly and minimise its potential risks.

After much debate – involving proposals to provide banking capital by means of mortgages on land, future tax revenues, pawnbroking or finance from companies with royal charters enabling them to carry on overseas trade – a parliamentary committee finally approved a scheme to found a national bank capitalised by subscription and in 1694 the Bank of England was born.

In fact, its creation had little to do with banking and everything to do with a new government's pressing need for money. The so-called Glorious Revolution of 1688 had overthrown Charles's successor, the Catholic James II, and brought to the throne James's Protestant daughter, Mary, and her husband William of Orange, who would reign after his wife's early death as William III. Though in England the revolution had been bloodless, there had been considerable violence to be suppressed in Ireland and Scotland – the infamous Glencoe

Massacre dates from this period – and the new reign was marked by a succession of wars on the Continent, chiefly against the France of Louis XIV. As ever, this military activity caused a tremendous drain on the exchequer and the general euphoria that had greeted William's arrival in Britain soon turned to dismay as taxes rose in line with a fighting fund that would eventually reach an estimated £150,000,000.

Of course, such a staggering sum, the equivalent of almost a hundred years of ordinary government expenditure in times of peace, could not be raised by taxes alone or, indeed, as rapidly as it was required, given that Parliament had to debate and approve each new imposition or tax rise. Government borrowing had become commonplace, but the lenders' recent experience with Charles II made it unlikely that the sums needed could be obtained through normal financial-market channels. In desperation, Parliament turned to a scheme for a public bank suggested by a Scotsman named William Paterson and, on the back of legislation designed principally to raise duties on shipping and wine, the Bank of England came into existence in June 1694 and was incorporated by royal charter the following month.

Paterson is a controversial figure, the sort of man we would now dignify with the title of entrepreneur but seen by many in his own day and later as a reckless buccaneer and even something of a confidence trickster. Born in Dumfriesshire in 1658, he founded his fortune in the West Indies and vastly increased it through successful trading in London, where he became one of the luminaries of the developing financial market and as such was the prime mover of the Bank of England scheme. His own involvement, however, ended abruptly and in recrimination after only a few months when he tried to set up a rival banking operation. These were not his only contributions to financial history. He will reappear a little later as the man who brought the fledgling Scottish banking system to its knees – and incidentally contributed to the union with England – through his promotion of a risky business adventure in Panama, one of the earliest scandals of the new world of money.

In the eyes of the government the purpose of the Bank of England was to create a new form of national debt, a perpetual loan on which interest would be paid at eight per cent but the capital was never due for repayment. The original sum raised from the Bank's subscribers was £1,200,000 but, governments being what they are, it had topped £10,000,000 by 1760. Meanwhile, the 1500 businessmen who had subscribed – the great majority of them at less than £2000 each – had seized the opportunity for the Bank to take on the business of the goldsmiths by accepting deposits, making loans, handling bills of exchange and issuing its own notes which, unlike those of the goldsmiths, were fully negotiable. These notes, handwritten and signed by a Bank cashier, were made out in the exact sum of the deposit, expressed in pounds, shillings and pence, and promised to pay the bearer that sum on presentation of the note. No longer were the signatures of the depositor and the creditor required. This was portable cash of an entirely new variety.

The initial success of the Bank of England and its paper equivalent of ready money provoked a rash of similar schemes, mostly supported by the state but also in the private sector. In 1695 the Bank of Scotland became the first joint-stock company created in Europe without government sponsorship and it immediately issued currency notes to make up for the country's traditional shortage of coins. Other schemes, such as the National Land Bank incorporated in London in 1696, were short-lived, and fears about the growth of credit and the emergence of other banks that might damage the standing of the Bank of England and its Scottish cousin prompted the government to grant note-issuing monopolies to them. Even the reluctant goldsmiths found themselves issuing only 'official' banknotes.

However, a new coinage crisis, which resulted in the replacement of all of England's silver currency and growing public support for the convenience of pieces of paper that could be immediately exchanged for cash, drove banking headlong to the forefront of financial transactions. The day of the pound note was at hand.

12

Paper Chase

Let us aske the aged, whether five hundred pounds
Portion with a Daughter sixty Years agoe, were not
esteemed a larger Proportion than Two thousand
pounds is now.

Josiah Child, *Brief Observations Concerning Trade and*
Interest of Money, 1668

The idea of using pieces of paper instead of coins was not exactly new. The Chinese are thought to have been the first to introduce paper currency in the ninth century, during the reign of the Emperor Hien Tsung, when they ran out of the copper from which their coins were made. The basic Chinese coin, incidentally, was called a 'cash', hence the term we have long used to refer to ready money. However, there was a problem with currency notes in that it was only too easy to produce them in nominal values unrelated to the stocks of bullion on which the value of the currency was based – even easier than the coinage debasements so regularly practised in Europe. When the money supply ran low, China simply issued more paper, with the result that by the middle of the eleventh century inflation was running out of control and each successive issue of currency was worth less than the previous one. As in the West, there were repeated attempts to rescue the system, but paper money was finally abandoned towards the end of the fifteenth century when a note with a face value of a thousand cash would actually change hands for only three.

Five hundred years later the inflationary tendency of paper money still presented difficulties, as witness the hyperinflation in Germany after the First World War and in countries such as Brazil even today. During the early 1990s in particular, for instance, it was not unusual for Brazilian prices to rise daily, with shops pasting up new lists every morning and customers handing over growing bundles of cruzeiros for their goods. It is only in very recent times that the debate over whether to value currencies in terms of assets or trade seems to have been settled, with trade winning out, so that inflation can in theory be controlled and the money supply manipulated largely by means of the interest charged on credit. Indeed, as will become apparent in the last chapter of this book, we may soon find in our age of instant communications and electronic transfers that the fundamental idea of a 'supply' of currency is no longer relevant.

In the eighteenth century, of course, the picture was very different. Then, and for many years to come, the value of the pound and other currencies was still inseparable from the amount of bullion in circulation, so that even if some coins contained no gold or silver at all, the fractions they referred to depended ultimately on the bullion content of the unit with higher denominations. The sole purpose of the complete recoinage undertaken in 1696, during the reign of William III, was to restore to the traditionally accepted standard the silver content of the pennies, shillings and other pieces that formed the bulk of the British stock of money – a total of nearly £7,000,000. This was putting into practice the 'sound money' theory of influential philosophers such as the sage of Somerset, John Locke, who wrote in 1696:

> Silver is the Instrument and Measure of Commerce in all the Civilized and Trading parts of the World. It is the Instrument of Commerce by its intrinsick value. The intrinsick value of Silver consider'd as Money, is that estimate which common consent has placed on it, whereby it is made Equivalent to all other things, and consequently is the universal Barter or Exchange which Men give and receive for other things they would purchase or part with for a valuable consideration . . .
>
> Silver is the Measure of Commerce by its quantity, which is the Measure also of its intrinsick value. If one grain of Silver has an intrinsick value in it, two grains of Silver have double that intrinsick value, and three grains treble, and so on proportionably. This we have daily Experience of, in common buying and selling. For if one Ounce of Silver will buy, i.e. is of equal value to one Bushel of Wheat, two Ounces of Silver will buy two Bushels of the same

Wheat, i.e. has double the value.

Hence it is evident, that an equal quantity of Silver is always of equal value to an equal quantity of Silver.

This common Sense, as well as the Market, teaches us. For Silver being all of the same nature and goodness, having all the same qualities, 'tis impossible but it should in the same quantity have the same value.

The recoinage of William III, then, was Britain's vote for sound money, which in Locke's view underpinned everything else: 'Money is necessary to the carrying on of Trade. For where Money fails, Men cannot buy, and Trade stops. Credit will supply the defect of it to some small degree for a little while. But Credit being nothing but the expectation of Money within some limited time, Money must be had or Credit will fail.'

This narrow, traditionalist view of money was to survive well into the twentieth century in a slightly different form through adherence to what became known as the Gold Standard, under which the monetary unit was based on the value of a fixed weight of gold. In fact, even as late as the 1970s there was a strong body of political and economic opinion in Britain that demanded, in the face of rampant inflation and fluctuating foreign exchange rates, a return to the Gold Standard, which had been finally abandoned in 1931. Locke had not been a particular supporter of gold in currency terms – after all, the pound was really nothing more than a gold coin representing a weight of sterling silver. Many other thinkers would later argue that keeping monetary units tied to the Gold

Standard served to limit trade, inhibiting economic growth in less developed regions of the world, which in consequence prevented the opening up of potential new markets. Yet, in its time, the Gold Standard was of enormous benefit to the pound, an advantage recognised by the great mathematician and natural scientist Isaac Newton, who became Master of the Royal Mint in 1699. Under his guidance the production of silver coinage declined sharply, while that of gold coins soared to unprecedented heights and the pound – though at the time it was still generally referred to as a 'guinea' – became established on the basis of its quality as an international measure of value. It would not be until 1918 that sterling began eventually and irrevocably to lose its place as the money that ruled the world.

In the meantime, as the eighteenth century progressed, the fundamental flaw in the 'intrinsic value' theory of money was becoming ever more obvious. Linking the value of currency to gold bullion was one thing, but insisting – as Locke had done – that each coin should contain a particular weight of silver, whether or not it was mixed with other metals, both limited the amount of coinage that could sensibly be produced and encouraged people to hoard the coins merely because of their intrinsic value, which further reduced the amount of hard cash in circulation. Newton's virtual invention of the Gold Standard was more visionary, but of course it depended upon the adequate provision of convertible currency to meet the growing everyday demands of trade and industry, especially the overseas markets. Inevitably, that meant the use of paper but the question then arose: could the banknote really be regarded as money? The debate would be a long and bitter one.

As far back as 1682 the polymath and entrepreneur Sir William Petty had published a pamphlet extolling the virtues of banking and the use of bank-issued paper as the best means of developing trade. Petty, a one-time teacher of anatomy and army doctor, became a leader of the new breed of businessman who saw that national wealth could be created rather than simply acquired. The inventor of a primitive copying machine, he also started a series of industries, including lead mining, iron founding and fisheries, on estates he had bought in Ireland and he believed that his own ambitions could be translated into a successful national policy if the correct financial structure were created to support it. A properly constituted public bank, Petty suggested, could issue paper that would effectively double Britain's money supply and give the country the opportunity to trade on a scale never before imagined.

Petty's ideas were at least partly taken up in the creation of the Bank of England, but even before his *Quantulumcunque Concerning Money* had appeared, the American colonies had taken the lead. As we saw earlier, the settlers in Virginia had overcome the difficulties of a shortage of currency by inventing the 'tobacco note' and other bills related to stocks of agricultural commodities, but in 1681 the Massachusetts Bay colony went further by founding the first public bank to issue credit notes similar to those provided by the goldsmiths in London. Nine years later such banknotes were used in fixed amounts to pay troops fighting the French in Canada and it was officially recognised that they could subsequently be used to pay taxes. Before long the notes had become legal tender to be exchanged freely – the first ever real 'pound notes' – and the Massachusetts example had been followed throughout British North

America, with Virginian tobacco notes, for instance, also being recognised as legal tender.

Back in England, the amount of paper in circulation had topped £15,000,000, exceeding coinage by £4,000,000 and making up some fifty-six per cent of the total money supply, but the now negotiable Bank of England and goldsmiths' notes, bills of exchange and other financial instruments were still not legal tender and therefore could not really be counted as paper money. In Scotland, where bullion had always been in short supply and the bulk of the inadequate coinage was made up of foreign pieces, the popularity of paper had even outstripped that in England. The new Bank of Scotland had rather too boldly, as it turned out, opened branch offices in the trading centres of Glasgow, Dundee, Montrose and Aberdeen, yet its notes were in essence still nothing more than credit slips and the branches had to be closed when too many people demanded cash in exchange. Paper might be convenient and portable, but Britain was not as prepared as its overseas colonists – or perhaps just not as desperate – to make the leap of faith required to recognise promissory notes as money.

As with the creation of the Bank of England, it was a Scotsman, John Law, who in 1705 pressed the case for embracing paper money, though his intervention proved to be less successful than that of William Paterson in the case of the Bank. Born in 1671, Law was the son of a wealthy Edinburgh goldsmith-banker but spent his early twenties on the Continent, having been forced into exile himself after killing a man named 'Beau' Wilson in a duel in London. He supported himself in several European capitals by means of a natural talent for gambling and speculation, but he also took the opportunity to study the methods of the Amsterdam bank in issuing credit notes and, like Sir William Petty, he became convinced that paper was the money of the future.

Coinage, Law argued, could not meet the needs of a world functioning more and more on the profits of trade. As business expanded the mints would never be able to keep pace with the explosive growth of demand unless they routinely debased the coinage, which defeated the object of having it in the first place. In consequence, trading would inevitably stagnate and wealth creation would cease. On the other hand, with properly managed paper money issued by a public bank the market would always determine that a sufficient supply of currency was available and 'by this Money, the People may be employed, the Country improved, Manufacture advanced, Trade Domestic and Foreign be carried on, and Wealth and Power attained'.

His treatise *Money and Trade Considered: With a Proposal for Supplying the Nation with Money* was published after his return to Edinburgh, where he lobbied the Scottish Parliament to adopt his ideas. In spite of the growth in the circulation of bills and notes, issued not only by the Bank of Scotland but also by various wealthy trading companies, Law was rebuffed and took himself off to France, where he and his brother William set up their own bank, the country's first such public institution, which became known as the Banque Générale. This was so successful that in 1718 the Duke of Orléans, declared Regent of France after the death of Louis XIV, presented Law with a charter to turn his bank into a state enterprise, the Banque Royale, with responsibilities similar to those of the Bank of England in managing the national debt.

Unfortunately, Law had failed to anticipate the difficulty

always cited by the advocates of sound money and issued excessive quantities of notes, which the bank's capital could not sustain when an economic crisis struck. As Locke had written, 'Money must be had or Credit will fail' and money still meant gold or silver. Bold as ever, Law attempted to repay depositors and creditors in more notes, but the panic was such that even the support of the Regent and a new law could not persuade people to accept what might turn out to be even more useless pieces of paper and the Banque Royale collapsed. Law died nine years later in Venice, alone, poor and in perhaps undeserved obscurity.

Such experiments did nothing to further the cause of paper money, though it still had its fervent supporters. In Scotland, while Law's scheme had been rejected by Parliament, the Bank of Scotland, after the Act of Union in 1707, began to issue its own notes in fixed denominations of sterling – ten, fifty and a hundred pounds – and in 1716 the first putative one-pound note appeared in Edinburgh, although for people unfamiliar with the value of things in sterling, because of the previous difference of their currency, the note indicated that it was 'twelve pounds Scots'. The emergence of the fixed sum and the promise to pay 'the bearer' gave these notes some of the characteristics of the modern banknote, but genuine paper currency was still a long way off. Apart from anything else, the Bank of Scotland reserved to itself the right to pay either on demand or, with interest, six months later. These notes remained in effect letters of credit and were not yet legal tender.

Among the now greatly expanded colonies, however, banknotes were by this time generally accepted as being the same as cash, a cause of concern to the sound money brigade.

The British government tried to stabilise the American money supply by imposing a maximum exchange rate of six shillings to one Spanish dollar but the colonists took little notice and cheerfully continued to finance their activities through the issue of paper. With the wealth of natural resources at their disposal and ample supplies of gold from the Spanish territories to the south, the residents of Massachusetts Bay, Virginia, Connecticut, New Jersey, Rhode Island, New York, Nova Scotia, New Hampshire, North and South Carolina, Georgia and Maryland had no reason to be nervous that the basis upon which their currency system was built might be unsound. That was far from the case among their supposed masters in London.

In 1740 a belligerent, deeply conservative, hard-money economist named William Douglass, who had wide experience of the colonies in North America and the Caribbean, lashed out at the reckless ways of the settlers in a pamphlet entitled *A Discourse concerning the Currencies of the British Plantations in America. Especially with Regard to their PAPER MONEY*. Singling out Massachusetts as the chief miscreant, Douglass thundered:

> Depreciating the Value of nummary Denominations, to defraud the Creditors of the Publick and of private Persons; by Proclamations of Sovereigns, by Recoinages, and by a late Contrivance of a depreciating Paper-Credit-Currency; were never practised but in notoriously bad Administrations.
>
> It is not easily to be accounted for, how England, France and Holland, have tacitly allowed

their several American Colonies; by Laws of their
several Provinces, by Chancerings in their Courts of
Judicature, and by Custom; to depreciate from Time
to Time, the Value of their original Denominations,
to defraud their Principals and Creditors in Europe.
The British Plantations have not only varied, from
Sterling, but have also very much varied from one
another; to the great Confusion of Business, and
Damage of the Merchant.

Though he took no pains to conceal his outrage, Douglass gave
an interesting description of how the currency system worked
in the various colonies. In Nova Scotia, for example, sterling
bills of exchange were used to pay the garrison and also for
small dealings, which were otherwise transacted in French
currency. In North Carolina, the debased coinage was
exchanged for sterling at the rate of ten to one, while in South
Carolina it was eight to one. Douglass gave a nod of faint praise
to Virginia, which had managed to maintain the value of its
silver at seventy-five per cent of sterling. But as for
Massachusetts:

At the first settling of the New England Colonies;
their Medium was Sterling Coin at Sterling Value,
and Barter; some Part of their Taxes was paid in
Provisions and other Produce, called Stock in the
Treasury. When they got into Trade a heavy piece of
Eight passed at 5s. A[nno]. 1652, They proceeded to
coin Silver Shillings, six Pences, and three Pences,
at the Rate of 6s. to a heavy Piece of Eight; Silver

continued current at this Rate by sundry subsequent
Acts of Assembly till A. 1705, by a Resolve of the
General court Silver was to pass at 7 s. per Oz. A.
1706 the Courts of Judicature chancered Silver to 8s.
per Oz. in satisfying of Debts, being nearly after the
Rate of 6s. a light Piece of Eight as then current. At
this Rate Silver and Province Bills continued upon
Par until A. 1714, the Assembly or Legislature fell
into the Error of making from Time to Time large
superfluous Sums of Paper Money upon Loans, and
the Emissions for Charges of Government not
cancellable for many Years, so that these Publick
Bills have been continually depreciating for these
last 26 Years, and are now arrived to 29s. per Oz.
Silver.

In Douglass's view, this cavalier attitude to the currency, a new
and particularly pernicious form of debasement, was unforgiv-
able. He wrote: 'The King's Instructions to the commissioned
Governments are evaded, by the popular Charter Governments,
rendring them of no Effect, having as it were no Dependance on
the Crown. A Parliamentary Regulation is the only adequate
Remedy.'

Then we reach the heart of the opposition case:

The Merchants of Great Britain Adventurers to New
England, because of their largest Dealings have
suffered most. Their Goods are here generally sold at
a long Credit, while the Denominations of the Money
in which they are to be paid, continues depreciating;

so that they are paid in a less Value than was contracted for: thus our Bills have successively depreciated from 8 s. per Oz. Silver A. 1713, to 29s. in this Year 1739; that is, if we could suppose the same Person to have constantly followed this Trade (without extraordinary Hits) for that space of Time, he must have reduced his Estate after the rate of 8s. only for 29s. For every Shilling in the Pound that Silver rises in Price, or, which is the same, for every Shilling in the Pound that the Denominations of our Paper Money depreciates, the Creditor actually looses 5 per Cent. of his Debt.

There was also a moral imperative involved: 'The Shopkeepers are become as it were Bankers between the Merchants and Tradesmen, and do impose upon both egregiously. Shop Notes, that great and insufferable Grievance of Tradesmen, were not in Use until much Paper Money took Place: this Pay in goods which generally are of no necessary Use encourages Extravagance in Apparel and Furniture much above our Condition.'

In the face of such a vituperative attack, it is hardly surprising that in 1764 the British government forbade the American colonies to issue notes as legal tender. It proved to be an act both unjust and stupid, limiting the ability of the colonies to grow and prosper on their own terms and taking its place among the causes of the American Revolution of 1775, which would rob Britain of what was potentially the richest and greatest part of its empire.

Curiously, it was not the use of banknotes in itself that aroused such opposition. Adam Smith, the father of political economy, whose seminal work *Wealth of Nations* is one of the most influential books ever written in English, supported the provision of paper as a means of liberalising trade and expanding markets, yet he celebrated the ban on colonial notes because he could not accept that paper money should be legal tender. His fellow Scot and friend, the philosopher David Hume, explained why:

> It is better, it may be thought, that a public company should enjoy the benefit of that paper-credit, which always will have place in every opulent kingdom. But to endeavour artificially to encrease such a credit, can never be the interest of any trading nation; but must lay them under disadvantages, by encreasing money beyond its natural proportion to labour and commodities, and thereby heightening their price to the merchant and manufacturer.

This was a different argument from the one used by Locke, a more sophisticated one but equally effective. The assumption was that there was a sort of natural level of money in the economy depending upon the condition of the commodity and labour markets. It was a fallacy, according to Hume, to suggest 'that any particular state is weak, though fertile, populous, and well cultivated, merely because it wants money'. In his opinion, 'It appears, that the want of money can never injure any state within itself: For men and commodities are the real strength of any community. It is the simple manner of living which here hurts the public, by confining the gold and silver to few hands, and preventing its universal diffusion and circulation. On the contrary, industry and refinements of all kinds incorporate it with the whole state, however small its quantity may be.' Thus, increasing the money supply in itself upset the equilibrium of the market and forced up the prices of commodities and labour, or in other words produced inflation: 'The greater plenty of money, is very limited in its use, and may even sometimes be a loss to a nation in its commerce with foreigners.' That, said Hume, made him doubt the wisdom of, as he saw it, artificially increasing the money supply by issuing banknotes.

There were other, less theoretical demonstrations of the dangers of unlimited distribution of paper which played into the hands of the sound money brigade. The first occurred in Scotland at the turn of the century and involved the same William Paterson who had been instrumental in the foundation of the Bank of England. Expelled from the Bank board for trying to create what was seen as a rival to it, Paterson returned to Edinburgh and attempted to set up another financial institution in opposition to the Bank of Scotland. In principle, the 'Company of Scotland trading to Africa and the Indies' was to mount an expedition to Panama and establish an international trading centre at Darien, then regarded as the hub of trade routes around the world. But Paterson was also keen to get back into banking and what became known to the public as the Darien Company soon began to issue its own notes, based on public subscription to the Panama scheme, which eventually amounted to £153,000 in Scotland and some £300,000 from England – though the latter never materialised on account of legal action by the East India Company in defence of its trade monopoly.

The venture proved to be a total failure, however, with

three costly expeditions failing to establish a permanent presence in Darien. Not only did the Scottish investors lose all their money, but Paterson's company also left £80,000 worth of debt unpaid, which added up to a serious blow to the Scottish economy and the country's desire to establish a stake for itself in international trade. There were many reasons why the Scots entered into union with England in 1707, but one of them was the realisation that in the feverish spread of mercantilism, and the huge investments involved, their country was unlikely to be able to go it alone. It also meant that the victims of the Darien Company crash finally got their money back. Paterson himself received £18,000 and went on to become a Scottish member of the Union Parliament.

Twenty years later England itself was hit by a cloud of worthless paper in very similar circumstances. The so-called South Sea Bubble of 1719–20 has become one of the legendary scandals in the annals of financial history, an example of mass hysteria, fraudulent financial activities, insider dealing and political corruption that still offers lessons for the modern world of increasingly complex and arcane speculative transactions.

The South Sea Company, chartered in 1711, was the creation of a group of more or less unscrupulous characters who were directors of a somewhat unreliable private bank called the Sword Blade. The chief mover was a former scrivener – a sort of quasi-legal practitioner who was also often a moneylender – named John Blunt, son of a fairly wealthy shoemaker in Rochester, Kent. Blunt and his associates had sleazy political connections that helped them to establish the company for the purpose of competing with Spanish and Portuguese merchants in South America and, though its early operations were only moderately profitable, the directors' ministerial and Court contacts helped persuade King George I to become its governor.

So far so good. The South Sea Company might have gone on to become a large and successful trading concern, except that Blunt, his colleagues and his influential backers were not prepared to wait for their creation to develop. They wanted quick profits and, at a time when economic boom and investment fever were producing new companies almost every day, they saw the way to achieve their aims in promoting the prospects of the South Sea to the point where so many people would buy shares that the insiders could dispose of theirs at a handsome premium.

With the outlook for the trading venture at best limited in the short term, Blunt hit upon the idea of taking on the Bank of England by bidding to privatise the national debt, which at that time accounted for as much as a fifth of government revenues and stood at some £31,000,000 in addition to the portions already held by the Bank and by the East India Company. Blunt's offer was to convert the debt into South Sea shares, to repay it over a period of years at initially five per cent and later four, and to pour more than £7,000,000 into the Exchequer for the privilege.

It sounds ridiculous, and it was, but like all confidence tricks it held out the prospect of glittering prizes. The talking up of potential dividends had already caused the company's share price to rise, but the prospect of also buying into government stock so excited investors that by the summer of 1720 the shares were changing hands at more than a hundred times their original value. Not only that, but virtually the whole of the populace who could afford it – and very many who certainly could not – had taken advantage of cheap paper credit to invest in a whole raft of similar new companies with equally exaggerated dividend forecasts. On the back of the South Sea phenomenon any half-baked industrial or trading scheme acquired the ability to raise money without question, in at least one case even when the promoters would not reveal what it was the company would actually do.

Of course, it was bound to end in tears and it did. Concerned that too much of investors' money was going into other ventures, the South Sea Company took legal action against eighty-six others and promoted an addition to an Act of Parliament that imposed severe penalties for operating joint-stock companies without crown authorisation. It was a spectacular own goal. As investors rushed to try to turn their paper into real money, scores of companies went bankrupt, among them the Sword Blade bank. As many investors lost almost everything they possessed, having mortgaged or sold land and property in their desperation to become part of the great investment boom, the South Sea Company was exposed for the sham it had become. The government wobbled and fell.

John Blunt, now a baronet on the basis of his earlier 'success', was arrested and ordered to forfeit all but £5000 of his assets, which amounted to about £140,000. He retired to Bath, where he lived quietly until his death in 1733. His habit of deception continued in a small way, however – the Court of Chivalry accused him of fraudulently using the coat of arms of another Blunt family.

As for the South Sea Company, it staggered on for more than a century, having abandoned its trading ambitions in

1750, on an annuity from the Treasury for servicing the £10,000,000 of national debt it had been allotted to keep it going in the aftermath of the Bubble. It had been a short-lived phenomenon, but the effect of its brief and inglorious history was to be felt for many years. The regulations imposed in the wake of the South Sea Bubble would hold back commercial development in Britain, while the impression left by the scandal would reinforce the traditional reliance on hard currency and perhaps even help to justify a resistance to change that was to serve the country ill in succeeding centuries.

Banking and paper substitutes for currency had not gone away – they were too convenient for that. By 1745 the Bank of England was issuing part-printed notes in fixed denominations on the Scottish model, for sums ranging between twenty and a thousand pounds. Fifty years or so later, as a result of gold and silver shortages caused by the American Revolution and the Napoleonic Wars, denominations of one pound, two pounds and five and ten pounds would help to alleviate the drastic shortage of coins that was inevitable in any bullion-based system.

But it was not until 1833 that the Bank's notes became legal tender, and then only for sums over five pounds, and it would be more than twenty years before fully printed notes appeared, removing the necessity for the name of the presenter to be inscribed by a cashier. The pound note had arrived, but the day when it could be handed over in payment for a purchase was still a long way off.

13

The People's Pound

> *'Annual income twenty pounds, annual expenditure*
> *nineteen nineteen six, result happiness. Annual*
> *income twenty pounds, annual expenditure twenty*
> *pounds ought and six, result misery.'*
>
> Mr Micawber in Charles Dickens' *David Copperfield*

U p to this point the story of the pound has been mainly one of warlords and monarchs, landed aristocrats and wealthy merchants. About the middle of the eighteenth century, however, something began to change fundamentally in the nature of the British economy and that change would have profound implications for the currency. Already we have seen monetary power move away from the crown and into the hands of the newly fledged financial markets as the requirements of an agrarian economy were overtaken by the demands of a system of wealth creation based on trade and overseas investment.

What happened next was of even greater significance. The Industrial Revolution altered for ever the face of Britain, where it began, and of the world. What it also did, for the first time, was put the power of the pound into the pockets of the people.

Already in 1724 the novelist and social commentator Daniel Defoe was writing: 'As frugality is not the national virtue of England, so the people that get much, spend much; and as they work hard, so they live well, eat and drink well, clothe warm, and lodge soft; in a word, the working manufacturing people of England, eat the fat, drink the sweet, live better, and fare better, than the working poor of any other nation in Europe; they make better wages of their work; and spend more of the money upon their backs and bellies than in any other country.' From the 1730s onwards, despite the dislocations and alarms of financial and social change, the conditons of those who worked hard would improve significantly and the gradual spread of national wealth among the labouring classes would endow them with a political and economic power that proved to be irresistible.

In the words of the leading nineteenth-century economic historian and social reformer Arnold Toynbee, the Industrial Revolution – and he himself coined the phrase – was 'the substitution of competition for the mediaeval regulations which had previously controlled the production and distribution of wealth'. Just as, in Defoe's analysis, the new gentry was composed not of traditional landowners but of people who had made fortunes 'behind the counter' and in manufacturing and trade, so the trickle-down effect produced a new class that had its own commodity to sell at the highest price it could get – labour. Advances in technology and transport, and the emergence of new industries depended for their success on a ready pool of labour, from craftsmen and those who could learn the new skills demanded by machinery, to floor sweepers, watchmen and, increasingly, women and children. With labour now more directly an element of the market, its price was subject to supply and demand, while families that had perhaps relied in the past on one or two breadwinners now found they could raise their standard of living because there was work available for all of them.

Between 1700 and 1790 the generally increasing demand for labour prompted a variable but appreciable rise in the money wages most workers could expect. For instance, the day rate for a London builder went up from two shillings and sixpence to three shillings and fourpence, a rise of more than thirty per cent. In the north of England, day rates for labourers doubled from ninepence to eighteen pence, largely because of strong competition for workers among manufacturing, mining and farming. Throughout most of the same period prices of staple commodities such as wheat actually fell, though there was a sharp increase after 1796 as a result of shortages caused by war. In any case, the wider use of potatoes as a starch substitute for wheat and the growing popularity of root vegetables meant workers were able to feed themselves at least adequately even if flour was beyond their reach. As Ralph Leycester reported in the *Annals of Agriculture* for 1798: 'It is with great satisfaction that I can report that wages are now 8s. per week, having only increased 1s. in twenty-five years, and that, considering the use of potatoes and turnips, the labourer is better off than before. Potatoes are in great use here, which necessarily lessens the consumption of bread.'

Echoing Defoe's earlier claim about the relative prosperity of the British – or at any rate English – worker, Arthur Young, the secretary to the Board of Agriculture and a prolific writer on the subject, noted in 1794 that the average national wage for farm labourers was eight shillings and fivepence a week, which he believed left them seventy-six per cent better off than their counterparts in France. Since the call of the factory reduced the pool of labour for agriculture, wages in the sector were bound to rise, too, as a result of industrialisation – together with the drive to increase farm production in order to feed a growing population, which in itself was brought about by the growth of industry.

'In the cotton trade,' commented the Member of Parliament and future Prime Minister Sir Robert Peel in 1806, 'machinery has given birth to a new population. It has promoted the comforts of the population to such a degree that early marriages have been resorted to, and a great increase of numbers has been occasioned by it, and I may say that they have given rise to an additional race of men.'

With the benefit of employment for wives and children, even a rural family traditionally at the bottom of the pay scale might expect to earn at the end of the eighteenth century up to forty pounds a year, though the average was nearer twenty-five pounds.

This did not mean, of course, that people had much to spend on luxuries. A study entitled *The State of the Poor*, undertaken by Sir Frederic Eden and published in 1797, revealed that the average rural family spent between one pound fifteen shillings and two pounds a year on rent and from one to just over two pounds a year on fuel. Food generally cost about nine shillings a week for the working family with more than three children, though that figure varied depending on whether wheat, oatmeal – popular particularly in the north – or potatoes were the main sources of starch. Few families ever ate meat and for those that did, ninepence or a shilling tended to be the maximum expenditure, while the study found milk hardly used at all. Tea is recorded as a popular drink and most people seem to have eaten small amounts of butter. Clothing and shoes were very low on the list of spending, varying from as little as ten shillings a year to as much as twelve pounds for a relatively well-off working family with an income of fifty pounds a year.

In the now growing towns, where the arrival of steam power and a variety of new mechanical inventions allowed the development of factories for the woollen and cotton industries, for iron founding and for a range of other industries, wages were spectacularly higher, especially in the 'cotton belt' of the north-west. The output of cotton trebled between 1788 and 1803, providing well-paid work for virtually anyone who could do it. Such was the demand for labour in Bolton, Lancashire, that wages for weavers reached twenty-five shillings a week, which meant that the average family with three or more children might achieve a weekly income in times of full employment of two pounds, with an extraordinary six pounds recorded in some weeks when the demands of production were high and many extra hours were worked.

Small wonder that urban populations grew exponentially, particularly after the introduction of turnpike roads in the 1730s and the beginning of the canal system forty years later made for the easy transport of goods into an expanding market of new consumers. The number of people in Liverpool increased tenfold during the century after 1685 and in the following hundred years swelled to more than half a million. Birmingham went from 4000 to 400,000 during the same two centuries. Overall, the urban population of England and Wales increased by 1,800,000 between 1700 and 1800.

Much is made of 'dark satanic mills' and appalling housing conditions in the factory towns, but the fact is that many people were better off as a result of the Industrial Revolution, at least in its early phase. Rising wages meant an improvement in diet, even if protein remained lacking, and urban housing was often actually better thanthe tied cottages of rural workers. These two factors contributed to a dramatic fall in death rates, especially among children, as did the necessary improvements to water supplies and drainage occasioned by urbanisation. As bad as things might still look to our eyes, industrialisation brought about an equally significant revolution in public health, which in itself contributed to the overall rise in population to something over 9,000,000 in England and Wales by 1801.

Inevitably, though, it was not all good news. While skilled workers continued to do well, their wages rising from about a pound a week in 1790 to as much as one pound and sixteen shillings by 1813, others found their livelihoods suppressed by mechanisation or at best damaged by the fluctuations in trade that naturally resulted from overproduction, war and sudden changes in levels of demand. The introduction of the power loom early in the nineteenth century forced cotton weavers' pay down to thirteen shillings a week, little more than half what they had been earning a couple of decades earlier, and they would almost halve again as employers sought to cut prices through the greater use of machinery.

Toynbee commented: 'The old relations between masters and men disappeared, and a "cash nexus" was substituted for the human tie. The workmen on their side resorted to combination, and Trades-Unions began a fight which looked as if it were between mortal enemies rather than joint producers . . . The effects of the Industrial Revolution prove that free competition may produce wealth without wellbeing . . .'

Yet the very fact that workers could combine in an attempt to force change or improve their conditions, and that the government found it necessary to pass laws to try to stop them, indicates an important shift of economic power. The wealth created by industrialisation and market expansion – especially in exports, which reached a value of £55,000,000 in 1800 – was not being evenly spread by any means, but it was at least being distributed in a way that would have been impossible before market forces shouldered aside the oligarchy that controlled the money supply. And labour, as we have noted, was one of those market forces, which could be harnessed through trades unions. At the same time the working classes had access to money in a way that had never happened before, earning in the good times, at any rate, virtually as much as they wanted to in the hours available. They were beginning to be important customers as well as producers.

Before long, workers were also starting to become capitalists in their own small way. During the high-wage period of the early days of industrialisation many people found that by increasing their expenditure on necessities only moderately they could accumulate cash surpluses. Gradually, groups were formed called Friendly Societies to function more or less as poor men's banks, operating primarily to gather and protect savings, which might be deposited in a proper bank, but also to provide limited credit in an emergency, such as unexpected medical costs or temporary absence from work through illness or injury.

These Friendly Societies were initially treated with some suspicion by the authorities because they had no official authorisation or legal standing, as the Act limiting the formation of companies had demanded in the fall-out from the South Sea Bubble. They gradually gained acceptance, however, as the less welcome effects of the Industrial Revolution provoked a rise in the taxes levied to support the poor from £1,250,000 a year in 1760 to £3,000,000 and rising by the 1790s. Prompted by an assortment of the great and the good – among them the prominent political economist Thomas Malthus, the anti-slavery campaigner William Wilberforce and the 'Utilitarian' thinker Jeremy Bentham – Parliament passed in 1793 an Act to legalise Friendly Societies and protect their members from possible fraud.

Encouraging thrift among the working classes, it was thought, would help to relieve the burden of the Poor Rate. Although that did not happen, and by 1818 the annual levy was just under £8,000,000 or thirteen shillings and threepence for every man, woman and child, workers were encouraged to save in a variety of organisations so that by the latter part of the nineteenth century Toynbee was calculating that 'the savings of the working classes . . . probably amount to about £130,000,000'. Although this was estimated at only a little more than half of the nation's annual growth of capital in 1875, it nevertheless represented a significant stake in the country's wealth by people who would have had no such share just over a century earlier.

A few of the better-paid workers had also begun to save to buy their own houses by the end of the eighteenth century. Probably the movement started with shopkeepers and self-employed master craftsmen, who for between £200 and £500 could set up their own businesses and workshops. The first recorded venture of its kind was in Birmingham, where in 1775, at the Golden Cross Inn, Snow Hill, landlord Richard Ketley persuaded a group of his customers to form a mutual society into which they would pay regular amounts for the purpose of financing the purchase of properties. It was the beginning of a movement that would eventually see Britain leading Europe in the numbers of homes owned by their occupiers and make property the most important source of capital for two-thirds of the population.

By the second decade of the nineteenth century there were perhaps as many as 250 'building societies', of which the funds of many were actually used to construct new housing rather than buying existing stock. They were known as 'terminating' societies, because their function ceased when property was acquired by all the members, but in the 1840s there appeared 'permanent' building societies, which operated more like banks in that they accepted deposits from savers on which they paid interest and used their funds to lend money to others for the express purpose of buying homes. Unlike banks, the permanent building societies were owned by their members – whether savers or borrowers – and sought to amass assets rather than to make profits, which made them literally as safe as houses for investors. First in the field was the Woolwich Equitable Benefit, Building and Investment Association, registered in 1847, and it was quickly followed by the Leeds, the Abbey, the Halifax, the Co-operative (later the Nationwide) and more than 2000 others, mostly operating locally.

From the end of the nineteenth century until the end of the twentieth, the mutual building society was the sine qua non for economic development and security among people without capital of their own or any other means of raising it. In a sense they were deeply unfair. The relative absence of risk made them most attractive to middle-class investors, who could thus increase their wealth without pain, whereas the high interest rates they charged, and the fact that their mortgages were always recoverable because they never reflected the full value of a property and they could always repossess the home of a defaulter, discriminated against less well-off borrowers. Equally, the building society concept was highly inefficient in macro-economic terms because it ultimately encouraged over-investment by the public in property at the expense of the wealth-creating financial markets, which meant that British industry tended always to be under-resourced. Britain preferred to be a property-owning democracy rather than a share-owning one, such as the USA, a choice for which it would pay dearly.

Nevertheless, the building society and the opportunity it offered to step on to what became known as the 'housing ladder' – which offers owners the prospect, however illusory, of profits from progressive selling and buying as property prices increase – proved to be one of the most potent single forces militating in favour of a redistribution of wealth in Britain. Toynbee, noting that his figure for the savings of the working classes took no account of their investments in property, commented: 'The facts make it clear that the working classes can raise their

position, though not in the same ratio as the middle classes.'
Yet he also quoted a writer in the *Contemporary Review* of
February 1882 as calculating that during the previous forty
years 'the average wealth of the rich family has decreased from
£28,820 to £25,803, or 11 per cent; that of a middle-class
family has decreased from £1,439 to £1,005, or 30 per cent;
while that of a working-class family has *increased* from £44 to
£86, or nearly 100 per cent'.

The rich, incidentally, were regarded as those who spent
more than £5000 a year, the middle classes as spending
between £100 and £5000 and the working classes as people
with an annual outlay of less than £100.

As an indication of what these changes represented in
terms of wages and expenditure, Toynbee quoted the case of a
senior ploughman on a Scottish estate whose pay rate had risen
from twenty-eight pounds two shillings a year in 1840 to forty-
eight pounds nine shillings in 1880. This was by no means a
case of inflation, for the ploughman of 1880 'complained, in a
letter describing his position, of his increased expenditure,
increased not because things were dearer, but because he now
needed more of them'.

This explosion of relative prosperity among the large
numbers of workers favoured by the Industrial Revolution after
about 1750 – leaving aside a similar eruption of poverty in the
case of those cast aside by it – also had a dramatic effect on the
money supply. At the Royal Mint Sir Isaac Newton's policy of
concentrating on gold had continued apace, while the amounts
of the standard silver and now copper coins had been reduced
to little more than a trickle. By the turn of the century even the
gold coinage was severely restricted, largely because of a

shortage of bullion arising from the disruptions of the French Revolution and subsequent Napoleonic Wars, and the outflow of gold and silver overseas to support the spreading British Empire.

The Bank of England, as we have already seen, began to issue notes in smaller denominations, as did a handful of new provincial banks and a by now extensive network of bank branches in Scotland, which of course had long been accustomed to a shortage of coins. But these were of little use in meeting demand from what were becoming the largest domestic users of currency and especially small change, the wage-earning workers. Desperate employers went to extraordinary lengths to obtain cash with which they could pay their workers, even opening retail businesses unrelated to their own in the hope of acquiring ready money. Others obliged their employees to accept payment in 'truck', or goods – cotton, for instance, or coal in the case of miners – or gave them 'shop notes', which could be exchanged for everyday items in stores operated by their companies. Some of these company stores later developed into what became the notorious 'Tommy' shops, the name being slang for provisions, where unscrupulous employers virtually recouped the amounts of their wage bills by charging extortionately high prices and imposing heavy discounts on the face values of the workers' notes. The unfortunate customers had no choice other than to be thus exploited, since there was no cash available for wages that would have allowed them to shop on the open market.

Once again foreign coins began to circulate widely in Britain, a curious reversion to almost mediaeval practices against a background of the thrusting modernity of an industrial powerhouse the like of which could not have been imagined during the Middle Ages. In spite of the fact of war with the French, silver sous were pressed into service as sixpenny pieces and shillings. Even the government joined in, instructing the Bank of England to raid its reserves and overstamp the head of King Carlos IV on Spanish silver dollars with the image of King George III and issue them as legal tender. 'The head of a fool stamped on the neck of an ass,' said the wags.

It made little difference and neither did an appeal to the private sector in the shape of the steam engine pioneer Matthew Boulton, a partner of James Watt, who began to produce penny and tuppenny pieces in copper from his factory at Soho, near Birmingham, under contract from the government. Boulton was an appropriate choice since, in addition to his engineering skills, his father had been a silver stamper. His coinage proved to be extremely popular, although in the end not as widely available as it might have been because large amounts ended up in seaports or towns containing military depots, where it was used to pay the armed forces and those who made their living from supplying them.

Another throwback to ages past was the reappearance of privately produced tokens, but unlike their predecessors those of the early Industrial Revolution actually resembled coins and in many cases looked and felt better than the real thing, as did Boulton's more official pieces. Since they were supposedly for internal circulation – even if that meant in the shops of an entire locality, as well as the company stores – the tokens were, perhaps pragmatically in the circumstances, not considered illegal, but some producers did rather overstep the mark of respectability. When the hugely successful industrialist John Wilkinson decided to make his own coins to serve the communities that kept his Welsh ironworks going, he had them stamped with his own head, an act of supreme arrogance that would probably have caused him to lose it not long before.

Somewhat late in the day the Bank of England itself went into the token business, issuing below-par silver pieces nominally worth three shillings and one shilling and sixpence in a reflection of the debasement policies adopted by the likes of Henry VIII. It turned out to be a rash move. The example of the state bank taking over what had long been the function of the Royal Mint merely served to encourage private operators to do the same, not always with the fastidiousness such a serious enterprise demanded. While most silver tokens were at pains to establish their temporary and limited nature, some producers were tempted to apply the same techniques to make counterfeit Bank of England pieces and even coins of the realm. Not a few were hanged, since the mediaeval death penalty for counterfeiting still applied, as it would until 1832, when it was superseded by transportation to the colonies, usually Australia.

All this made it difficult for working-class families to take full advantage of the degree of prosperity they had achieved through the revolution in trade and manufacturing, in addition to which they had suffered something of a reverse because of financial and commercial crises related to the French war. With some exceptions, wages had continued to rise during the conflict, often quite steeply, but prices had also increased and in any case the general recourse to 'funny money', from tokens to banknotes upon which cash payment was suspended by law, and the appearance of the Tommy shop had made it difficult to judge whether people were better off or not. Following the final victory over Napoleon in 1815, a new trade boom should have been the signal for ordinary people to test their new purchasing power.

The social reformer and indefatigable pamphleteer Patrick Colquhoun estimated in 1814 that the total income of the 9,000,000-strong working-class households in Britain, including those of the by then dwindling numbers of agricultural workers, amounted to some £82,000,000. That figure represented approximately a third of the sum earned – or in some cases, such as royalty, the nobility, the gentry and the senior clergy, acquired in other ways – by the whole community. How those numbers were arrived at is something of a mystery and it is unlikely that they are entirely accurate. None the less, Colquhoun's dedicated and painstaking research does give a generally acceptable indication of the way in which the national income was trickling down. The bulk of the country's wealth, a proportion expressed in income terms as about £159,000,000, still resided in very few hands. But when we consider that in Colquhoun's view only about £37,000,000 went to non-wage-earners, that is employers, in trade and industry, the workers as a whole – although definitely not individually – made up a substantial income group. They might lack capital, but their spending power had to be taken into account in the new market economy.

Unfortunately for them, the ability really to exercise that power was to be delayed somewhat, first by a heavy burden of taxation and second by a deep economic recession that forced wages down again.

In 1799 the novel imposition of income tax was

introduced by William Pitt, the prime minister who would be fêted as the saviour of Europe after the French defeat at Trafalgar. More important, so far as this story is concerned, Pitt was one of the earliest political followers of Adam Smith and his free trade theories, which would eventually spawn the laissez-faire capitalism of the nineteenth century, which took the pound sterling to the apogee of its financial power.

Before the war, Pitt had been an enthusiastic free trader, but at a time when a French invasion force was daily expected to land on British shores he guided through Parliament the Act that suspended cash payments on Bank of England notes and thus made it possible to quadruple the national debt over the succeeding twenty years. His next move was to raise £6,000,000 a year through a ten per cent tax on annual incomes over £200, with lower percentages applied to those earning as little as sixty pounds. This caught to some extent the more affluent members of the working classes, but more important it represented a cash drain on their employers, who often sought to compensate for it either by laying off workers or by reducing wage rates.

Of even more significance for working people was the extension of indirect taxation to cover almost everything they might buy – 'upon every article that enters the mouth, or covers the back, or is placed under the foot . . . upon warmth, light, locomotion . . . on the poor man's salt and the rich man's spice,' wrote the cleric and journalist Sydney Smith. This forced up prices even further than inflation had already done and, according to Toynbee, helped contribute to the spread of pauperism that forced the sharp increases in the Poor Rate referred to earlier in this chapter.

Looking at the wider picture, the aftermath of the French Revolution and Napoleon's wars had combined with a series of severe winters and cool, wet summers to produce bad harvests, which further increased food prices and provoked a general economic recession in both Europe and the USA. The sum of £10,000,000 was wiped off the value of British exports in 1816, with a further £10,000,000 three years later as financial panic gripped America following a period of excessive speculation.

Since workers laid off or forced to accept lower pay as a result of the recession did not understand the principles of international trade or political economy – and neither, according to Toynbee, did the intellectuals who extolled their virtues – this was the epoch of the Luddites, who blamed mechanisation for their misfortune and, particularly in north-west England, broke into factories and wrecked their equipment. The business lobby became so worried that it began to issue special popular editions of pamphlets on the benefits of industrialisation and the common purpose of capital and labour. Others, such as an influential though somewhat eccentric Birmingham banker named Thomas Attwood, demanded an immediate increase in the money supply and the lifting of the ban on cash payments against Bank of England notes.

At first the government did little, apart from passing a law to reassure people that Bank notes would be guaranteed at face value and could effectively be used as currency. It still resisted the idea of a genuine paper currency to make the money supply more flexible and renew economic confidence, but in May 1816 it did officially embrace the Gold Standard, by which the value of sterling was fixed at 123.25 grains of gold to the pound. To celebrate this, the pound itself acquired a new face in the form of the gold sovereign, which would become the standard-bearer of the economic ambition of nineteenth-century Britain.

To the workers, none of this made an immediate difference. In 1816 and again in 1819 there were strikes and riots against pay cuts, in favour of a minimum wage and in support of trades unions, the formation of which had been forbidden by law. Even the abolition of the income tax could not turn aside public anger, since falling wages had by this time placed most tradesmen and labourers outside its scope anyway. In the cotton industry, for instance, a skilled spinner's pay had dropped from a peak of thirty shillings in 1810 to a little over a pound by 1820. Scottish miners were trying to live on wages hardly better than those they had been receiving in the 1790s. In the English provinces, carpenters had lost four shillings a week.

The situation was better in London and the Home Counties, where pay had at least stabilised, although price rises and indirect taxes had substantially reduced the amount it could purchase, and the trades in the capital were generally not those seriously affected by the arrival of new machines. But there, too, the next decade would see no material improvement even in highly skilled jobs such as printing.

Economists attempted to justify the situation by citing what was called the Wage-Fund Theory, which held that at any stage in an economic cycle there was a limited amount of wealth that could be devoted to labour, which neither the employer nor the worker had the capacity to increase: the only way in which an employee could see his pay rise was if a balance was maintained by means of a reduction for other trades. Toynbee was to describe this nonsense as 'an offence to the whole working class'. The new breed of industrial workers instinctively knew this, and were beginning to seek redress. They had enjoyed the first fruits of the people's pound in the heady days of the 1760s and, sooner or later, they were going to pick them again. One way or another, the money supply would have to take them into account from now on.

14
Sterling Work

Everyone is aware that England is the greatest moneyed country in the world; everyone admits that it has much more immediately disposable and ready cash than any other country.

Walter Bagehot, Editor of *The Economist*, 1826–77

Towards the end of the nineteenth century, when the British Empire was approaching the height of its power, the politician, statesman and noted racehorse owner Lord Rosebery explained imperial policy to a meeting of the Royal Colonial Institute in London. 'We are engaged', he said, 'in "pegging out claims" for the future. We have to consider, not what we want now, but what we shall want in the future. We have to consider what countries must be developed either by ourselves or some other nation . . . We have to look forward . . . to the future of the race of which we are at present the trustees . . .'

By that time, of course, Britain had already pegged out pretty extensive claims, the race Lord Rosebery was concerned to protect had spread itself across the world and the pound sterling had become the most potent force in international trade and finance. The countries, territories, trading centres and concessions over which London held sway – and in many cases governed directly – had been acquired in a variety of ways.

Some, such as Australia and the West Indies, had been more or less uninhabited regions that the British government had simply annexed to the mother country through legal process. Others, including New Zealand, had fallen under British 'protection' at the 'request' of native rulers. Hong Kong had been seized by force from the Chinese, Canada and Jamaica had been among the fruits of victory over the French in Europe, a number of West African territories had been bought from the Dutch and the Danes. Perhaps the greatest prize of all, India, had come Britain's way by means of dowry – with the Portuguese Catherine of Braganza, wife of Charles II, who had inherited Bombay – and also as a result of military conquest and the activities of the East India Company, granted its charter by Elizabeth I.

There had been some failures, of course, most notably in North America, where the arrogance and ineptitude of the government in London provoked the British settlers to rebel in 1775 and subsequently to found the United States, which in the twentieth century would grow up to become Britain's nemesis in terms of international influence. Nevertheless, by the 1820s the British were well on their way to creating one of the greatest economic and political confederations history has ever recorded.

The words 'economic' and 'political' are placed in that order quite deliberately. Although the British Empire was ultimately administered from London, there never was a unified governmental or political structure for it. That is because, although it would assume in a geopolitical sense something of the identity of a 'Greater Britain', its roots were really commercial. Just as colonial expansion was haphazard, so the systems of organising the imperial possessions developed in an ad hoc manner, depending on local circumstances, the size and complexity of the territory, the nature of the imperial interest and the level of British immigration. In many cases it was the commercial interests that had taken the initiative in developing the region which largely determined how it should be run.

Thus Cecil Rhodes, the diamond prospector from Essex who founded the mighty De Beers company in South Africa, went on to become prime minister of the Cape Colony and at the same time was managing director of the British South Africa Company, which extended Britain's control into neighbouring Bechuanaland and eventually turned that native state into Rhodesia. Similarly, the manic depressive Robert Clive, who was to be immortalised in Britain as Clive of India, was essentially doing the business of the East India Company – where he had originally been employed as a writer – when he forcibly took over as ruler of Bengal in 1757 and incidentally acquired for himself the then vast income of £40,000 a year.

'The country of Bengal', Clive told a parliamentary select committee in London in 1773, 'is called the paradise of the earth. It not only abounds with the necessaries of life to such a degree, as to furnish a great part of India with its superfluity, but it abounds in very curious and valuable manufactures, sufficient not only for its own use, but for the use of the whole globe. Let the House figure to itself a country consisting of 15 millions of inhabitants, a revenue of four millions sterling, and a trade in proportion. By progressive steps the Company have become sovereigns of that empire.'

That commercial considerations were the main reason for developing systems of government is well illustrated in the *Act for Establishing Certain Regulations for the Better Management of the Affairs of the East India Company*, passed by the Parliament in London in 1773. Its preamble noted:

> Whereas the several powers and authorities granted by charters to the united company of merchants in England trading to the East Indies have been found, by experience, not to have sufficient force and efficacy to prevent various abuses which have prevailed in the government and administration of the affairs of the said united company, as well at home as in India, to the manifest injury of the public credit, and of the commercial interests of the said company; and it is therefore become highly expedient that certain further regulations, better adapted to their present circumstances and condition, should be provided and established.

As we have seen, the desirability of amassing 'treasure' by means of 'forraign trade' had become firmly established by the middle of the seventeenth century. Every financial and economic development after then made it inevitable that European countries would compete with each other to find, first, new sources of raw materials and commodities and later, as industrialisation dramatically raised domestic output, new markets into which they could sell. In this competition Britain had two distinct advantages, which help to explain both the extent of its imperial success and the underlying pressures that drove it: the early onset of industrialisation and, especially after the adoption of the Gold Standard in 1816, the integrity of the pound.

The link between industrialisation and colonial expansion was explained by the philosopher John Stuart Mill in his 1848 essay 'On Colonies and Colonization'. Mill observed:

> Much has been said of the good economy of importing commodities from the place where they can be bought cheapest; while the good economy of producing them where they can be produced cheapest, is comparatively little thought of. If to carry consumable goods from the places where they are superabundant to those where they are scarce, is a good pecuniary speculation, is it not an equally good speculation to do the same thing with regard to labour and instruments? The exportation of labourers and capital from old to new countries, from a place where their productive power is less, to a place where it is greater, increases by so much the aggregate produce of the labour and capital of the world. It adds to the joint wealth of the old and the new country, what amounts in a short period to many times the mere cost of effecting the transport. There needs be no hesitation in affirming that Colonization,

231

in the present state of the world, is the best affair of
business, in which the capital of an old and wealthy
country can engage.

In the previous chapter we saw how industrialisation was at
once a response to and a promoter of population growth, but as
it progressed it became much more the latter. Between 1801
and 1901, the great century of the Industrial Revolution, the
population of Britain rose from 10,500,000 to 37,000,000,
increasing at the rate of about 2,000,000 a year to begin with
and then, during the final thirty years of the period, recording
an annual rise of 3,000,000 or more. All these people had to be
fed, housed, clothed and – most important – given work to do so
that they could support themselves. Industry therefore had to
feed off industry, always expanding and, in order to continue
that expansion, forever seeking new sources of materials and
new markets, both of which could only be supplied by Britain's
overseas territories.

Whereas in the early days of settlement the prime motivation was to supply the home market with novel commodities
and the domestic economy with both profits and tax revenues, it
became increasingly important, as Mill pointed out, to develop
the colonies to the point where they could accommodate the
burgeoning output of British industry, from basics such as coal
and iron to the sophisticated products such as the typewriter
and the sewing machine that could now be made using the
power sources of steam and later electricity and the new
technical processes that the Industrial Revolution also made
possible.

Mill's 'old and wealthy country' therefore profited at both

ends of the equation, importing goods, raw materials and commodities at prices it controlled and selling back to the colonial producers the industrial wares they could not make themselves, also at prices controlled in Britain. Equally, the overseas territories could be developed to the point where they had industrial output of their own, from factories and machinery supplied by British companies, transported along roads and railways constructed with British expertise and exported to neighbouring countries in ships built in Britain. While it lasted, it seemed to be the perfect economic scenario.

Those who profited most of all were the bankers and financiers who made possible this vast foreign expansion. The amount of capital required was enormous and the returns equally staggering. By the close of the nineteenth century, Britain had some £4 billion invested abroad, mostly in the empire – almost twice the combined total of foreign investment for the USA, Germany and France. From these investments the revenues were something of the order of £750,000,000, helping to make London, in the words of Walter Bagehot – the great Victorian editor of *The Economist* newspaper and the 'father' of Britain's unwritten constitution – 'by far the greatest combination of economical power and economical delicacy that the world has even seen'.

In a book on the London money market, entitled *Lombard Street* after the banking centre in the City, Bagehot wrote in 1873:

> Everyone is aware that England is the greatest
> moneyed country in the world; everyone admits that
> it has much more immediately disposable and ready

cash than any other country. But very few persons are aware how much greater the ready balance, the floating loan-fund which can be lent to anyone or for any purpose, is in England than it is anywhere else in the world. A very few figures will show how large the London loan-fund is, and how much greater it is than any other. The known deposits of banks which publish their accounts are:

	£
London (31st December, 1872)	120,000,000
Paris (27th February, 1873)	13,000,000
New York (February, 1873)	40,000,000
German Empire (31st January, 1873)	8,000,000

Backed by the profits of empire, the pound, its value pegged to gold, had become the international currency, offering a fixed rate of exchange anywhere in the world.

We, [Bagehot noted] are asked to lend, and do lend, vast sums, which it would be impossible to obtain elsewhere. It is sometimes said that any foreign country can borrow in Lombard Street at a price: some countries can borrow much cheaper than others; but all, it is said, can have some money if they choose to pay enough for it. Perhaps this is an exaggeration; but confined, as of course it was meant to be, to civilised Governments, it is not much of an exaggeration. There are very few civilised Governments that could not borrow considerable sums off us

if they choose, and most of them seem more and more
likely to choose.

Having started late compared with other European cities,
especially Amsterdam, London had developed a system of
merchant banking and financial services that now ruled the
world. It had begun in 1762 when two sons of a German clergy-
man set up Baring Brothers bank, which was to crash so
spectacularly nearly 250 years later after a rogue trader in the
Far East exposed it to commitments the bank could not
possibly meet. Barings it was that advanced the money which
allowed the American government to buy Louisiana from the
French and the French themselves to embark on a vital
reconstruction programme following the overthrow of Napoleon
in 1815. The Barings were followed by the Rothschilds, who
specialised in government loans, foreign exchange and bullion
dealing, the Kleinworts and the Hambros – all foreigners and
all attracted to British banking by the opportunities of the
Industrial Revolution and rapidly expanding overseas trade.

The fact that most of these new bankers were both
foreigners and originally merchants, or from mercantile
families, also helps to explain why they flourished and why
London flourished with them as an international financial
centre. On the one hand they understood the needs of trade and
were used to the risks associated with it, and on the other their
horizons tended to be wider than those of many British bankers
because they had come from somewhere else. But perhaps the
most crucial factor in London's emergence as banker to the
world was the pound itself.

As we have seen, it was the almost traditional shortage of

hard currency in Britain that encouraged the spread of paper and a variety of non-cash financial instruments. Credit had become a way of life, often based on the deposit for safe-keeping of high-quality coinage because the people into whose hands it had come saw its comparative rarity as a reason for not using it in everyday exchange. At the same time the policy of minting mostly gold rather than silver, begun by Sir Isaac Newton – a sort of undeclared Gold Standard – had maybe unconsciously served to protect the integrity of the pound, even if it did little to maintain the quality and availability of the silver coinage that supported it. There were two main consequences.

First, sterling was seen throughout the world as a reliable currency because it had, in recent times at any rate, adhered firmly to the bullion theory, although it most often appeared in the form of bills and notes. That made it an ideal medium for financing overseas investment and for advancing loans to foreigners as well as domestic borrowers. The only other currency to come anywhere near – and still a long way behind – in that respect was the restored French franc in the early part of the twentieth century, before the American dollar began to make its presence felt in the aftermath of the First World War.

Second, the lack of attention paid to silver coinage and the substitution of 'light' silver, copper, foreign coins and tokens had encouraged the habit of saving among those people who could afford it. What gold and silver coinage they did have was routinely deposited in the scores of joint-stock banks that sprang up throughout the country as notes became more widely accepted and ordinary transactions could be accomplished by means of the substitute metal currencies. The new banks made their own deposits at the Bank of England, which in turn issued credit to commercial companies and merchant banks. It was what Bagehot called the 'democratisation' of the banking system.

'The Joint Stock Banks of this country are a most remarkable success,' he wrote, listing the combined capital of the hundred or so leading players at well over £40,000,000 in 1866. 'Concentration of money in banks, though not the sole cause, is the principal cause which has made the Money Market of England so exceedingly rich, so much beyond that of other countries . . . A place like Lombard Street, where in all but the rarest times money can be always obtained upon good security or upon decent prospects of probable gain, is a luxury which no country has ever enjoyed with even comparable equality before.'

It was the efficiency and flexibility of this banking system that gave Britain its industrial edge. By the early nineteenth century there were some 800 banks throughout England and Wales, with a further thirty or so in Scotland. The money they took in deposits could therefore be easily redistributed as credit where it was needed. Bagehot noted:

> Deposits are made with the bankers and bill brokers in Lombard Street by the bankers of such counties as Somersetshire and Hampshire, and those bill brokers and bankers employ them in the discount of bills from Yorkshire and Lancashire. Lombard Street is thus a perpetual agent between the two great divisions of England, between the rapidly-growing districts, where almost any amount of money can be

well and easily employed, and the stationary and the declining districts, where there is more money than can be used.

There are whole districts in England which cannot and do not employ their own money. No purely agricultural county does so. The savings of a county with good land but no manufactures and no trade much exceed what can be safely lent in the county. These savings are first lodged in the local banks, are by them sent to London, and are deposited with London bankers, or with the bill brokers. In either case the result is the same. The money thus sent up from the accumulating districts is employed in discounting the bills of the industrial districts.

The habit of saving in banks that allowed the London money market to function was not to be found to anything like the same degree in countries 'not of British descent', as Bagehot put it.

If a 'branch', such as the National Provincial Bank opens in an English country town, were opened in a corresponding French one, it would not pay its expenses. You could not get any sufficient number of Frenchmen to agree to put their money there. Cheque-books are unknown, and money kept on running account by bankers is rare. People store their money in a caisse at their houses. Steady savings, which are waiting for investment, and which are sure not to be soon wanted, may be lodged with bankers; but the common floating cash of the community is kept by the community themselves at home.

This was, Bagehot admitted, hardly a sign of British vision and imagination, but arose instead out of the deficiencies of the coinage. 'The first banks were not founded for our system of deposit banking, or for anything like it. They were founded for much more pressing reasons, and having been founded, they, or copies from them, were applied to our modern uses.'

Not that the system was perfect, however. The frenetic pace of industrialisation and the expansion of trade, together with a general lack of regulation arising from the ad hoc development of banking, led to overenthusiasm among provincial banks in particular and large numbers of notes were issued without adequate capital assets. Since the only legal tender was coinage, there was always a danger that too many people would require redemption of their notes at the same time. The smaller banks relied on being able to discount their own bills at the Bank of England, which was responsible for maintaining their reserves, but when liabilities exceeded assets there was a risk that sudden calls by the joint-stock banks could bring down the whole system.

It almost happened in 1825, when a crisis of financial confidence and a system-wide excess of banknotes caused a run on the Bank of England. 'When only coin was a legal tender, and when there was only one department in the Bank, the Bank had reduced its reserve to £1,027,000 and was within an ace of stopping payment,' Bagehot commented. Instead, it merely withdrew the facility of instant discounting, but that was enough to force seventy provincial banks to suspend their payments and put sixty of them out of business. This only served to deepen the crisis and the following year a hundred banks suspended payments on their notes. A great deal of liquidity was thus taken out of the monetary system and as something of a panic measure the Bank of England issued £1,000,000 worth of one-pound and two-pound notes as currency while the Royal Mint hurriedly stepped up the production of gold sovereigns. The merchant bank Rothschilds also stepped in with loans to the Bank and, in the view of the Duke of Wellington, then a Cabinet minister, helped to prevent a general collapse.

After that, Parliament tried to stop the issue of banknotes with a face value of less than five pounds as a means of restricting the amount of paper in circulation. It succeeded in England and Wales, but the Scots objected and won their case. The branch banking system was more highly developed in Scotland and the banks there had, as long ago as 1727, introduced a 'cash-credit' facility that permitted approved applicants to withdraw more than their deposits and pay interest only on the excess. It was the earliest example – first offered by the Royal Bank of Scotland – of what we now call an overdraft and it helped to reduce reliance on short-term and small-denomination bills, in turn decreasing the need for discounting and improving liquidity.

In 1833 a second precautionary measure was taken to protect the Bank of England reserve when, as we noted earlier, Bank notes were made legal tender in England and Wales, though not in Scotland – where they can still be refused as payment even today – for all sums over five pounds. It meant that banks could repay depositors on demand with Bank of England notes rather than cash and it was the first step towards recognising paper as real money without depending on its instant conversion into gold.

To stabilise the system further the Bank Charter Act was guided through Parliament in 1844 by the Tory Prime Minister, Sir Robert Peel, who incidentally also reintroduced income tax at sevenpence in the pound for a three-year period. Peel, who had previously been chairman of the Bank Committee of the House of Commons, split the Bank of England into two parts. The Issue Department was responsible for the new legal tender notes, of which it could authorise up to a total of £15,000,000 worth on the basis of government debt and securities, while any amount exceeding that had to be supported by bullion reserves. The banking operations – taking deposits, issuing credit, supervising the national debt and so on – were undertaken by a separate Banking Department.

At the same time the issue of notes by joint-stock and other banks, which were not legal tender, was restricted to those that had been approved before the 1844 Act. New banks had to seek twenty-year charters on the basis of a minimum capital investment of £100,000, with at least half of it fully paid up. 'Peel's Act' caused fury among pro-banking economists but was supported with equal vehemence by the so-called Currency School, which like the bullionist tendency that preceded it believed that gold and notes supported by gold were the only forms of 'real' money. Bagehot, however, looking back from 1873, regarded it as a slight irrelevance and pointed to something governments even now appear not to have fully appreciated – that the market will always win in the end.

The Tories were lucky with their Bank Act, which in essence underpinned the Gold Standard, because the California gold rush of 1849 and a similar phenomenon in Australia three years later significantly increased the available supply of bullion. This allowed currency expansion in line with surging demand, but it also had the effect of encouraging price inflation and, worse still, of maintaining high consumer prices throughout the 1860s and into the 1870s, at a time when producers' costs were falling as a result of the constant flow of new and more efficient technologies. Equally, the confidence in sterling promoted by the new 'sound money' policy soon spilled over into a fever of speculation similar to that which had caused the South Sea Bubble.

A rash of highly suspect share schemes and bogus companies led to a crash in 1847, prompted mainly by the great railway boom. Men such as the so-called 'Railway King', George Hudson, a linen draper from York, promised large dividends to investors in the rush to expand this exciting new form of transport following the opening of the first railway lines in the late 1820s. By 1845 Hudson controlled a third of the 3000 or so miles of track that linked London with other important cities and he had been elected Member of Parliament for Sunderland. His business methods were highly dubious, however. Overpromotion of his projects led to oversubscription of shares in the companies and overcapitalisation. All those investors were impatient to receive their promised dividends, which forced Hudson to raid the capital of new companies as they were formed in order to meet his commitments. Inevitably the strategy was self-defeating and the whole scheme collapsed. Charged with false accounting, Hudson lost his fortune almost overnight and retreated into self-imposed exile – although he soon bounced back to resume his place as the Sunderland MP, holding the seat until 1859.

The 1847 panic caused another run on the banks and once again the Bank of England found itself drained of reserves. The Bank Act was suspended in order to allow the issue of notes not supported by gold and interest rates rose sharply. The £224,000,000 invested in railways was returning only a little more than £11,000,000, and speculation suddenly went out of fashion. The banking lobby blamed the unjustifiably restrictive nature of the 'Peel Act' and their case was strengthened by a further crisis with the news of the Indian Mutiny in 1857, when the Act had to be suspended again and the Bank was obliged to prepare £2,000,000 worth of its by now printed notes in the face of a further run by depositors. The government, by this time more inclined towards free trade, gave in to some of the lobbyists' demands by repealing the laws limiting the formation of joint-stock banks.

In 1866, panic again gripped the financial markets as a leading firm of London brokers, Overend Gurney, failed and for a third time the Bank Act was suspended. Unless the law had been broken, Walter Bagehot commented sourly, the Bank of England could not have survived. He blamed the cash reserve requirement of the Bank Act, which meant that in a period of high demand, credit was always far in excess of assets:

There is no country at present, and there never was any country before, in which the ratio of the cash reserve to the bank deposits was so small as it is now in England. So far from our being able to rely on the

proportional magnitude of our cash in hand, the
amount of that cash is so exceedingly small that a
bystander almost trembles when he compares its
minuteness with the immensity of the credit which
rests upon it.

All would be well, Bagehot went on, if the proportion of cash to
credit could be reliably managed, but it was not.

There is the astounding instance of Overend,
Gurney, and Co. Ten years ago that house stood next
to the Bank of England in the City of London; it was
better known abroad than any similar firm known,
perhaps, better than any purely English firm. The
partners had great estates, which had mostly been
made in the business. They still derived an immense
income from it. Yet in six years they lost all their own
wealth, sold the business to the company, and then
lost a large part of the company's capital. And these
losses were made in a manner so reckless and so
foolish, that one would think a child who had lent
money in the City of London would have lent it
better. After this example, we must not confide too
surely in long-established credit, or in firmly-rooted
traditions of business. We must examine the system
on which these great masses of money are
manipulated, and assure ourselves that it is safe and
right.

Bagehot's response was a proposal to strengthen the

governance of the Bank of England and to maintain its reserves at a minimum of £11,000,000. In order to do that, he suggested, the Bank should raise its interest rates when the reserves dipped to between £14,000,000 and £15,000,000. It was only a superficial remedy, he conceded: the real answer was to require all banks to have a certain level of cash reserves, rather than relying on Bank of England deposits. But such a suggestion was fruitless. 'No one who has not long considered the subject can have a notion how much this dependence on the Bank of England is fixed in our national habits,' Bagehot wrote.

Fixed it might be, but by the 1870s the market had already changed a great deal in the banking system. The practice of settling bills by means of banknotes in commercial transactions had been overtaken by the chequebook and it would not be long before even people who were not businessmen would be using cheques to settle larger accounts. The pound sterling might still be pegged to gold, but it was gradually transforming itself into a substitute for hard cash, which could take more than one form. In 1881 sterling-denominated postal orders would be introduced and would subsequently become legal tender. The 'cash' pound note would make its appearance in 1914 and the gold sovereign would begin to be withdrawn from circulation.

In due course the phrase on the Bank of England note that promised 'to pay the bearer on demand the sum of . . .' would become little more than a promise. What the bearer would receive would not be the equivalent value of gold, but another note, or perhaps a cheque. The pound was becoming less of a currency and more of a symbol.

As if to emphasise the point, the ancient 'pound of sterlings' was no more. The silver penny, mainstay of the

English currency for more than a thousand years – esterlin, sceat or whatever – ended its active life in 1820, when the Royal Mint stopped producing it. The pound would never be the same again.

15

Cashing In

From now on the pound abroad is worth 14 per cent or so less in terms of other currencies. It does not mean, of course, that the pound here in Britain, in your pocket or purse or in your bank, has been devalued.

Prime Minister Harold Wilson, 18 November 1967

The British tend to look back on the Victorian era, with all its flaws, inequalities and iniquities, as a golden age in their history, and in terms of the pound sterling that is certainly and literally the case. The official adoption of the Gold Standard in 1816 had, by the early years of Queen Victoria's reign, become codified as the British Imperial Standard, from which in the 1870s it would develop into the International Gold Standard. With sterling the most powerful currency in the world and Britain the unchallenged leader in political, economic, financial and commercial terms, any nation wishing to be taken seriously had to peg its monetary system to the value of gold as defined by the pound. It was a curious position for a measure that had traditionally been based on silver, but with the disappearance of the silver penny after 1820 the direct link between the pound and its past was broken and the gold sovereign became firmly established as the standard of value.

These were vintage years, too, for the coinage as regards not only its quality but also its quantity and variety. In addition to the sovereign there was the half-sovereign, obviously worth ten shillings and also cast in gold. A five-shilling coin, known as a crown, was made of silver, as was the better known and more useful half-crown, at two shillings and sixpence. The shilling, sixpence and threepenny pieces were also silver and for a time there continued to be a silver fourpenny coin, the old groat. A shilling had become known in common parlance as a 'bob', for reasons that are obscure, and the sixpenny piece was called a 'tanner', though again the etymology is unclear. The term 'Joey' was applied to the silver groat, during its brief life from 1836 to 1855, because it had been introduced on the suggestion of a well-known radical Member of Parliament called Joseph Hume, who felt such a coin was useful for paying taxi fares. Later the 'Joey' was the silver threepenny piece, which could still be found in circulation in the 1940s.

The penny, which had been converted to copper and then, after 1860, to bronze, remained a significant feature of the coinage, along with the halfpenny, which even survived for a few years after decimalisation in 1971. Farthings were also widely used in the nineteenth and throughout much of the twentieth centuries, but half-farthings quickly disappeared because of their small size. Meanwhile, the guinea coin had ceased to be minted in 1813 and within five years had gone out of circulation, even though the sum of one pound one shilling it represented continued to be a common feature of certain payments. Barristers, for example, were always paid in guineas, keeping the pounds for themselves and handing the shillings to their clerks. For some reason the guinea acquired an air of social distinction that set it above even the gold sovereign and the use of this unusual amount did not really cease until after decimalisation.

This variety of coinage had much to do with the quaint value system of sterling, which still counted twelve pence to the shilling and twenty shillings – or 240 pence – to the pound. Other currencies outside the sphere of British influence had already opted for the decimal system, using numbers to the power of ten, which had been introduced to Europe as early as the fourteenth century. The British £.s.d. arrangement, however, had a perceived advantage in its greater divisibility. Decimal money, with one hundred units to the principal coin, can only be divided into halves, quarters, fifths, tenths, twentieths, twenty-fifths, and fiftieths. The old British currency, on the other hand, permitted in addition thirds, sixths, eighths, twelfths, fifteenths, sixteenths, twenty-fourths, thirtieths, fortieths, forty-eighths, sixtieths, eightieths, and one-hundred-and-twentieths.

Such flexibility was important when it came to pricing goods, especially manufactures that could be costed down to the smallest component, and also in calculating profit margins from producer to wholesaler to retailer and eventually to consumer. There is undoubtedly a case to be made that the divisibility of pounds, shillings and pence tended in ordinary times to militate against excessive inflationary shocks, since an almost imperceptible price rise from the point of view of the customer could make a significant difference to the balance sheets of companies producing mass-market goods. Some people argue, indeed, that the hyperinflation of the 1970s was provoked in part at least by the decimalisation of the pound.

Nevertheless, the decimal system had long had its supporters in Britain. It was first proposed in Parliament in 1824 and in 1849, following another attempt to introduce it, the silver florin first minted by Edward III made its reappearance with a face value of two shillings, or one tenth of a pound. Unfortunately, there was an error in the minting process and the 'Dei Gratia' (by God's grace) that normally appeared in the royal inscription was omitted, along with the initials F.D. (meaning Defender of the Faith) after the queen's name. This unwitting piece of supposed blasphemy was blamed by the superstitious for a sharp outbreak of cholera in Britain that year and the offending coins were withdrawn, which led to the abrupt departure from the Royal Mint of its Master, Richard Lalor Sheil, amid dark mutterings about the fact that he was a Roman Catholic.

Once reissued in its correct form, however, the two-shilling piece proved to be very popular and finally entered the decimal system as ten pence 122 years after its inception for that purpose.

The first half of the Victorian era, with Britain reaching the height of its power, was also generally a boom time for the economy, apart from a couple of financial crises in 1857 and

1866, both of which served first to halt what had been sharp price rises and in the end to cause prices to fall. Wages still fluctuated according to the condition of trade, but on average there were substantial rises between 1850 and 1874, with even the vulnerable agricultural trades earning some fifty-five per cent more at the end of the period than they had been receiving at the beginning. In the cotton trade, wages doubled in twenty-five years, while for builders, mining engineers and shipyard craftsmen the rises were seventy per cent and thirty per cent respectively, though these groups did gain a reduction in their working hours from ten and a half a day to nine by the early 1870s.

According to contemporary observers, the average worker's wage across the United Kingdom – including lower-paid Ireland – was about nineteen shillings a week, with the incomes of working-class families, with women and children also in employment, totalling some thirty-one shillings in England and Wales, and about twenty-eight shillings in Scotland. In Ireland the average family income was estimated at about twenty-three shillings and sixpence a week. Higher up the social scale non-manual workers such as shop assistants, messengers and junior office staff would earn less than two pounds a week, while older and more senior office staff and shop managers might receive between £100 and £300 a year. Middle management and small shopkeepers might earn up to a £1000 a year and for the professional classes, salaries or fees could provide an annual income of about £5000.

To give some idea of the numbers involved, by 1881 more than 4,000,000 people were employed in manufacturing, against just under 2,000,000 in agriculture and about the same number in domestic service. A further 2,000,000 worked in trade and transport, just over 500,000 in mining and quarrying, and a little under 1,000,000 in the construction industry.

That most people felt themselves prosperous during this period may be judged from noticeable changes in food consumption. According to a series of surveys, the use of bread and flour declined in the later nineteenth century, as did that of potatoes, while consumption of meat, fats and sugar rose sharply. By the 1890s people were eating on average a pound of meat per week and the same amount of sugar – 'bread is the staple food of poverty and . . . people eat much less of it when they can afford to buy meat and to indulge in the type of dish with which sugar is eaten,' commented the authors of perhaps the first dietary history of the country, *The Englishman's Food*.

In some ways, however, the general air of prosperity and power was illusory. By 1886, Britain was already being overtaken in macro-economic terms by the more productive economies of the United States and Germany, while imports were eating into the profits of domestic manufacturers and farmers alike. At the same time London's position as the world's greatest financial centre resulted in a steady outflow of capital abroad, not all of it to the empire. In 1890, for example, £150,000,000, or nearly half of Britain's total overseas investment, had gone to Argentina, a fact that brought the venerable merchant bank Barings to the brink of collapse for the first time when the Argentinian people rose up in rebellion. This taste for foreign investment naturally served to limit the amount of capital available to finance business at home and for generations economists have argued that the City of London did the country no favours by scouring the world for the most attractive returns. It is perhaps only now, as trade and investment become truly global, that Britain is beginning to reap the rewards of its traditionally wide horizons.

As the century neared its end, new pressures emerged to threaten the 'golden age'. Abroad, France and Russia had joined the USA and Germany to rival Britain's economic dominance, and the Germans in particular harboured serious imperial ambitions. At home, radical thinkers and socialist politicians were questioning the liberal free trade economics that had helped the country forge ahead, pointing among other things to the persistent scourge of poverty as the theory of a welfate state began to form. In the workplace trade unionism was on the march, as a campaign gathered pace to reduce the working week further to forty-eight hours and strikes were threatened in support of it. The very foundations of this first ever industrial society were a subject for debate as intellectuals such as the art critic and commentator John Ruskin and the designer William Morris started a fashion for harking back to a supposedly idyllic rural past, while the writers George Bernard Shaw and H. G. Wells helped to found the left-wing Fabian Society, arguing that laissez-faire economics was not only socially unjust but also deeply inefficient.

In 1899 the South African War against the Dutch Afrikaner settlers, or Boers, who dominated the colony, both exposed Britain's underlying imperial weakness – the fighting lasted until 1902 and a peace treaty was only signed after a series of atrocities on the part of the British – and pushed government spending far above its traditional levels, setting a precedent for the future. The great power was beginning to totter in the face of a gathering process of change, both internal and external. Not only were foreign rivals knocking at the gates of empire, but the very nature of the state itself was being challenged.

When we look back, the years between the death of Queen Victoria in 1902 and the outbreak of the First World War in 1914 may look like something of a pause, the 'long summer afternoon' that ushered in the first dark night of carnage in a century that would be remarkable for the extent and nature of its violence. In reality, much was changing. The Liberal government elected in 1905 heeded the concerns of social reformers by introducing free school meals, the National Insurance scheme that protected workers during periods of illness, old age pensions and labour exchanges to help the by now growing numbers of unemployed people. There were rows over ways to raise finance for a new fleet of battleships to restore the supremacy of the British navy, and in 1909 the House of Lords threw out David Lloyd George's budget because it sought to impose new taxes on land and a special 'supertax' on the incomes of the richest section of society. The depth of the political divisions is demonstrated by the calling of two general elections in 1910, which left the Liberals in power but only with the support of the nascent Labour Party and Irish members.

After 1908 prices began to rise again while wages remained static and, as the trades union movement grew towards a membership of 4,000,000, a series of strikes erupted in important industrial sectors, often prompting the government to send in troops much as it might have done during the very early years of the Industrial Revolution a century and more before. And as tensions rose among the European powers, even Britain as the greatest of them all could not prevent the slide into what would become the bloodiest war in history.

The 1914–18 war, though essentially a European affair, was one of America's great defining moments, even though the United States was a late entrant. For the first time it demonstrated to the world both the extent of American power and the nature of American ambitions. President Woodrow Wilson used the American-aided victory of Britain and its allies to serve notice that the days of the old imperial powers were numbered and that a new form of economic empire was in the making. Thanks to the defeat of Germany, Britain would retain its superpower status for a further two decades or so, and parts of its empire for thirty years after that, but it would be constantly looking over its shoulder towards the colony it had lost, which was now rising to succeed it as leader of the world.

When the war started it was the first serious threat Britain had faced from an important European power since the days of Napoleon and in a sense the government panicked, borrowing money for the war effort wherever and as quickly as it could without using London's financial muscle to obtain the most favourable rates of interest. Lloyd George, then Chancellor of the Exchequer and later to be Prime Minister, wrote in his war memoirs:

> By November 1914, it was obvious that the additional expenditure caused by the War would far outrun anything provided for by the peace-time Budget I had introduced in the spring. Already on 8th August the House of Commons had voted the Government a credit of £100,000,000 for War purposes, and it was now necessary to ask it for a

further credit of more than twice that amount. If the
War were to continue into 1915, much greater sums
still would be required. The issue before the country
. . . was whether these huge sums should be raised
entirely by loans . . . or whether we should aim at
paying our way as far as possible by current taxation,
and thus reduce the debt burden to be handed on to
the next generation.

In the event, Lloyd George immediately raised taxes, increasing government revenues by £60,000,000 a year. Income tax doubled to two shillings and eightpence in the pound and the Chancellor's new supertax on the rich also doubled, to an additional tenpence in the pound on incomes over £3000 a year and an extra two shillings and eightpence for those earning more than £11,000. Today, it is interesting for us to note that such people were regarded in 1914 as the very rich, but then the average wage for a railwayman at that time was only about one pound ten shillings a week.

The remainder of the £325,000,000 the Chancellor required immediately – and that sum represented double the government's normal annual expenditure – came from a War Loan, with government securities offered at three and a half per cent, redeemable at par in 1925–28. Within less than a year a second War Loan had to be raised, this time with an upper limit of £910,000,000 and in 1917 a third issue became the world's first billion-pound loan, at what proved to be a crippling five per cent. And that was only the beginning.

In his first wartime budget speech Lloyd George forecast that when the war ended there would be a brief economic boom,

. . . but when that period is over we shall be face to face with one of the most serious industrial situations with which we have ever been confronted. We shall have exhausted an enormous amount of the capital of the world which would otherwise have been available for industries. Our purchasers, both here and abroad, will be crippled. Their purchasing power will have been depressed. Let us make no mistake. Great Britain will be confronted with some of the gravest problems with which it has ever been faced.

His prediction proved to be dismally accurate. Writing in 1933 he observed:

The adoption of the principle that the British Government had to pay the commercial rate for money needed to defend the country had a costly sequel . . . The War had added a further £4,000,000,000 to our National Debt. It cost the country a dozen years of remorseless deflation and concomitant depression to bring interest rates down again to a level that would enable this vast sum to be reconverted to 3½ per cent. Throughout the interval, not only was the country taxing itself to pay a sum ranging at one time as high as £100,000,000 a year more than it would otherwise have done, but the high yield of a gilt-edged Government security kept up rates all round, and made money dearer for all enterprises, industrial, commercial and national.

It is probably no exaggeration to say that Britain never fully recovered from the financial effects of the First World War. The short boom Lloyd George had anticipated gave way in 1929 to the worst economic depression the world has ever seen, after a speculative bubble burst to cause the infamous Wall Street Crash, and although Britain would remain a leading industrial, financial and political power, its glory days were over. So long as the empire lasted the pound remained the leading international currency, but competition from the dollar continued to intensify and, beneath the surface, a long period of decline set in that would not begin to be reversed until the 1980s.

From the point of view of the currency the First World War had other important effects. Within months of its outbreak the Bank of England quietly started to withdraw gold from domestic circulation, the sovereign and half-sovereign being replaced by one-pound and ten-shilling notes, though at first these were issued by the Treasury rather than the Bank. It was the beginning of the end of the Gold Standard and of full conversion to paper money. Officially Britain returned to the Gold Standard in 1925, but within seven years – in the depths of the Depression – it was finally abandoned. Meanwhile, the Bank of England took over the issuing of banknotes, with the first coloured examples at a pound and ten shillings (also the first to be printed on both sides) appearing in 1928. The issue of notes by commercial banks in England and Wales had ceased in 1921, although Scottish banks retained the privilege and continue to produce their own distinctive notes today.

Curiously, it was as the seeds of macro-economic decline were taking root that the influence of sterling reached its widest limits. Between 1919 and the outbreak of the Second World

War twenty years later, the British Empire was at its most extensive, thanks partly to the acquisition of former German-held territories. But, as the military historian Anthony Clayton pointed out in his book *The British Empire as a Superpower*, 'Global presence did not mean global power' and that applied both politically and economically. In these post-imperial times it is fashionable to think of the purpose of the empire as a money-making scheme on a vast scale, ensuring both cheap imports from dependent countries and a ready market for British exports. The truth is that, while such might have been the case for a time, it was not long before the costs of empire outweighed the trade benefits.

By 1930, for instance, only about a third of Britain's annual billion pounds' worth of imports came from British possessions and approximately half of the £570,000,000 in exports from Britain went to India, the dominions and the colonies. It was a similar story in terms of overseas investment, which even before the First World War was evenly split between the Empire and other countries, with the largest proportion – a fifth – of the almost £4 billions worth of capital employed invested in the United States. Nor were the returns on imperial investment particularly good, since they consistently underperformed those from the USA, Latin America and elsewhere. As just one example, the British South Africa Company failed to pay dividends to investors for more than thirty years. So while sterling continued to control or influence a large part of the world, it was not necessarily doing so to its own long-term benefit.

The economic decline of Britain pursued its course slowly and, to a large extent, imperceptibly throughout the 1920s and

1930s, or what has become known to historians as the Age of Anxiety, when everything appeared to be in flux. For a time there seemed to be reasons for optimism. By 1932 the Bank of England had managed to reduce its base interest rate to two per cent, which in turn enabled the conversion of government loan stock from the panicky five per cent of the war years to its pre-1914 level of three and a half per cent. The resulting loss suffered by War Loan holders was compensated for by a general fall in long- and short-term borrowing rates, and a surge in share prices prompted by a boom in housing construction and the development of new light industries – car making, electronics, chemicals and so on.

Industrial production rose sharply, outstripping that of the United States and all other developed countries in the years between 1929 and 1937. The Bank of England interest rate was to remain virtually unchanged for twenty years and, although inflation began to set in after 1935, it was kept to modest proportions until the price and wage explosion of the 1970s. There was even some long-awaited redistribution of wealth, with changes to taxation in the mid-1930s spreading an estimated £91,000,000 from the richer to the less affluent sections of society.

The average working man's wage was, by 1938, between three pounds and three pounds ten shillings a week, while for women it had reached about one pound fourteen shillings. Surveys showed a vast expansion of the middle classes, with nearly twenty per cent of the workforce earning between £250 and £1000 a year, against just over half making up the so-called working classes and receiving less than £250. The cost of living was judged to be about thirty shillings per head per week for a working-class family enjoying an adequate diet and reasonable shelter and comfort, while the subsistence line was set at fifteen shillings per head per week – and research showed that up to a third of families were living below that line. Apart from that persistently poor section of society, life was relatively prosperous and pleasant for people who had regular work. Although most still rented their homes, ownership was increasing at least among the middle classes. For almost everyone gradual reductions in working hours meant either more leisure or the opportunity for overtime earnings, and paid holidays were becoming common.

This plateau of modest affluence masked for most Britons the changes in the rest of the world that were slowly undermining the nation's economic position: the power of America, which had merely been temporarily checked by the Depression; spreading industrialisation across what, by 1937, had become the commonwealth rather than the empire, and a consequent reduction in the importance of imports from Britain; the birth of independence movements in the colonies, especially India; and the stirrings of trade competition in the Far East, notably Japan.

But it was the Second World War that dealt the final blow to the dominance of sterling. Britain entered it as leading creditor nation and in the very hour of victory had to begin to come to terms with the fact that the war had cost the country up to a quarter of its wealth. By 1945 the United Kingdom was running a deficit of £10 billion, owed more than £5 billion to the United States, had sold £1 billion worth of foreign investments and was obliged to repay nearly £4 billion in short-term borrowings. On top of all that were the costs of post-war

261

reconstruction. Small wonder that the late 1940s and early 1950s became known as the era of austerity as governments struggled to deal with the debt mountain, replace infrastructure destroyed by German bombing, find jobs for hundreds of thousands of demobilised service personnel, end the rationing of food and other essential items, divest itself of overseas commitments it could no longer afford – a process that began with the granting of independence to India and Pakistan in 1947 – and, most of all, to re-establish Britain as a trading nation.

The Labour government that swept to power in the 1945 election saw state control and central planning as the essential tools of reconstruction – and to meet its cherished commitment of establishing a National Health Service and the other elements of a welfare state. About twenty per cent of British industry – along with the Bank of England – was taken into 'public ownership' in 1947, which meant that its operations were directed by government appointees. It was seen as a positive development at the time, but it was one the country would live to regret as productivity stagnated, the trades unions grew ever more demanding and the levels of public subsidy necessary to keep failing industries alive rose inexorably. Financing government spending, rather than wealth creation, seemed to become the main objective of economic activity.

The next thirty years were to be a period of continuing economic failure, whether Labour or the Conservatives were in power: a cycle of unsustainable boom followed by recession, of currency crises and devaluations, of growing unemployment, of trade deficits and rising public borrowing, of industrial strife and collapse.

Why, asked the economist Sidney Pollard in 1982, when other countries including devastated Germany were enjoying a post-war 'economic miracle', did Britain not join in? In his book *The Wasting of the British Economy* he wrote sardonically: 'The only economic miracle was the British failure to take part in the progress of the rest of the industrial world. Surely it must have required a powerful and sustained effort or most unusual circumstances to prevent the world boom from spilling over into Britain as well.'

Even when the government was congratulating itself on four per cent growth rates in economic output and fixed domestic investments of fifteen per cent, Britain was lagging well behind the rest of the world, with its overall thirteen per cent rates of output growth and level of domestic capital investment at twenty per cent.

In 1949 the pound was devalued by thirty per cent against the dollar, falling from $4.30 to $2.80. It was the start of a series of exchange rate fluctuations, which involved a further devaluation to $2.40 in 1967 and, at one stage during the 1980s, a free fall that left sterling hovering just above parity with the dollar. Attempts to stabilise exchange rates both before and after Britain joined the European Economic Community in 1972 – which had prompted the decimalisation of the currency the previous year – all failed so far as sterling was concerned.

By 1978 the political commentator Peter Jenkins was writing in the *Guardian*: 'No country has yet made the journey from developed to under-developed. Britain could be the first to embark upon that route. That is what it would mean to move away from a century of relative economic decline into a state of absolute decline.' Within two years of that article, Britain's gross national product, the measure of the country's productive wealth, when calculated per head of population, had fallen below that of not only the United States, Japan and West Germany but also of countries such as Finland, New Zealand and Iceland. In 1985 'even Italy', as outraged newspapers pointed out, was doing better than the United Kingdom.

But absolute decline never happened, although it sometimes felt as if it was taking place. The arrival in power of the Conservative Party under Margaret Thatcher in 1979, with the Prime Minister's commitment to modernise the economy, caused the collapse of large sections of the older British industries and even some of the newer ones. Coal mining virtually ceased, steel making and shipbuilding were reduced to a fraction of their former extent and the automotive industry, which had been expensively and fruitlessly subsidised by a succession of previous administrations, was allowed to fall – at least what was left of it – into foreign hands. What did happen under Thatcher was that controls on the export of capital were removed, large-scale foreign investment was encouraged, and the London money markets were completely reformed to encompass electronic trading and freer competition, so that the financial services sector became the dominant force in economic growth. Even a Wall Street crash in 1987 and a subsequent slump on the London Stock Exchange that far exceeded the falls of 1929 failed to turn a crisis into a disaster, though it did provoke a sharp economic recession throughout the world in the late 1980s and early 1990s. The aftermath, however, was a sustained rise in world markets that continued more or less unchecked even through a general financial and industrial collapse in Japan and the rest of Asia in 1998.

As Britain's old nationalised industries were either allowed to sink into history or sold off into the private sector, another wide-ranging social restructuring similar to that of the Industrial Revolution began to take shape. At first unemployment soared to frightening levels, with official figures recording some 3,000,000 people out of work and critics of the government suggesting the total might be nearer 5,000,000, but the explosion of the now deregulated telecommunications industry, the rapid growth of the service sector and a flood of investment by foreign car makers and technology companies had, by the mid-1990s, given Britain one of the lowest rates of unemployment in Europe and the economy was growing again, albeit slowly.

After a series of alarums and excursions, the pound came out of the regulated European Exchange Rate Mechanism – which was designed to allow currencies to fluctuate in value only within predetermined limits – and settled down at a relatively stable rate against the dollar somewhere within the $1.60 range. Interest rates began to fall and so did inflation as the social democratic consensus introduced by the Labour government of 1945 was finally replaced by a new concord that placed economic competence, financial prudence, tight control over government spending, competition, individual responsibility and effort, and the encouragement of enterprise at the top of the political agenda. When, in 1997, Labour was re-elected after eighteen years in opposition, it could hardly be distinguished in many essentials of its economic policy from its Conservative predecessors and one of its first acts, in recognition of the apparent triumph of market forces, was to make the

Bank of England an independent arbiter of monetary policy, along the lines of the Federal Reserve in America. The Bank's brief was above all else to maintain low inflation by means of manipulation of base interest rates.

It began to seem as if Britain had finally started to manage its decline from the pinnacle of economic power, that it had passed through the trough of despair and regained confidence in its new, if somewhat reduced, place in the world. As the eminent economist Sir Alan Walters commented in 1998 in his foreword to *An Illustrated Guide to the British Economy*, written by Bill Jamieson, Economics Editor of the *Sunday Telegraph*: 'Britain is no longer the poor relation of continental Europe. Now Britons have more income to spend, net of tax, than any other country in Europe, save for West Germany.'

The pound might no longer enjoy the absolute power it once had – in 1972 it ceased to be a currency in which other countries maintain reserves – but, as we shall see in the final chapter of this book, sterling remains a significant influence on the international economic structure. It has adapted itself to survive many crises since the far-off days when it represented a pile of silver pennies. The question is, can it, or indeed should it, come through a series of new challenges in a world where the very nature of currency itself may face its first fundamental change since the invention of coins more than two millennia ago?

16

The Last Days of the Pound?

Electronic money resembles the diverse forms of primitive money – cowrie shells, animal teeth and beads – in that it permits individuals more control over its creation and use. It has far more flexibility than governments or banks have allotted to metal or paper currency in the last two millennia.

Jack Weatherford, *The History of Money*, New York, 1997

Although the Worshipful Company of Goldsmiths in London still checks the quality of the United Kingdom coinage each year, the pound coin of today is obviously a very different piece from the first one minted on the instructions of King Henry VII. Made from an alloy of nickel and brass, it is produced by the Royal Mint at Llantrisant in South Wales on some of the most advanced casting machinery in the world. Regarded, like Henry's sovereign, as a particularly fine coin for the modern age, the pound has an intrinsic value that is negligible and purchasing power to match. It will not even buy you the cheapest fare on the London Underground, which is why it has recently been joined by a two-pound coin with an outer rim of nickel-brass and a core of cupro-nickel.

At the last count there were more than 1 billion pound coins circulating in Britain, supplemented by the relatively few surviving pound notes still produced by banks based in Scotland and Northern Ireland. Fifty-pence pieces numbered about ½ billion, twenty- and ten-pence coins 1.5 and 1.3 billion respectively, and five-pence pieces just under 3 billion. The bulk of the coinage, as it has always been, is made up of pennies – now minted in copper-plated steel – with nearly 7 billion circulating, while twopenny coins number a little more than 4 billion.

The total face value of the 18 billion or so coins in use is approximately £2 billion, which equates to about thirty-five pounds for every man, woman and child in Britain. It seems little enough in an age that has seen the rate of inflation hit twenty-five per cent at its peak, so that a salary of £5000 a year in 1970 had multiplied tenfold, in purely numerical terms, by the mid-1990s. But of course the use of and demand for coinage is not what it was. Banknotes are now the main medium of cash exchange, with some £25 billion worth circulating at any one time, while non-cash transactions have reached the point where even for the purchase of food in supermarkets special check-outs are identified for people who do not wish to use cheques and credit or debit cards. The amount of credit advanced to ordinary people by banks generally hovers around the £1 billion mark and the overdraft, invented by the Royal Bank of Scotland in the eighteenth century, is now a way of life. Money in the modern world has become much more of a notional commodity, which must cause the old supporters of the bullion theory to turn in their graves.

Most people in Britain actually see only a tiny fraction of their incomes in cash, with salaries most often paid by electronic transfer, bills paid by cheque or direct debit or bank standing order and purchases made by means of a small piece of plastic. Even those forms of transaction are rapidly being overtaken as use of the Internet develops, revolutionising both banking and shopping. It will soon be possible for some people to live, theoretically at least, without ever handling a pound coin, buying and paying for goods through computers and eventually digital television sets. Throughout the developed world bank branches are closing in large numbers and many of those that remain increasingly contain only machines.

So far the take-up of non-cash forms of transaction, though impressive, has remained limited. While in value terms the vast majority of transactions in countries such as Britain are undertaken without the exchange of real money, the proportion is reversed when dealings are assessed by volume. People still like to have cash in their pockets and purses, and to use it at least for small everyday purchases. That will change as computers and the machines they spawn take over more of our lives – ticket machines at rail stations, for instance, now often accept credit cards – but, more important, such change will be driven by the market because of the costs involved in handling cash and cheques, which are clearly much greater than for electronic and other 'notional' transfers that can be processed automatically without human intervention. In the twenty-first century it is highly likely that in many parts of the world the use of cash will cease altogether.

Does that mean the end of the pound, after 1000 years? Well, it depends. Remember that money came into being to represent a unit of account, a measure and a store of value and a medium of exchange. Even if the last function is removed, the other three remain, and in fact seem to have become more important rather than less so as the idea of an intrinsic value in currency has declined. There is no longer any point in hoarding pounds for the metal they contain or, in the case of banknotes, that they represent. Go to the Bank of England bearing a note inscribed 'I promise to pay the bearer on demand the sum of . . .' and you will not be given pieces of gold in exchange. Yet as the Scottish philosopher Thomas Carlyle noted at the height of the Industrial Revolution, we live in an epoch 'when Cash Payment has become the sole nexus of man to man' – except that in our day, unlike Carlyle's, money does not necessarily mean cash. What the cash nexus means now is that people are judged by the value of the houses they live in, by the amount of their salaries, by the size of their bank balances or investments, in short by the numbers of pounds that can be attached to them. It often seems that money is the sole measure of value and therefore the only legitimate store of value.

From that point of view, then, it might appear that the pound will be safe for some time to come. How else are we to assess the worth or status of people around us? Perhaps more to the point, how otherwise can we determine the condition of the country if not through its wealth? Alternatives have been suggested and different ways of calculating national performance, but they tend to be more complex and perhaps more subjective than the gross domestic product or the balance of trade expressed in pounds sterling.

Equally, the pound remains an important international currency and London one of the greatest and most productive financial centres in the world. Britain's overseas assets amount to some £2000 billion and its investment income from them more than doubled between 1986 and 1996 to £96 billion, or nearly £4000 for every adult. This is the new British empire, the second largest after that of the US, and it has been built upon the foundation of sterling, which at the time of writing remains a highly valued currency in spite of a steady decline in British interest rates that would generally be assumed to make the pound less attractive to foreign investors. Nevertheless, the annual flow of foreign investment in Britain is currently about £20 billion, thirty-four per cent of the total for the whole of the European Union of which Britain is a member, or more than that of Germany and France combined. In 1997 the total amount of foreign capital invested in the United Kingdom reached £168 billion, which represents a current market value many times greater than that capital sum.

The London Stock Exchange is among the top three such institutions in the world, along with New York and Tokyo, and sterling ranks alongside the dollar and the yen as one of the most frequently traded currencies on international markets. In terms of capitalisation, the markets in the United States and Japan are significantly larger than that in Britain and increasing globalisation of finance and trade means that the City of London is more dependent than in former times on market movements in other parts of the world, especially the United States. The value of shares on the Stock Exchange is frequently influenced by rises or falls in New York, which in turn may reflect events in Tokyo. However, London continues to enjoy the position it achieved in the nineteenth century as the principal centre for international financial activity. It ranks first in global banking and foreign exchange trading, and comes second only to Tokyo in the scale of investment funds under management.

London's importance as a global financial centre is emphasised by the fact that Britain remains an important member of the so-called Group of Seven, formed in 1967 as a forum for the world's leading industrial and economic powers. The other members are, of course, the United States, Japan and Germany, along with Canada, France and Italy. More recently it became a Group of Eight, with Russia a sort of honorary member more for political than economic reasons, given its decline in financial terms since the fall of the Communist system.

All this suggests that, whether or not people continue to use banknotes and coins in the future, the pound sterling will continue to be a powerful economic and monetary symbol, however notional it might have become. Or will it? There are two important forces at work, one pressing and the other more long-term, that could result in the pound's disappearance within a few short years.

The immediate challenge to the future of sterling is the arrival of the European Single Currency, the euro, which has been designed to replace the national currencies of all fifteen members of the European Union. As of 1 January 1999 the euro is the legal currency in the eleven European nations – Austria, Belgium, Finland, France, Germany, Ireland, Italy, Luxembourg, the Netherlands, Portugal and Spain – that signed up to the first wave of what is called Economic and Monetary Union, or EMU for short. The treaty that established EMU assumed that the United Kingdom, Denmark, Greece and Sweden, together with other countries now awaiting membership of the EU, would also eventually agree to see their currencies subsumed into the euro.

There can be no doubt that the birth of the euro is the most significant monetary development since the creation of the American dollar. It was originally planned to come into being in 1980, just eight years after Britain joined what was then known as the European Economic Community, but a series of economic crises and political difficulties delayed EMU for nearly twenty years beyond its target date. Now, though, the nations that have adopted the euro have agreed to delegate what used to be thought of as economic sovereignty to the European Central Bank, which co-ordinates monetary policy across the euro zone, fixing exchange rates and levels of interest, and controlling the money supply to match prevailing economic conditions.

To supporters of the euro, Economic and Monetary Union is a logical outcome of the single market created by the European Union – indeed, they say there is little point in having this internal trading block if it is to be disrupted by fluctuating exchange rates among competing national currencies. Apart from the aim of exchange rate stability, the euro has been designed to reduce the costs of business transactions among member states; to introduce price transparency, which means that businesses and customers can see at a glance whether one country is charging more for goods or services than its partners and can therefore apply pressure for price reductions; and to harmonise monetary and fiscal policy in ways that will lead to an even pattern of prices, wages and economic growth. From a political point of view, europhiles say the single currency will increase co-operation among European states and eliminate economic rivalries that throughout history have tended to result in disastrous wars.

Of course, the scheme is not without its critics, of which many have been in Britain. One of the most fundamental objections to EMU has been the fact that it is not accompanied by proper, accountable political institutions and it is therefore seen as undemocratic. Eurosceptics point out that crucial economic, monetary and fiscal decisions traditionally managed by elected governments have been devolved to the European Central Bank, which cannot be removed or challenged by voters. The single currency cannot work, the critics contend, without the creation of a European superstate involving a multinational central parliament and bureaucracy, which would have the effect of reducing current national governments to the status of regional authorities.

That is a political argument, but there are also economic objections to the euro. Opponents suggest that the economic stability EMU was designed to create is artificial and could lead to stagnation as tight monetary control by bankers stifles growth and drags all the European economies down to a sort of tick-over rate that would see them underperforming on the international stage against the dynamic, market-led economy of the United States. In brief, the claim is that lack of competition among the members of the EU will make the whole block less competitive. There are also fears about the harmonisation of fiscal policy, given wide social differences among the various European countries. One of the criteria for entering the euro zone is a cap on government borrowing, which sceptics believe will force some governments to raise taxes to punitive levels in order to meet their commitments on such matters as health, education and social security. Doubts have emerged, too, over whether the single currency will do anything to relieve what appears to have become almost structural unemployment across Europe, representing the Union's most urgent economic and social problem.

Underlying all these reservations, though, is the suspicion that a one-size-fits-all economic policy tied to a single currency simply will not work across the range of varying conditions in the diverse EU membership. What suits Spain, for example, might well be damaging to Germany and, says the anti-euro lobby, the monetary straitjacket could well leave individual countries more vulnerable to recession and economic crises such as the Asian collapse of 1998 because they will be unable to react in their own best interests, obliged instead to follow what is perceived to be good for the Union as a whole. Some economists have forecast darkly that in such circumstances disgruntled populations could rise up and force their governments to take actions that might cause the euro to collapse, split the Union apart and possibly provoke one of the very wars the single currency is intended to render impossible.

And finally there is the view that the euro cannot succeed

because as a currency it is designed primarily, perhaps solely, as a unit of account and not as a real standard of value – especially in terms of existing contracts in the currencies it replaces – or as a realistic medium of exchange because it attempts to control markets rather than being modified by them.

So far as the United Kingdom is concerned, there are several particular arguments that militated against the country joining the single currency at its outset. The main one is that the British economy operates in a very different way from the economies of most of its European partners, causing some commentators to suggest that it cannot properly be called a 'European' economy at all.

Partly because of huge UK investment in the United States, the economic cycle in Britain tends to shadow that of America far more closely than the German cycle, which is the main indicator for the rest of Europe. Unlike all its EU partners, the United Kingdom is a net exporter of primary energy and an important exporter of oil. Britain also relies less than other EU countries on trade within the Union. Trading with itself accounts for sixty-one per cent of the Union's activities, whereas in the case of Britain only forty-nine per cent of its trade credits come from within Europe and it relies on the US and the rest of the world to make good its balance of trade deficit with its European partners. In addition, the vast financial services industry on which the UK economy depends sets it apart from its European neighbours and tends again to bring it closer to America.

Looking at the picture in more detail, one notes that Britain has a higher level of household borrowing than its partners, which means that the economy is more vulnerable to changes in interest rates, but at the same time British public expenditure and taxes are lower overall than in most EU countries. Similarly, the overall cost of production in the UK is considerably lower than it is in the other main European economies of Germany, France and Italy, because although wages are relatively high they are not matched by proportionate non-wage costs such as payroll taxes and employers' social security contributions, as they are elsewhere. The last comparison might also help to account for the fact that, as this book was being written, the level of unemployment in the United Kingdom was running at less than half that for the European Union as a whole.

Many British business leaders – perhaps even a little more than half of them – have expressed support for entry into the single currency, but as the euro burst upon an apparently less than wildly enthusiastic world there was little evidence of public support in the United Kingdom, especially in England. There are cultural, political and emotional reasons for this. One is that the 'island race' has tended always to view itself as being apart from the Continent, as we have seen even in this fairly narrowly focused history of its currency. In a recent public opinion poll that asked the question, 'Do you feel as much a European as you do a citizen of your own country?' only twelve per cent of Britons answered 'yes', against an average of a third for all fifteen countries.

Then, as the first great trading nation of the modern world, Britain has seen the European Union principally as a free trade area rather than a global economic block. The pan-EU harmonisation of such things as business practices, health and safety standards, food regulations, the minimum wage, working hours and social provision have been accepted rather reluctantly as the price of remaining a member of the club.

Yet in purely economic terms, it is hard to see where Britain has really benefited from its membership. For consumers, the European Common Agricultural Policy has resulted in the steady rise of food prices to meet continental levels. The fisheries policy of the EU has done immense, possibly terminal damage to the British fishing industry. During the decade from 1986 to 1996 the United Kingdom has – with the exception of 1991 – suffered substantial deficits in trade with the EU relating to goods, services, investment income and cash transfers, while as the third-largest net contributor to the Union budget it had paid in £30 billion (at current prices) by 1997, more than £1 billion a year for the privilege of receiving grants and subsidies that generally do not match contributions.

Since this is not an economic treatise we do not need to rehearse the arguments of the potential risks and rewards arising from taking part in the single currency or, otherwise, rejecting it. At the time of writing, public opinion in the United Kingdom appeared to be hardening against the euro, whose performance as an international currency had in any case been less than spectacular so far. The British, it seemed, overwhelmingly wanted to hold on to their pound, which had served them so well for a millennium or more. Noting this groundswell of opinion, the government dithered, allegedly adopting a wait-and-see policy and muttering about the possibility of joining 'when conditions are right' and certain economic tests had been analysed. If one had had to vote on the matter in 1999, it seemed pretty obvious that Britain would not be joining the single currency soon – and it was almost possible to predict that it would not join at all.

Yet political imperatives are not always exactly the same as economic ones, and some observers on both sides of the euro fence, not to mention those sitting on it, were suggesting that just as it was felt to be politically correct to join the old European Economic Community in 1972, there might be compelling non-economic reasons for adopting the euro at some point in the future.

That, of course, would mean the end of the pound after a long and more or less glorious reign. It might be seen as just another evolutionary step in the history of the currency. Almost everything has changed, after all, since King Offa struck his first pennies, since King Henry II originally raised the English currency to international prominence, since Henry VII introduced the sovereign and Charles II the guinea, since the Gold Standard was finally abandoned. In spite of fierce opposition, the venerable £.s.d. system, dating back to the Roman Empire, was thrown out in 1971, which fundamentally altered the character of the pound for ever, along with the complex arithmetical gymnastics enjoyed by generations schooled in the arcane calculations of the old money. Yards, feet and inches have been officially replaced by metres and their decimal divisions, pounds have been converted into kilos, and maybe all of those will eventually be superseded by some as yet unarticulated piece of computer-speak. It is perhaps unrealistic, in a world where the pace of change seems to accelerate year on year, to expect the pound to continue even in its current altered state.

But the best argument against Britain's adoption of the

euro is that it is likely to prove an expensive irrelevance as the globalisation of trade and what has been aptly described as 'the death of distance' brought about by communications technology drive us towards rethinking the way we buy and sell, and generally how we organise economic life. In its way the European single currency is nothing more than an extension of the existing national currencies that have been competing with each other almost since their inception. Its introduction might bring marginal benefits to European Union members trading with each other, but it offers little if any gain in terms of transactions with the rest of the world.

Just like the pound itself, the euro faces a long-term challenge from the establishment of global markets that will eventually begin to demand a truly international unit of account. The nearest thing we have to that at present is the dollar which, for example, is used to denominate the worldwide price of oil even though the main producers are a long way from America. That, however, is something of an historical accident, related to the fact that so many of the big oil companies are American, and the mighty dollar, too, could well find itself overtaken as the volume of electronic commerce increases and currency exchange rates become something of an irritation.

At a time when vast sums of money can cross frontiers electronically in a matter of minutes, exchanging those sums into a variety of currencies for local use is unproductive and incurs cost. For large multinational companies, those costs can be significant – as in the case, for instance, of a business with headquarters in London and substantial branches in, say, Italy, South Africa, the United States, Japan, Singapore, Australia and Brazil. The company's capital and earnings will be accounted for in pounds, but the income and expenditure of its branches will involve the use of lire, rand, US and Australian dollars, yen and so on and the revenues earned back in London will be affected by exchange rate fluctuations that have nothing to do with the health of the company's trading position.

The losses and uncertainties arising from all these currency transactions are one of the main reasons why European business leaders in particular are in favour of the euro, but the advantages of the single currency apply only to intra-European trade. It is logical, therefore, to assume that as globalisation increases the spread of multinational companies, demand will grow for some worldwide unit of account – the 'mondo' perhaps. And if such a currency becomes the universal medium of business transactions it will not be long before companies balk at converting it into pounds, dollars or euros in order to pay wages and taxes.

Nor can we dismiss such a development as one that only applies to business. The electronic revolution also makes it possible for many individuals to globalise their work, and that process is likely to spread as companies start to appreciate the benefits both of having employees work from home – such as the removal of the need for large and expensive offices – and the ability to find workers in countries where labour is cheaper than in their domestic market. British Airways, for instance, now locates much of its passenger revenue accounting operation in India, while American insurance and financial services companies site such things as bill-processing in Scotland and other places. Meanwhile, the Internet offers consumers the opportunity to shop internationally: how much more convenient and transparent it would be if they did not have to convert from their own currencies into those of the countries in which they were making their purchases, and even more so if they were also paid in an internationally recognised medium of exchange.

From the point of view of governments, too, the idea of a world currency makes sense. Few seem yet to have realised fully that global trading and instant communications mean that in future it will become increasingly difficult for them to collect taxes unless there is some universal system that can deal with, let us say, an individual living in London and working remotely for the Malaysian branch of a company registered in the Cayman Islands, which pays his salary electronically into an Internet banking system anywhere else he chooses. If such a person were to rent his London property, have a non-resident bank account in the Republic of Ireland and do all his shopping either through his computer or by means of an international credit card, how would the Inland Revenue be able to assess his tax liabilities? Would the authorities even be aware of his existence? Our newly invented mondo and an international system of taxation would solve the problem.

Perhaps all this sounds far-fetched, but what is incontrovertible is that the uses of currency, in the developed world at least, are changing rapidly. The introduction of the euro is merely a sign that new units of account are going to be required as the patterns of trade and of advanced economies themselves develop beyond the bounds of traditional monetary thought. But what about the use of money as a measure of value?

As the twentieth century neared its end, one of the fashionable phrases among forward-thinking economists was 'the dematerialised economy', which refers to the fact that, for the one-time industrial giants of the West, the idea of buying raw materials, transforming them into manufactured goods and selling those products across the world will soon no longer apply. In the United Kingdom, for example, while the export of goods still accounts for fifty-two per cent of trading income, by 1997 the revenues from services and investment income were nearly matching it at forty-six per cent – and manufactured exports were actually running at a deficit, with sales of £166 billion against imports of £179 billion.

Against this background economists of the 'dematerialisation' school argue that Western post-industrial societies should in future concentrate on selling services, skills, design and ideas, while the manufacturing sector is left to less developed countries with a need for labour-intensive activities. That has already happened to a large extent in businesses such as textiles, where Western designers have the fruits of their creativity realised in places such as Pakistan, and in the technology industries, with much computer hardware being manufactured in Taiwan, China, Malaysia and South Korea on the basis of concepts and designs from America and Europe. But in both cases we are looking at tangible products, whereas in the dematerialised economy it is knowledge and the uses of it that will have to be quantified, and whether that can be done in monetary terms must be open to question.

How much is an idea worth? It is a question that is being seriously considered among the growing band of academics who are turning their intellectual prowess towards theories on the future of business. How does a company reward someone whose contribution is based entirely on what is in his or her head? The answer that seems to be emerging is that the reward system has to concentrate less on salary and more on quality of

life – flexibility of working hours, holidays, retirement arrangements and so on. Interestingly, in 1998 the advertising
industry, which had for many years constructed its pitches to
potential customers on market segments based on income,
began to revise its categories along much broader lines, concentrating more on benefits rather than pay. Thus teachers, for
instance, came out much higher in the advertisers' social
structure than previously because of their long holidays, job
security and generous pension provision. This could be something of an indication that we might move into a third wave of
value judgements about people – first birth, second property
and financial status, and now that horrible modern term
'lifestyle'.

It is an entirely plausible development. After all, people
were once accorded status on the basis of who their parents
were, then on the amount of land or livestock they owned, and
later on their assets and income. Suppose, then, that in future
social status is conferred not by how much one has to spend but
by how little one needs to spend. In a cashless society, which is
what we seem to be moving slowly towards, salaries become
entirely notional and rewards may instead be offered in kind –
free housing, holidays, children's education, insurance and so
on. So as not to remove choice and independence entirely, and
to allow for daily needs, a system of electronic credits might be
developed as a sort of extension of Internet banking practices
in which the individual can 'spend' and 'borrow' and 'save'
according to predetermined limits. There are already crude
prototypes of this sort of thing in supermarket loyalty cards and
the frequent-flyer programmes operated by airlines, where
credits can be exchanged for goods or services, and even some

conventional bank accounts come with similar facilities.

But if currency as we understand it is no longer required as a unit of account and a measure – and therefore a store – of value, does it still have a role as an everyday medium of exchange? Well, in 1990 Tim Jones and Graham Higgins of the NatWest banking group produced an electronic exchange mechanism that bids fair to replace the use of notes and coins. Called Mondex, the system employs a so-called smart card containing a microchip on which 'cash' can be loaded directly from the user's bank account, even by telephone, and can then be spent in exactly the same way as with a debit card, except that no signature or authorisation is needed and the transaction is instantaneous. Money can also be transferred between individuals by means of a device known as the Mondex Wallet, which allows users to load credits from their cards directly on to other people's.

Following public trials in Swindon, Wiltshire, the Mondex system was sold to at least fifty countries with a potential market of 3 billion people and in 1999 plans were well advanced for its launch throughout the United Kingdom, and in the United States, Canada and Hong Kong. Other types of digital money had been tried before, but Mondex appeared to be the first one with all the attributes and none of the disadvantages of tangible forms of currency.

And so, at what may be the end of the story of the pound, we could be arriving more or less back at the point from which we started: a society without any pressing need for real money. Maybe, when all is said and done, the bullionists were right and there is no point in a currency that does not have its own intrinsic value. The pound today is just a number and if it continues to exist at all it will never be anything else. It would probably be foolish to replace it with the euro, even in the unlikely event that the single currency did manage to survive all the pitfalls awaiting it. Like the Gold Standard, the idea of a single European currency is one whose time has passed. Beyond that, however, it is hard to see unwavering attachment to the pound as much more than sentiment.

We might finally have to recognise that, the poor euro notwithstanding, the pound really has reached the end of its useful life. If so, it will almost certainly be part of a general abandonment of what we have learned to call currency. And at least we will be able to take justifiable pride in the fact that, after 1000 years or more, the pound has had an exceptionally good run for its money.

Chronology

Key Dates for the Pound

- 765–96   King Offa of Mercia begins to mint the first English silver pennies.

- 871–99   Alfred The Great reforms the coinage with three new series of pennies. Use of the term 'pound' for a quantity of coins begins.

- 928   King Athelstan unites the Saxon kingdoms of England and decrees a single national currency.

- 973   Edgar The Peaceable institutes a regular cycle of recoinage to establish and maintain a reliable standard for the silver penny.

- 978–1016 The minting of pennies vastly increases as the Saxons pay Danegeld to Viking invaders.

- 1085   William The Conqueror orders the survey that will become known as the Domesday Book, laying the foundation of the English tax system.

- 1124   Half the moneyers in England suffer mutilation as a punishment for producing sub-standard and counterfeit coins. Pennies become known as 'starlings' or 'sterlings'.

- 1158   Henry II orders a complete recoinage, producing the best quality pennies so far. He also constructs a highly efficient system of tax collection.

- 1279   Edward I mints halfpennies, farthings and the fourpenny groat.

- 1282:   First recorded Trial of the Pyx, which verifies the quality of the coinage.

- 1327–77   Edward III introduces the gold florin and later the noble, valued respectively at six shillings and six shillings and eightpence, the first larger-denomination coins.

- 1465   A ten-shilling coin is produced for the first time, called the rose noble.

- 1489   Henry VII produces the first ever pound coin, called a sovereign.

- 1504   The first English shilling is minted on the orders of Henry VII.

- 1542–51   The Great Debasement of Henry VIII forces the penny down to its lowest ever silver content, just over ten grains.

- 1560   Elizabeth I restores the value of the coinage with new gold pieces worth a pound, ten shillings, five shillings and two shillings and sixpence. The silver content of pennies is increased and coins worth sixpence and threepence are minted, along with new small change worth one and a half pence and three farthings.

- 1613   Private minting of the first copper farthings.
- 1663   The first guinea coin is produced, worth a pound to start with but later accepted as one pound one shilling.
- 1672   First ever government-approved English copper coins are introduced.
- 1694   Founding of the Bank of England.
- 1695   The Bank of Scotland founded.
- 1716   First pound note appears in Scotland – although it is also marked 'twelve pounds Scots' and is not legal tender.
- 1797   Copper pennies and twopenny pieces go into circulation.
- 1816   British government adopts the Gold Standard and a new pound coin is produced.
- 1820   Last minting of silver pennies.
- 1833   Bank of England notes become legal tender for sums above five pounds in England and Wales, but not Scotland, which continues to produce its own banknotes.
- 1855   The first fully printed Bank of England notes appear.
- 1914   The first true one-pound and ten-shilling notes are issued by the Treasury and gradually replace gold coinage. Later, printing will revert to the Bank of England.
- 1928   Bank of England prints the first coloured pound and ten-shilling notes.

- 1931   Britain abandons the Gold Standard.
- 1949   The pound is devalued thirty per cent against the US dollar.
- 1957   The first blue five-pound note is issued.
- 1960   For the first time, the portrait of the monarch appears on banknotes.
- 1971   The pound is decimalised, as one hundred new pence.
- 1999   Eleven European Union countries, excluding Britain, adopt the euro, which is to replace their national currencies.

What a Pound Was Worth

980

During the reign of King Aethelraed the Unraedy, the cost of a cow was about twenty pence, or four shillings. At sixty shillings to the pound, as it then was, you could buy fifteen head of cattle for a pound.

1086

According to the Domesday Book, the survey of English land-holding ordered by William The Conqueror, the rent on about 200 acres of good farmland in Norfolk was one pound a year.

1208

For a farmer in southern England, a pound would have met the wage bill for a whole year of one herdsman, one carpenter, a dairy maid and two carters.

1500

For a pound, a woman could buy two yards of best black velvet, which was used for lining cloaks. To spend that much on her clothes, she would have to have been wealthy.

1630

At the market, a pound would buy you 28lb of peas or beans, or six kilderkins (108 gallons) of ale, or 60lb of best butter, or 280lb of beef.

1759

A guinea, or one pound one shilling, was the cost of a wig, while a pound would buy four sacks of coal or about a dozen bottles of good port.

1780

A good seat – that is, inside rather than outside – in a coach between London and Salisbury, a distance of about eighty miles, would cost a guinea. An outside seat was half the price.

1805

A young outside servant in a modest country house received wages of two guineas a year, a footman eight guineas.

1832

Contemporary surveys put the average working man's wage in the cotton industry at one pound four shillings and sixpence per week. An artisan in London would earn about thirty shillings a week and in Glasgow only some fourteen shillings.

1898

The highest wage for a professional footballer was £208 a year.

1902

One pound per week was the average wage of a factory labourer. The working day was nine hours, six days a week with, in some industries, a week's paid holiday per year.

1933

The cost of a ninety per cent mortgage, over twenty-five years, on an average three-bedroom terrace house in England and Wales was approximately one pound ten shillings and eight pence per month. At that time only about a third of all homes were owned by their occupiers, the rest rented.

1947

A pound would buy you dinner for four people in a hotel. As a result of post-war food shortages, hotels were not permitted to charge more than a maximum of five shillings per head for meals.

1966

An average provincial three-bedroom semi-detached house, newly built on a small estate, cost between £3100 and £3800, depending on type and area.

Purchasing power of the pound

According to tables compiled by the Government Statistical Service and adjusted for the decimal value of one hundred pence to a pound:

- A pound spent in 1914 would have bought only two pence worth of goods in 1997.
- The pound of 1930 was worth just three pence in 1997.
- In 1950 the pound of 1914 was worth only thirty pence, but a 1950 pound was worth just six pence in 1997.
- Spending a pound at its 1960 value was the equivalent of twelve pounds in 1997.
- Between 1980 and 1997 the pound lost sixty per cent of its purchasing power.
- Between 1990 and 1997 the amount the pound would buy fell by twenty per cent.

Index

Aethelberht, King, 37
agriculture, 20, 27, 126, 138,
    181–2, 211
Alfred, King, 24, 44–50
angel, 140, 141, 145, 157
Angles, 27–8
Arabs, 30–1, 34, 37–8, 54, 81
armed forces, 18, 45–6, 63, 66,
    83–4, 97, 100, 101, 124,
    186
Athelstan, 50, 51–3

Babylonians, 32
banking, 171–88, 233, 237
    merchant, 235–7, 258
banknotes, 166, 173–5, 181,
    187, 189–207, 219, 223,
    224, 239–40, 245, 268
Bank of England, 185–8, 194,

205, 207, 219, 221, 223,
    239, 241–3, 258, 266
Bank of Scotland, 187–8, 195,
    197, 203
barter, 11, 27, 75, 164
    see also payment in kind
bimetallism, 2–8
Black Death, 14, 130–5, 143
blanched coins, 105, 121
building societies, 216–17
bullion, 3, 7, 25–6, 93, 125,
    139, 141, 144, 150, 163,
    172–3, 189–207
busts on coins, 18, 35, 36–7,
    47, 53, 95, 99, 108, 111,
    116, 140, 179
    see also decoration

capitalisation, 271–2

cash economy, 112, 116–17, 127, 151
cashless society, 282–6
cash transactions, 11, 19, 41- 2, 268–70
see also non-cash
Charles II, 166, 171, 184
cheques, 174, 245, 269
church, Roman, 63–4, 114
civil war, 93, 119–20, 135, 137, 161–2
Cnut, King, 63–6
coinage systems, 26–7, 29–30, 33–5, 46–8, 50, 52–3, 64- 6, 69–70, 109,150, 157- 8, 180–1
see also foreign coins
coins, 4, 15–17, 28, 105–6, 123, 193, 196, 236, 268
see also minting, mints
colonies, 155, 160–1, 163–4, 194, 197–9, 227–31, 259, 228–33
see also British Empire
Commonwealth, 261, 262
copper coins, 180
counterfeiting, 61, 85–6, 221
credit, 111, 127–9, 174–7, 190, 236–7, 269
crown coin, 158, 248
crusades, 76, 110–12, 122
customs and excise, 21, 122

Danegeld, 60–3, 67, 70–1, 98
David, King of Scotland, 95
debasement, 5–6, 15, 55, 66- 7, 84–7, 88, 107, 118, 142, 144–6, 148–9, 151, 157, 196, 221
see also Gresham's Law
decimal system, 16, 26, 249
decoration of coins, 108, 118
demesne revenues, 19–20, 99
denarius, 56–7
denier, 35
deposits, 236–8
devaluation, 62
dinar, 'Offa's', 38
dirhem (dinar), 31–3, 38–40
dollar, US, 165–6, 258, 280
Domesday Book, 71–4, 80

East India Company, 167, 203, 205, 228–30
economic decline, 254–62
Economic and Monetary Union (EMU), 273–80
economic stability, 15
Edgar the Peaceable, 54–6, 63
Edward I, 120–5, 127
Edward III, 129–35
Edward IV, 140
Edward VI, 146–7
Edward the Confessor, 66–7
Edward the Elder, 50–2
Edward the Martyr, 55
Egbert, King of Wessex, 42–3
Elizabeth I, 10, 148–55
esterlin, design of, 99
euro, 78, 272–3
exchange rates, 263

exchequer, 19, 85, 102–4
  see also treasury
exports, 12, 20, 62, 224, 264

farthing, 11–12, 55, 122, 151,
  162, 248
fines, 21–2, 27
First World War, 255–8
FitzNigel, Richard, 101–8
five shilling piece, gold, 150
florin, 13, 129, 250
foreign coinage in England, 13,
  15, 17, 84, 121, 139, 148,
  165, 219–20
Franks, 34
free trade, 223, 243, 253
Friendly Societies, 214–15

gold, shortage of, 139, 258
gold-silver mix, 29, 32
  see also silver-gold ratio
goldsmith-bankers, 183–5
Goldsmiths' Company, 123, 173
goldsmith's notes, 173–5, 183,
  195
  see also banknotes; bills
Gold Standard, 3, 192–3, 224,
  236, 242, 247, 258
Gresham's Law, 6–7, 148
groat, silver, 13, 122, 140, 141,
  151, 248
guinea, gold, 179, 193, 249

half-crown, 248
half-farthings, 249
half-groat, 141

halfpenny, 11–12, 55, 86, 122,
  151, 248
half-sovereign, 248
Harold II, 67–8
'harps', 145
Henry I, 77, 82–9
Henry II, 94–109, 111
Henry III, 118–21
Henry IV, 139
Henry VII, 9–24, 141–2
Henry VIII, 10, 142–6, 174
heregeld (army tax), 62–3,
  65
hideage, 70–1, 73

industrialisation, 209, 211- 15,
  231–2, 261
inflation, 118, 130, 158, 190,
  250, 260, 265, 268
  see also prices; wages
interest rates, 176, 190, 245,
  257, 260, 265, 271
Internet, 269
investment, 183, 153, 167,
  252–3, 259, 264, 271
Ivar the Boneless, 44

James I, 157, 167
James III of Scotland, 140
John, King, 115–16
John of Gaunt, 136–8

labour, 130–4, 210, 225
landowners, 98, 135
laurel, 157
loans, see credit

loyalty bonds, 22
£.s.d. ratios, 62, 249
Lydians, 32

Macedonians, 33
mancus (Arab), 31, 33, 37,
    48–9, 65
manufacturing, 126, 183
mark, 12, 47, 49, 158
Mary I, 147
merchants, 12, 91–2, 183
minting techniques, 38–9, 54,
    67, 107–9, 123, 149, 163,
    178–9
mint-master, see moneyer
mints, 16–17, 36, 46, 61, 66,
    70, 99, 108–9, 123, 146-
    7, 150, 162–3, 165, 178,
    180, 193, 218, 268
    see also coin production
money
    earliest forms of, 31
    purchasing power, 106–7
    purposes of, 31, 270
    as power, 14
    sound, 15, 191–2
    supply, 87, 106, 118, 141,
        172, 190, 203, 218
    wages in form of, 11
moneyers, 17, 68, 85–6, 88
    Arab, 38–9
    Athelstan law on, 52–4
    charges, 17, 56, 68–70, 108,
        118, 121–2, 141
    regulation of, 87
money markets, 264

national debt, 152, 187, 255- 7,
    261
nationalisation, 262, 265
navy, 18, 46, 152, 254
noble, gold, 13, 129–30, 139
non-cash transactions, 268
Norsemen, see Vikings

obols, gold, 104
Offa, King of Mercia, 34–40
offices, sale of, 20
Oliver Cromwell, 161
ora, 31, 65
overdraft, 240, 269

Parliamentary powers, 172
payment in kind, 11, 117
Peasants' Revolt, 138
penalties, 21
penning, 35
penny, 36
    bronze, 248
    copper, 151, 220, 248
    silver, 12, 13, 35–7, 46, 48,
        61–2, 70, 82, 93, 107–8,
        130, 141, 145, 245
    see also sterling
Persians, 33
peso, 165
Peter's Pence, 39–40, 46
postal orders, 245
pound, 3, 6, 11, 24, 25
pound coin, 11, 16, 142, 150,
    157, 193
pound sterling, 178, 228, 258,
    271

prices, 12, 130–3, 143, 146,
     151, 157, 159, 210, 249,
     254, 260
productivity, 252, 260, 264

recoinage, 16–17, 24, 49, 55- 6,
     67, 75–6, 86, 99, 107,
     145–6, 149, 191
revenues, royal, 99, 107
Richard I, 110–15
Richard II, 135–8
Richard III, 10
Robert of Normandy, 76, 82
Robin Hood Paradox, 115
Romans, 25–6, 32, 33
Royal Exchange, 148
rural economy, 46
ryal, gold, 13, 140, 141

savings, 215, 236
Saxons, 27–30, 32, 33–4
sceat (scat), 30, 33, 37, 65
scilling, 37
Scotland, 83, 95, 124, 134,
     157–8
scutage, 100
Second World War, 261–2
shilling, 12, 47, 49, 141, 145,
     147, 248
silver-gold ratio, 3, 33, 47, 65
     see also bimetallism
sixpenny pieces, 147, 150, 158,
     248
skimming of coins, 4–7, 86,
     118, 121
social services, financing of,

99–100, 254, 262
South Sea Bubble, 204–7
sovereign, gold, 141, 145, 225,
     245, 248
     see also pound coin
spur-ryal, 157
Stephen, King, 90–3
sterling, 77–9, 80–1, 258
St Paul's (London), 29
stycca, 33

tallage, 100–1, 115, 122, 136
tallies, 103–4, 111
taxation, 17, 20, 71–4, 84–5,
     99–100, 113–14, 152
taxes, 27
  crusading, 122
  on English church, 122
  income, 21, 222–3, 225, 241,
     256: *see also* tallage
  indirect, 223
  land, 136, 254
  for military campaigns, 115
  poll, 135–7
  Poor Rate, 215, 223
  wealth, 56, 254, 256
  William I, 70–1
  see also customs; Danegeld;
     Domesday; heregeld;
     hideage; tolls
ten shilling piece, gold, 150
testoon, silver, 17, 141, 145
     see also shilling
Thatcher, Margaret, 14, 264
three-farthings coin, 151
three-halfpenny coins, 151

threepenny pieces, 150, 248
thrisma, 31
tobacco notes, 166, 194–5
tokens, trading, 158, 220–1
tolls, 56–7
trade, 14, 32, 39, 66, 75, 92
    balance of, 169, 172, 183
    international, 166–8, 229- 31
    see also barter
trades unions, 214, 225, 253,
    254, 262
treasury, 101–4
    see also tallies
Trial of the Pyx, 123–4, 173

Unite (coin), 157, 162
United States, 255
urbanisation, 46, 112, 182

value
    'crying-up' of, 145, 157
    of gold and silver, relative,

37–8, 47–9: *see also* silver-
    gold ratio
    of man, 50
Vikings, 40–7, 59–66

wages, 130–4, 143, 146, 159,
    182, 210–11, 219, 221,
    224, 225, 251, 260
Wales, 83, 124, 129
Wars of the Roses, 10, 13, 14,
    18
wealth redistribution, 217–18
wergild (blood-money), 50
William I (the Conqueror),
    68–75, 80
William III, 185, 191
William Rufus, 75–6
wool and cloth, 97, 122, 126,
    138–9, 157, 159
working people, 209–15, 222,
    252, 260–1